Focus Groups

Focus Groups

Second Edition

A Practical Guide for Applied Research

Richard A. Krueger

SAGE Publications
International Educational and Professional Publisher
Thousand Oaks   London   New Delhi

For information address:

SAGE Publications, Inc.
2455 Teller Road
Thousand Oaks, California 91320
E-mail: order@sagepub.com

SAGE Publications Ltd.
6 Bonhill Street
London EC2A 4PU
United Kingdom

SAGE Publications India Pvt. Ltd.
M-32 Market
Greater Kailash I
New Delhi 110 048 India

Printed in the United States of America

Library of Congress Cataloging-in-Publication Data

Krueger, Richard A.
    Focus groups : a practical guide for applied research / Richard A.
    Krueger.—2nd ed.
        p. cm.
    Includes bibliographical references and index.
    ISBN 0-8039-5566-9 (cl.)—ISBN 0-8039-5567-7 (pb)
    1. Focused group interviewing. 2. Social sciences—Methodology.
    I. Title.
    H61.28.K78   1994
    361.6'1068—dc20   93-43665

96 97 98 99 00 12 11 10 9 8 7 6 5

Sage Production Editor: Astrid Virding

Contents

Preface

This second edition of *Focus Groups: A Practical Guide for Applied Research* adds to the materials presented in the earlier edition. I wrote the first edition after agonizing over the lack of literature available to the evaluation researcher on focus group interviewing. At that time, most of what was known about focus group interviewing had been in the hands of a guild of practitioners, with the technique passed down from master to apprentice. Unfortunately, this inefficient process of information transfer resulted in limited availability for those research-ers who are unable to watch the masters.

Since the publication of the first edition of this book it has been my good fortune to continue watching, conducting, analyzing, and teaching about focus groups. I've had the opportunity to participate in a variety of roles, such as teacher, coach, mentor, and student. This second edition grows out of these experiences and is a better book because it draws on the wisdom and insight of hundreds of students and colleagues.

This book is specifically intended for the public and nonprofit sector, including multiple layers of government at the local, state, and national levels. It includes professional associations and societies, religious and charitable organizations, philanthropic agencies, as well as hundreds of organizations charged with our health, safety, education, and public service.

With the exception of the landmark effort of Robert Merton and colleagues (1990/1956), most of the energy invested in focus groups for three decades had come from private sector market research. The pragmatic, practical, and innovative environment of market research nourished the concept of focus group interviewing. By the 1980s, decision makers in the public and nonprofit sectors were increasingly aware of the need for qualitative information and consequently began to embrace focus groups.

Focus groups within the public and nonprofit sector are different from those in the private, commercial sector because the circumstances are different. Within public and nonprofit organizations the following factors operate and influence focus group research:

1. Budgets are limited and often shrinking; consequently monies for research are often severely restricted.
2. Policies and procedures often limit, and occasionally prohibit, the use of funds to pay participants in focus groups.
3. Traditions, values, and policies may be in opposition to several principles essential to focus groups, namely these beliefs:
   - All meetings should be open to anyone who wants to participate.
   - Individuals with certain characteristics capably represent others with similar characteristics.
   - Information gathering must include all interest groups from a broad section of the population.
4. The topic of inquiry is complex. In the public/nonprofit sector, focus groups are used to examine areas of concern that have considerable complexity and are typically dependent on motivational forces and characteristics of human behavior.
5. Various stakeholders typically hold diverse perceptions on critical areas of concern. There is regularly limited understanding of customer/client motivation, multiple interpretations of the organization's mission, and limited insights as to the organization's competitors.
6. Considerable credibility is given to individual testimony. As a result, focus group interviewing is given considerable face validity.
7. Decision makers are diverse and nonspecific. Decisions are often slow because of multiple and overlapping audiences with decisions made by consensus.
8. Volunteers represent a valuable and often untapped resource. These volunteers may be able to take on specific tasks that would be difficult or impossible for staff.

This book describes a hybrid approach to focus groups. Some of the emphasis is traditional, such as a fidelity to original concepts that drive focus groups. Other modifications have pragmatic roots based on practices of exceptional moderators, approaches of skillful qualitative researchers, and features that build on the assets of the public and nonprofit sectors. Attention is placed on the value added by assistant moderators and the use of the internal resources of the agency. Furthermore, emphasis is placed on situational analysis and the selective use of nonresearchers.

What I've Learned and What's Changed

Focus group research is certainly not static, and the approach and methodology are constantly changing. Over the past decade several distinctive changes have become apparent.

Smaller groups show considerable potential. The old dictum of needing 10 to 12 participants for a focus group is largely unworkable with complex topics. Smaller groups of 5, 6, or 7 participants not only offer more opportunity for individuals to talk but are considerably more practical to set up and manage.

There is no one right way to conduct analysis. Ten years ago, I assumed that transcript-based analysis was the sine qua non of focus group research. Unfortunately, this form of analysis was extraordinarily slow and cumbersome, and researchers struggled to find a more efficient method of analysis. Analysis of transcripts that spanned weeks and months was often impractical. However, the lack of rigor associated with the oral debriefing report was unsettling. This book takes a more practical attitude in recommending a variety of analysis strategies that are appropriate to the situation.

A decade ago, little or no consideration was placed on the benefits of nonresearchers assisting with the process. Researchers considered these individuals not qualified. As a result, the nonresearchers were avoided because they had limited background in research strategies, asked questions that usually delayed action, and generally resulted in more work for the researcher. For many of us the paradigm has shifted and these nonresearchers are now considered an asset. They have skills, connections, energy, and ideas that when appropriately channeled can multiply the potential benefit of the study. Involvement of nonresearchers can not only improve the quality of the study but build commitment as well.

Focus groups in the public sector demand sensitivity to diversity. Although the white middle-class consumer has been the principal target of focus groups, the public and nonprofit sector reaches out to more diverse audiences. As a result, sensitivity is needed in adapting focus groups to build on the strengths of the target audience. Sensitivity is essential in environments where disenfranchised people are cautious to share views with those in power.

Fancy facilities and technological devices are generally overrated. The private sector market research environment often cites these electronic and physical features as benchmarks of quality. The true benchmark is the quality of the discussion, which can easily erode when participants are overly fascinated, annoyed, or distracted by such devices as one-way mirrors, television cameras, and knobs and buttons.

Focus groups are robust. When the moderator is sincere and the study is deemed acceptable to local participants, the focus group can be conducted in a variety of successful ways. The focus group is beneficial for identification of major themes but not so much for the micro-analysis of subtle differences. Major themes tend to surface in spite of difficulties with the environment, questions, or moderator skills. This is not a call for abandonment of systematic protocol but rather encouragement for researchers to experiment with the technique and process of focus groups.

More than anything else, this book presents an alternative means of obtaining information from people. Decision makers regularly encounter this problem as they seek to plan, administer, or allocate resources. It has been my experience that the first reaction of decision makers is to request a survey. In part, this reaction is prompted by two factors: the survey's scientific aura and the decision maker's lack of knowledge about alternative means of gathering information. Focus groups offer an alternative that capitalizes on the strengths of the decision makers: knowledge of the program and an ability to talk to clientele.

This book was written after an extensive literature search; observation of both masters and novices as they engage in focus groups; and experiences in classes, workshops, and seminars designed to help non-researchers develop the requisite skills for moderating focus groups. The tenor of the suggestions will emphasize the practical considerations of moderating more than the theoretical underpinnings of focus group interviews. I hope this book will also serve as a review to those researchers who are already grounded in the basics of moderating.

The Organization of the Book

The book is organized around three themes. Part I (Chapters 1 and 2) presents a general overview of focus groups that highlights distinctions between this methodological procedure and other seemingly similar group or individual research procedures. Within Part I, the reader will find a discussion of the development of focus group procedures, why focus groups work, characteristics of focus groups, uses of focus groups, validity of focus group interviewing, and advantages and limitations of this research procedure. This first part of the book is intended to provide the readers—both researchers and users—with the concepts that undergird focus group interviewing.

Part II (Chapters 3-9) suggests strategies for actually conducting focus group interviews. This section emphasizes the elements involved in doing focus groups and will likely be of greater interest to researchers as they prepare for the experience. Chapter 3 highlights the planning necessary for successful focus groups. Effective focus groups depend on developing quality questions. Chapter 4 is considerably expanded from the first edition. Also expanded is the discussion of involving the right participants in the focus group (Chapter 5). Moderating skills are discussed in Chapter 6. Analysis principles are presented in Chapter 7, and alternative processes of analysis are described in Chapter 8. Reporting focus group results is discussed in Chapter 9.

Part III (Chapters 10-13) surfaces several issues that are often of concern to both researchers and users, particularly those within the nonprofit sector. Chapter 10 presents a collaborative approach to focus groups. Chapter 11 provides suggestions on the use of focus groups with different audiences and Chapter 12 suggests several variations of focus groups that have proven to be effective. Chapter 13 provides suggestions for contracting for focus group assistance. The Postscript offers some thoughts on the future of focus groups.

Acknowledgments

I owe much to colleagues and friends who have assisted me with this effort. Although the title page bears the name of a single author, the contents would not have been possible without the contributions of others. Mary Anne Casey was a valuable advisor who helped me straighten out the logic and influenced my thinking on the valuable potential of volunteers. Jerry Migler has helped teach many focus group workshops and has made beneficial contributions in handling the logistics and budgetary aspects of focus groups. Tom Berkas contributed ideas and encouragement in the use of focus groups for empowerment and in developmental projects, both in this country and in others. Earl Bracewell added humor and a sensitivity that made focus groups fun. Theresa Ahles pulled together a comprehensive bibliography on focus groups and also used her many computer skills to explore analysis strategies and protocol. Michael Patton—scholar, teacher, and friend—has provided encouragement, sound advice, and enthusiasm for this book.

I have been fortunate to work with many extraordinarily capable people in the past decade. They have used focus groups and stretched my horizons and I have greatly valued their advice. Thanks to:

Donna Bagdan and her colleagues with Alberta Agriculture
Dale Blyth and his colleagues at Search Institute
Bonnie Bray, Marlys Peters, Barbara Jo Stahl, and their colleagues in education

Carol Bryant and her colleagues working in social marketing at the University of South Florida

John Collins at Seattle University

Barbara Duffy at the Federal Bureau of Investigation

Alan Griffin and his colleagues at the General Accounting Office

Gretchen Griffin and Karen Lawson and their colleagues at the Hennepin County Community Health Department

Michael Mangano and his colleagues with the Office of Inspector General, Health and Human Services

John Milatzo and colleagues with the U.S. Postal Service

Mary Montagne and Sue Gehrz and their colleagues at the Dakota County Public Health Department

David Morgan at Portland State University

Ed Nelson and his colleagues with the Wisconsin Department of Natural Resources

Gail Redd and her coworkers throughout the nation from the Office of Personnel Management

Ray Rist and his colleagues at the General Accounting Office

Mary Story and Pam McCarthy in the College of Public Health, University of Minnesota

Gidget Terpstra of Seattle, Washington

Colleagues within the College of Education at the University of Minnesota continue to provide encouragement and advice. Special thanks to professors Jean King, Gary Leske, Edgar Persons, and Roland Peterson and to the scores of graduate students who are willing to learn and apply concepts.

I am indebted to colleagues with the Cooperative Extension Service who were willing to try out the ideas and suggest refinements to the procedures described in this book. Through field application I have had the opportunity to learn from many individuals. Thanks to Pat Borich and Gail Skinner with the Minnesota Cooperative Extension Service, Greg Hutchins from Alburn University, and Tom Archer from Ohio State University.

My wife Sue believed from the start that this book would get finished and helped arrange a home life that would allow for uninterrupted writing. In addition, she provided encouragement, advice, and support to complete the manuscript.

RICHARD A. KRUEGER

PART I

Groups and Focus Groups

First Exposure to a Focus Group

Betty was relaxing at home after a hectic day at the office. She had just finished reading Section A of today's newspaper and was reaching for Section B when the telephone rang. She answered, expecting a call from her brother George.

"Hello."

"Good evening," the voice on the phone responded. "I'm conducting a survey of people in the community, and I would like to ask you a few questions. It will only take a couple minutes. Is it OK to begin?"

"Sure, go ahead."

"Do you have any houseplants in your home?" the caller asked.

"Yes," Betty answered.

"How many do you have? Would you say that you have less than 5 plants, 5 to 10 plants, or more than 10 plants?" the voice inquired.

"More than 10."

"In the past year, have you used any fertilizer or plant growth chemicals on your plants?"

"Yes, I have," she responded.

"Our company, which is Research Incorporated, is conducting a study of houseplant fertilizer. We would like to invite you to a special meeting to discuss fertilizer products. There will be no selling involved, and if you decide to attend we will provide you with a year's supply of plant fertilizer. The meeting will be held on January 12 from 7:00 to 8:30 p.m. It will be at the Hanover Motel in Minneapolis. Would you be able to join us?"

"Sure, count me in," she replied.

"Great. Now let me get your name and address . . . "

It all happened rather quickly, and after the call Betty began to wonder what it was all about. "A year's supply of fertilizer is great, but what's the catch? They said no selling was involved, but why would they want to hold a meeting to discuss fertilizer on houseplants? Oh well, I guess I'll just have to wait and find out."

Does this phone call sound familiar? The call was a telephone screening questionnaire for a focus group. Betty passed through the screens for selection and accepted the invitation to talk about houseplant fertilizer. If she didn't have houseplants or use fertilizer she would have received a polite "Thank you, we have no further questions," and the call would have ended.

Later, after the meeting, Betty's brother George asked her about the experience. She reflected: "The meeting was interesting, in fact enjoyable. There were about 10 people there, including a person who asked questions. The people all had houseplants and talked about different types of fertilizer. The discussion leader asked questions about fertilizer and was interested in the reasons we selected various brands, and what we liked about different types of fertilizer. At the end of the session, she told us the information would be used by the Northern Fertilizer Company to improve their product. Before I left she offered me either two gallons of liquid houseplant fertilizer or a five pound bag of dry fertilizer. I took the liquid. Do you want some?"

Betty experienced a focus group interview. It is one of the most popular tools in market research today. A growing number of people have participated in focus groups. Interestingly, however, many participants in Betty's group didn't know that the group discussion was a focus group interview or that the telephone survey was a screen for focus group participation. Rarely is the term *focus group* used at the group discussion, because the term might inhibit the spontaneity of participants. Also the term *focus group* is rarely used when invitations are made to potential participants. Instead, participants are invited to "discuss" or "share ideas with others," thereby conveying the informal nature of the discussion.

Focus groups are being used increasingly by researchers to discover preferences for new or existing products. The focus group discussion is particularly effective in providing information about *why* people think or feel the way they do.

The Quest for Information

Focus groups have been a mainstay in private sector marketing research. More recently, public sector organizations are beginning to discover the potential of this procedure. Educational and nonprofit organizations have traditionally used face-to-face interviews and questionnaires to get information. Unfortunately, these popular techniques are sometimes inadequate in meeting information needs of decision makers. The focus group is unique from these other procedures; it allows for group interaction and greater insight into why certain opinions are held. Focus groups can improve the planning and design of new programs, provide means of evaluating existing programs, and produce insights for developing marketing strategies. This book is intended to provide assistance in using focus groups to obtain information that will be helpful to decision makers.

1

Groups

Groups are a common experience. It would be difficult to find a human being who has not been in a group; indeed most of us are repeatedly confronted with a plethora of groups. We find ourselves invited, herded, or seduced into groups for planning, decision making, advising, brainstorming, support, and a host of other purposes.

It's not surprising that we think twice at the prospect of getting together in a group. Groups can be fun, exciting, or invigorating, but they can also be agonizing, time-consuming experiences that are both unproductive and unnecessary. In some organizational environments the group (task force, committee, etc.) is created because individuals are confused as to a future course of action. More often than not the pooled confusion results not in enlightenment but only more confusion. As a consequence, the group becomes our scapegoat—we blame the group for the inadequacies of the individuals in the group. The group is neither good nor bad but merely a reflection of our human capabilities. The group magnifies our individual wisdom and shortcomings. Our shortcomings are often the result of confusion about the purpose and process of the group.

Sometimes the purpose of the group is clearly understood, such as in a nominating committee where the end result is a slate of officer candidates. Other times the purpose of the group is vaguely understood, perceived differently by participants, or changes over time. We tend to engage in group experiences without careful thought or clarity of purpose. At times the function of the group may be to suggest ideas, to clarify potential options, to recommend a course of action, or to make a decision—each function considerably different from the others. Researchers regularly find themselves working with groups for purposes of planning or evaluating. Difficulties emerge when there is ambiguity around these endeavors. Lack of clarity in defining the group purpose can result in confusion, frustration, misunderstandings, wasted time, and—most likely—the wrong outcomes.

The second type of confusion relates to the group process. Group leaders may not have the necessary skills to guide the group process. Effective leadership is essential if the group is to accomplish its purpose. The group leader must not only be in tune with the purpose of the group but also have the necessary skills to effectively guide the group process. Furthermore, the skills necessary for one type of group experience do not necessarily transfer into other group settings.

The Focus Group: A Special Type of Group

The focus group is a special type of group in terms of purpose, size, composition, and procedures. A focus group is typically composed of 7 to 10 participants who are selected because they have certain characteristics in common that relate to the topic of the focus group. Furthermore, the focus group is repeated several times with different people. Typically, a focus group study will consist of a minimum of three focus groups but could involve as many as several dozen groups.

The researcher creates a permissive environment in the focus group that nurtures different perceptions and points of view, without pressuring participants to vote, plan, or reach consensus. The group discussion is conducted several times with similar types of participants to identify trends and patterns in perceptions. Careful and systematic analysis of the discussions provide clues and insights as to how a product, service, or opportunity is perceived.

In summary, a focus group is a carefully planned discussion designed to obtain perceptions on a defined area of interest in a permissive, nonthreatening environment. It is conducted with approximately 7 to 10 people by a skilled interviewer. The discussion is comfortable and often enjoyable for participants as they share their ideas and perceptions. Group members influence each other by responding to ideas and comments in the discussion.

The Story Behind Focus Group Interviews

Focus group interviews were born out of necessity. In the late 1930s, social scientists began investigating the value of nondirective individual interviewing as an improved source of information. They had doubts about the accuracy of traditional information gathering methods, specifically the excessive influence of the interviewer and the limitations of predetermined, close-ended questions. The traditional individual interview, which used a predetermined questionnaire with close-ended response choices, had a major disadvantage: The respondent was limited by the choices offered and therefore the findings could be unintentionally influenced by the interviewer by oversight or omission. In contrast, nondirective procedures began with limited assumptions and placed considerable emphasis on getting in tune with the reality of the interviewee. Nondirective interviews use open-ended questions and allow individuals to respond without setting boundaries or providing clues for potential response categories. The open-ended approaches allow the subject ample opportunity to comment, to explain, and to share experiences and attitudes as opposed to the structured and directive interview that is lead by the interviewer. Stuart A. Rice was one of the first social scientists to express concern. In 1931 he wrote:

A defect of the interview for the purposes of fact-finding in scientific research, then, is that the questioner takes the lead. That is, the subject plays a more or less passive role. Information or points of view of the highest value may not be disclosed because the direction given the interview by the questioner leads away from them. In short, data obtained from an interview are as likely to embody the preconceived ideas of the interviewer as the attitudes of the subject interviewed. (p. 561)

As a result, social scientists began considering strategies in which the researcher would take on a less directive and dominating role and the respondent would be able to comment on the areas deemed by that respondent to be most important. In effect, the emphasis of nondirective interviewing was to shift attention from the interviewer to the respondent.

Nondirective interviewing had particular appeal to social scientists and psychologists in the late 1930s and 1940s. Roethlisberger and Dickson (1938) cited it in studies of employee motivation and Carl Rogers (1942) in psychotherapy. During World War II, increased attention was placed on focused interviewing in groups, primarily as a means of increasing military morale. Many of the procedures that have come to be accepted as common practice in focus group interviews were set forth in the classic work by Robert Merton, Marjorie Fiske, and Patricia Kendall, *The Focused Interview* (1990/1956).

In the past 30 years most applications of focus group interviewing have been in market research. Those who develop or manufacture new products know the importance of advertising their products and are also well aware of the financial risks of introducing new products. Gone are the days when emphasis was placed on super salespeople who could sell anything. The sensible strategy is to stay in touch with the people. Focus group interviews have considerable value because they enable the producers, manufacturers, and sellers to understand the thinking of consumers.

Most recently, focus group interviews have been regarded by many as a crucial step in shaping marketing strategies for products. Coe and MacLachlan (1980) found that focus groups were the most popular technique for evaluating potential television commercials among the 37 largest users of television advertising. Some products have undergone major revisions in manufacturing, packaging, or advertising because of findings in focus groups. Advertising campaigns often focus on what the consumer considers to be the positive attributes of the product. For example, soft drink companies discovered via focus groups that consumers drink beverages not because of thirst but because of the sociability features associated with the product. It is no wonder then that slogans promoting these beverages highlight how "things go better" or increase personal popularity on the beach (Bellenger, Bernhardt, & Goldstrucker, 1976).

Focus group interviews are widely accepted within marketing research because they produce believable results at a reasonable cost. This technique is growing in popularity among other information seekers, such as social scientists, evaluators, planners, and educators. It is a particularly appropriate procedure to use when the goal is to explain how people regard an experience, idea, or event.

Social scientists have rediscovered the focus group. Merton's pioneering work has lain dormant in the social sciences for decades. The evolution of focus groups, and for that matter of qualitative research methods in general, has been delayed for a variety of reasons—a preoccupation with quantitative procedures, assumptions about the nature of reality, and a societal tendency to believe in numbers. For several decades the pendulum of evaluation research swung to the quantitative side with primary attention to experimental designs, control groups, and randomization. This sojourn with numbers has been beneficial in that we have gained in our experimental sophistication, but it also nurtured a desire for more understanding of the human experience. Too often quantitative approaches were based on assumptions about people, about things, or about reality in general that were not warranted.

The process of evaluating social programs is maturing, in part because of an environment that expects relevance, practicality, and utility. Increasingly, human service programs are requested to be more accountable for the resources they consume. Those directing educational, medical, and social programs are being asked to document what they are doing and the impact of their efforts on people. Failure to take accountability seriously can have deleterious consequences on future funding. As a result, public and private providers of services are increasingly interested in knowing more about how their clients (customers) view their programs. Strategic planning, needs assessment, and program evaluation are critical activities for human service professionals who want to improve programs and services. Focus groups can provide them information about perceptions, feelings, and attitudes of program clients. The procedure allows professionals to see reality from the client's point of view.

For example, the University of Minnesota College of Agriculture was concerned about its declining enrollment of rural youth. High school graduates from small rural Minnesota schools were enrolling in agricultural colleges in neighboring states. A series of focus groups with potential students revealed that the young people had some negative notions about the university, and, in fact, the university was unwittingly adding to their perceptions. Students from small rural high schools saw the University of Minnesota as too big and too impersonal. They felt that they would get lost in the thousands of students at the university and therefore they preferred smaller schools. With this insight the faculty in the division of agricultural education took another look at the promotional materials being distributed to prospective students. The descriptive brochures had numerous pictures of the university—pictures of the campus mall with thousands of students and pictures showing the grandeur of the university. The brochures told of the millions of books in the library, the thousands of students in the university, and the scores and scores of departments and majors. Clearly, the existing promotional materials reinforced the fears of potential students. As a result of focus group research, faculty members designed a special brochure that emphasized the "more compact" St. Paul campus, "friendly teachers who take an interest in you," and the benefits of attending college with other students from rural communities (Casey, Leske, & Krueger, 1987).

It is dangerous for a university, or for any public service agency, to take the customer for granted. Periodically, effort is needed to get in touch with the customer and see the agency, program, service, or institution from the perspective of the client. Patricia Labaw, in her text on survey design (1985), argues that the day of "seat-of-the-pants decision making" has ended. She writes:

> Whether we choose to recognize it or not, our society is basically marketing oriented. None of our institutions exists indefinitely on public sufferance; each must perform. Each must respond to need. As a consequence every policymaker must know what the need is and try to learn the best way of providing the service or product to meet the need. The days of seat-of-the-pants decision making are passing, if they have not indeed already passed. (p. 17)

A similar view is expressed by Daniel Katz, Barbara Gutek, Robert Kahn, and Eugenia Barton in *Bureaucratic Encounters* (1975). They argue:

> In private enterprise under competitive conditions, there is some direct feedback from the appropriate public when people exercise their discretionary power as consumers to purchase from one or another competing source. In private monopolies and public agencies, there is no such direct check on products or services. In such cases the need for systematic feedback from the people being served is all the more necessary. (p. 2)

Administrators of nonprofit institutions are taking their cues from the private sector and discovering that marketing the product is essential. Although some institutions are able to survive on their historic reputation, other nonprofit organizations are concerned about maintaining or increasing their audience and meeting client needs in the most efficient manner possible.

Why Do Focus Groups Work?

The focus group interview works because it taps into human tendencies. Attitudes and perceptions relating to concepts, products, services, or programs are developed in part by interaction with other people. We are a product of our environment and are influenced by people around us. A deficiency of mail and telephone surveys and even face-to-face interviews is that those methods assume that individuals really do know how they feel. A further assumption is that individuals form opinions in isolation. Both of these assumptions have presented problems for researchers. People may need to listen to opinions of others before they form their own personal viewpoints. Although some opinions may be developed quickly and held with absolute certainty, other opinions are malleable and dynamic. Evidence from focus group interviews suggests that people do influence each other with their comments, and in the course of a discussion the opinions of an individual might shift. The focus group analyst can thereby discover more about how that shift occurred and the nature of the influencing factors. An excellent discussion is presented by Terrance L. Albrecht (1993) and her colleagues in the chapter "Understanding Communication Processes in Focus Groups."

Often the questions asked in a focused interview are deceptively simple. They are the kinds of questions an individual could answer in a couple of minutes. When questions are asked in a group environment and nourished by skillful probing, the results are candid portraits of customer perceptions. The permissive group environment gives individuals license to divulge emotions that often do not emerge in other forms of questioning. Indeed, one of the hazards in getting information from people is that they often want to tell us how they wish to be seen as opposed to how they are.

The intent of the focus group is to promote self-disclosure among participants. For some individuals self-disclosure comes easily—it is natural and comfortable. But for others it is difficult or uncomfortable and requires trust, effort, and courage. Children have a natural tendency to disclose things about themselves but through socialization they learn the values of dissemblance. Over time, the natural and spontaneous disclosures of children are modified by social pressure. Sidney Jourard (1964) expands on this tendency:

> As children we are, and we act, our real selves. We say what we think, we scream for what we want, we tell what we did. These spontaneous disclosures meet variable consequences—some disclosures are ignored, some rewarded, and some punished. Doubtless in accordance with the laws of reinforcement, we learn early to withhold certain disclosures because of the painful consequences to which they lead. We are punished in our society, not only for what we actually do, but also for what we think, feel, or want. Very soon, then, the growing child learns to display a highly expurgated version of his self to

others. I have coined the term "public self" to refer to the concept of oneself which one wants others to believe. (p. 10)

A familiar story, especially for mothers, is that of a child running home to tell of an exciting and possibly a dangerous experience. Mom is horrified at the tale and tells the child to never, never do that again. Mom's unexpected response leaves an indelible impression and the child learns one of two things: Either never repeat the experience, or if you do, don't tell Mom!

A young mother was visiting the Sunday school class of her 6-year-old daughter. The lesson was on proper behavior in church. The teacher asked the children to name places where we should not run. Lots of hands were raised and the teacher called on the children one at a time. The children offered their answers: school, the library, grocery store— but church was not mentioned. The visiting mother proudly noticed that her daughter's hand was still waving in the air, undoubtedly armed with the answer sought by the teacher. Finally the teacher called on the daughter. With great enthusiasm the 6-year-old responded: "The liquor store—my dad said that I should never run in the liquor store because I'll knock down the bottles." The mother was momentarily stunned as liquor stores were held in disrepute by this church. The child had not yet developed a "public self," at least as far as the church was concerned.

Throughout life, human beings form ideas or concepts of how they want to portray themselves. These concepts may be conditioned by the family, social networks, social or religious organizations, or employment. People tend to be selective about what they disclose about themselves. Jourard suggests:

Our disclosures reflect, not our spontaneous feelings, thoughts and wishes, but rather pretended experience which will avoid punishment and win unearned approval. We say that we feel things we do not feel. We say that we did things we did not do. We say that we believe things we do not believe. (p. 11)

Jourard contends that this pattern of selective disclosure, or pseudo self-disclosure, leads to self-alienation where "the individual loses his soul, literally" (p. 11). People have a greater tendency for self-disclosure when the environment is permissive and nonjudgmental. In some circumstances people will reveal more of themselves. An experience that has occurred to a number of people is in long-distance travel— particularly by bus or plane. In these experiences, people are seated in close proximity to strangers over a period of time. It is not unusual for travelers to strike up a casual conversation where they share information about themselves. In some circumstances, the travelers begin to reveal information—rather personal attitudes and feelings about work, family, or life that they might not share with acquaintances. This self-disclosure occurs for several reasons: One or both of the travelers may have sensed that they were alike; the environment is nonthreatening; and even if one disapproved of what was heard, the travelers will likely never see each other again. Linda Austin, a psychiatrist at the Medical University of South Carolina, was interviewed by Julie Schmit (1993) in *USA Today*:

> If you reveal something about yourself to a stranger, so what? There are no consequences. Once you get off the plane, the relationship, which can become very deep very quick, is over. (p. 1B)

Effort is made to produce this permissive environment in focus groups. This is achieved through selection of participants, the nature of the questioning, and the establishment of focus group rules. The focus group is often composed of strangers or, on occasion, it will consist of people who are acquainted but have minimal contact with each other. The interviewer is not in a position of power or influence and, in fact, encourages comments of all types—both positive and negative. The interviewer is careful not to make judgments about the responses and to control body language that might communicate approval or disapproval. At the beginning of the discussion the interviewer purposefully sanctions and even encourages alternative explanations. For example: "There are no right or wrong answers, but rather differing points of view. Please share your point of view even if it differs from what others have said. We are just as interested in negative comments as positive comments, and at times the negative comments are the most helpful."

Another reason why the traveling partners readily disclose is that they perceive that they are alike in some ways. It may be that they have one or more characteristics in common, such as age, sex, occupation, marital status, or hold similar attitudes on a topic of discussion. Jourard (1964) found that individuals are selective in their self-disclosure and the decision to reveal is based on perceptions of the other person. In his studies of self-disclosure Jourard found that "subjects tended to disclose more about themselves to people who resembled them in various ways than to people who differ from them" (p. 15).

Focus groups are best conducted with participants who are similar to each other, and this homogeneity is reinforced in the introduction to the group discussion. The rule for selecting focus group participants is commonality, not diversity. Care must be exercised to be alert to subtle distinctions that are not apparent to the researcher, such as social status, educational level, occupational status, income, and the like. For example, one cannot assume that all clerical workers, all hospital workers, or all farmers consider themselves to be like each other. Within each category there are distinctions that may seem subtle to the researcher but are major differences to those who are in those situations. The danger is that people tend to be hesitant to share and will defer their opinions to someone else in the group who is perceived to be more knowledgeable, wealthy, or influential. For example, a college graduate (or heaven forbid, a Ph.D.) in a group of high school graduates, even if they have similar job responsibilities, can affect the extent of sharing. Farmers place considerable status on the number of acres they own. Regularly, farmers who own fewer acres will defer to a farmer with greater acreage. In part, this may be an unwarranted assumption that acreage, prosperity, education, or income equals knowledge and more valued opinions. In a focus group, the interviewer underscores the commonality of the group in the following manner: "We have invited people with similar experiences to share their perceptions and ideas on this topic. You were selected because you have certain things in common that are of particular interest to us."

Summary

As a society we have a predisposition to form groups and engage in collective interactions. This tendency may well be part of a common human experience that is not bounded by cultures or time. In spite of our millennia of experience and cumulative wisdom about groups, we still struggle along regularly confused about both the purpose and process of such interactions. Focus group interviews involve people and from outward appearances the technique resembles experiences that are familiar to all of us. Below this surface, however, there are a number of elements that are unique from other group experiences. The focus group interview is created to accomplish a specific purpose through a defined process. The purpose is to obtain information of a qualitative nature from a predetermined and limited number of people. Focus groups provide an environment in which disclosures are encouraged and nurtured, but it falls to the interviewer to bring focus to those disclosures through open-ended questions within a permissive environment. Chapter 2 provides a close-up look at this environment.

2

Focus Groups

Focus groups have evolved over the past few decades and have taken on a set of characteristics that are distinctive from other group experiences. Focus groups are useful in obtaining a particular kind of information—information that would be difficult, if not impossible, to obtain using other methodological procedures. This chapter begins with an overview of focus group characteristics and then provides examples of how decision makers have used focus group procedures. This is followed by a brief overview of qualitative and quantitative research procedures and a discussion of the advantages and disadvantages of focus groups.

Characteristics of Focus Groups

Focus group interviews typically have six characteristics or features. These characteristics relate to the ingredients of a focus group: (1) people, (2) assembled in a series of groups, (3) possess certain characteristics, and (4) provide data (5) of a qualitative nature (6) in a focused discussion. Other types of group processes used in human services (delphic, nominal, planning, therapeutic, sensitivity, advisory, etc.) may also have one or more of these features, but not in the same combination as those of focus group interviews.

Focus Groups Involve People

Focus groups are typically composed of 6 to 10 people, but the size can range from as few as 4 to as many as 12. The size is conditioned by two factors: It must be small enough for everyone to have opportunity to share insights and yet large enough to provide diversity of perceptions. When the group exceeds a dozen participants there is a tendency for the group to fragment. Participants want to talk but are unable to do so because there is just not a sufficient pause in the conversation. In these situations the only recourse is for participants to share by whispering to the people next to them. When this occurs it is clearly a signal that the group is too big. Small groups of 4 or 5 participants afford more opportunity to share ideas, but the restricted size also results in a smaller pool of total ideas. These smaller groups—sometimes called *mini-focus groups*—have a distinct advantage in logistics. Groups of 4 or 5 can be easily accommodated in restaurants, private homes, and other environments where space is at a premium.

Focus Groups Are Conducted in Series

The focus group interview is conducted in a series. Multiple groups with similar participants are needed to detect patterns and trends across groups. Solo focus groups are risky because occasionally moderators will encounter "cold" groups—groups in which participants are quiet and seemingly reluctant to participate. Furthermore, focus groups can be influenced by internal or external factors that may cause one of the groups to yield extraordinary results. For example, a dominant, demanding participant may unduly sway or inhibit other participants; a community emergency may divert attention away from the focus group; or an incendiary comment from a participant might provoke chaos. These features or others may not always be apparent to the researcher and the effect on the focus groups can be enormous. As a result, the prudent strategy is to plan focus groups in a series.

Participants Are Reasonably Homogeneous and Unfamiliar With Each Other

Focus groups are composed of people who are similar to each other. The nature of this homogeneity is determined by the purpose of the study and is a basis for recruitment. Participants are typically informed of these common factors at the beginning of the discussion. This homogeneity can be broadly or narrowly defined. For example, suppose an adult community education program wanted to know more about reaching people not now participating in their services. In this case, homogeneity is broadly defined as adults who live in the community who have not yet attended community education sessions. The group might vary by age, gender, occupation, and interest, but members have the commonality of being adults, residents, and nonusers. If, however, the community education programs are targeted for certain occupations, residents in defined geographic areas, or only during certain times, then the researcher would use a narrower definition of homogeneity in selecting participants. The issue essentially is this: Who do you want to hear from? The researcher should decide who the target audience is and invite people with those characteristics.

Focus groups have traditionally been composed of people who do not know each other—for years it was considered ideal if participants were complete strangers. More recently, however, researchers are questioning the necessity and practicality of this guideline, especially in community-based studies. In some communities it is virtually impossible to locate strangers. Caution should still be used when considering focus groups with close friends, family members or relatives, or work groups. People who regularly interact, either socially or at work, present special difficulties for the focus group discussion because they may be responding more on past experiences, events, or discussions than on the immediate topic of concern. Moreover, familiarity tends to inhibit disclosure. A related, yet equally important issue is the familiarity between the interviewer and the participants. When nonprofit organizations use focus groups they may wish to use staff persons or even volunteers to moderate the discussion. If the staff member or volunteer is readily identified with the organization or for that matter identified with any controversial issue in the community, the quality of the results could be jeopardized. For example, the top administrator of a statewide nonprofit institution was convinced that focus groups would provide valuable insights about the concerns of field staff. The administrator wanted to personally moderate these discussions with subordinates. The administrator was clearly in a hierarchical position of final decisions on salary, job responsibilities, and hiring and termination. In this situation, we encouraged the administrator to identify a neutral moderator outside of the organizational chain of command.

The concern about familiarity of participants is really an issue of analysis. The analyst is unable to isolate what influenced the participants. Were the findings related to the issue being discussed or could the comments have been influenced by past, present, or the possibility of future interaction with other group members?

Focus Groups Are a Data Collection Procedure

Focus groups produce data of interest to researchers. In this respect the purpose differs from other group interactions in which the goal is to reach consensus, provide recommendations, or make decisions among alternatives. Delphic processes and nominal groups differ from focus groups in that they attempt to identify consensus and agreeable solutions, an important objective but considerably different from the purpose of focus groups. Brainstorming techniques resemble the freedom and spontaneity of focus groups but once again differ in that brainstorming is often directed to solving particular problems. Brainstorming, nominal groups, and delphic processes are all used primarily with people who are experts or are knowledgeable in finding potential solutions. Focus groups, however, pay attention to the perceptions of the users and consumers of solutions, products, and services. Focus groups have a rather narrow purpose for which they work particularly well—that is to determine the perceptions, feelings, and manner of thinking of consumers regarding products, services, or opportunities. Focus groups are not intended to develop consensus, to arrive at an agreeable plan, or to make decisions about which course of action to take.

Focus Groups Make Use of Qualitative Data

Focus groups produce qualitative data that provide insights into the attitudes, perceptions, and opinions of participants. These results are solicited through open-ended questions and a procedure in which respondents are able to choose the manner in which they respond and also from observations of those respondents in a group discussion. The focus group presents a more natural environment than that of an individual interview because participants are influencing and influenced by others—just as they are in real life. The researcher serves several functions in the focus group: moderating, listening, observing, and eventually analyzing, using an inductive process. The inductive researcher derives understanding based on the discussion as opposed to testing or confirming a preconceived hypothesis or theory.

Focus Groups Have a Focused Discussion

The topics of discussion in a focus group are carefully predetermined and sequenced, based on an analysis of the situation. This analysis includes an in-depth study of the event, experience, or topic in order to describe the context of the experience and the ingredients or components of the experience. The questions are placed in an environment that is understandable and logical to the participant. The moderator uses predetermined, open-ended questions. These questions appear to be spontaneous but are carefully developed after considerable reflection. The questions—called the *questioning route* or *interview guide*—are arranged in a natural, logical sequence. One of the unique elements of focus groups is that there is no pressure by the moderator to have the group reach consensus. Instead, attention is placed on understanding the thought processes used by participants as they consider the issues of discussion.

The term *focus groups* is in such vogue that it is frequently used to apply to any group discussion experience. These group experiences may contain some or most of the characteristics of focus groups but be deficient in other features. Recently, a large metropolitan school district conducted a series of what were called "focus groups" in order to develop a strategic plan. The "focus groups" consisted of a prominent local resident standing in front of open meetings where the entire community was invited to attend. In fact, the meetings might have been better called a community forum, a discussion, or possibly a hearing. In spite of the confusion over the focus group label, there is value in careful and selective modification of focus group procedures. Modification of the focus group may even be preferred for some applications. Chapter 12 provides an overview of some modifications of the focus group interview, including repeated focus groups, multiple moderators, and focus groups on the telephone. When considering these and other modifications, it is of value to be aware of the traditions and the rationale that have been associated with focus group interviews. When describing the strengths of focus groups, Gerald Linda (1982) relates:

> I submit to you that there is no unanimity of goals or practice in these groups. Nor is there a uniform similarity in educational background among the moderators of these groups. The reason is that the focus group is to qualitative

research what analysis of variance is to quantitative research. The technique is robust, hardy, and can be twisted a bit and still yield useful and significant results. (p. 98)

The Uses of Focus Groups

Nonprofit organizations regularly perform services or conduct programs that touch the lives of a number of people. At times, decision makers in an organization seek to get a reading of how these activities are perceived by a variety of parties: staff, volunteers, program users, potential program users, and so on. Focus groups can be used to provide information to decision makers about these opportunities at three different points in time: before, during, or after the program or service provided.

Focus Groups Before a Program Begins

Focus groups can be used before an experience such as in planning (including strategic planning), needs assessment, assets analysis, program design, or market research. Each of these tasks typically draws on information from several sources, including focus groups with both current and potential clientele. Here are examples of how focus groups have been used at the beginning of a program or experience.

EXAMPLE 1: MARKET RESEARCH ON KIDS

Nickelodeon, the cable TV network for kids, does extensive market research with focus groups being a primary means of gathering information. It is likely that Nickelodeon does more focus groups with young people than any other organization with around 200 to 250 groups per year, many of which are at Universal Studios Florida in Orlando. Kids are recruited from tour groups and are offered a T-shirt if they join the focus group discussion. From these focus groups with pre-teens the researchers are discovering what kids like to watch on TV and why. Based on Nickelodeon's research, one of the key factors is providing escape and refuge. A number of pre-teens are not necessarily excited about becoming teens. Teens, according to the pre-teens, have lots of problems with drugs, alcohol, independence, violence, and sex. The research must pay off, because Nickelodeon has become the largest producer of original children's programming (Winski, 1992, pp. S1, S22).

EXAMPLE 2: NEEDS ASSESSMENT

The Minnesota State Board of Vocational Technical Education had been concerned about the declining enrollment in agricultural programs at the eight area vocational technical institutes. In an effort to assess needs, a mail-out questionnaire was sent to hundreds of farmers and agri-business personnel. Instructors at the area institutes then used this assessment to develop new courses based on expressed needs. Even though the respondents indicated that they would attend courses, the actual attendance was extremely low. What went wrong? In the next year of the study, Professor Roland Peterson and his colleagues at the University of Minnesota instituted a series of focus groups to discover what would influence attendance. The focus groups revealed important information about potential clientele. Promotional flyers of courses were informative but personal invitations were much more effective in promoting attendance. Knowledgeable and practical instructors plus relevant class experiences attracted students. Despite the depressed farm economy, farmers did not perceive course tuition as a deterrence to enrollment. When staff at the technical institutes implemented the recommendations from focus group interviews, the results were impressive. The new procedures resulted in a tenfold enrollment boost of over 1,000 new farmers (Peterson & Migler, 1987).

EXAMPLE 3: PROVIDING EARLY WARNING INDICATORS

The report of June 1990 on crack babies by the Office of Inspector General of Health and Human Services provided an early indication of the scope and severity of the problem with crack-affected children. The study used focus groups to gain insights into how such children are affecting the child welfare system. The focus groups, held with professionals who were among the first to have experience with these babies, had sobering messages. The problem was more severe than many had anticipated and the reports call for increased efforts at all levels of government (Office of Inspector General, 1990).

EXAMPLE 4: CLOSING THE GAP BETWEEN PROFESSIONALS AND THE PUBLIC

Economic professionals have a different understanding of the American economy than does the general public. Recently, the gap between the experts and the public was documented by the American Council on

Education. The findings, based in part on more than a dozen focus groups, found discrepancies between how experts and the general public interpreted economic signs. Although productivity and growth were seen by experts as the hallmark of a healthy economy, the public felt that a healthy economy was one in which everyone has a job. The experts wanted policies that increased productivity but the public wanted jobs. What are seen as major concerns to the public (buying American, shipping jobs abroad, and excessive foreign investments) are seen by experts as symptoms and side effects of a less competitive society. As a result, the sponsors of the study launched an awareness and educational campaign targeted to the general public (Business and Higher Education Report, 1991).

EXAMPLE 5: LAYING THE FOUNDATION FOR
A SOCIAL MARKETING CAMPAIGN

According to Judith Brown and her colleagues, nutrition intervention programs in the United States have tended to use a "top-down" approach, in which health professionals identify the problem and determine the solution. In contrast, they recommend a more workable "bottom-up" approach that builds on practical behavior strategies that are acceptable to, and preferred by, the target audience. Brown and her colleagues contend that the needs, wants, and preferences of the target audience are critical factors in the design of the program. Focus groups have been instrumental in these social marketing campaigns in several ways. Initial focus groups help the researchers get the "lay of the land" and improve their general understanding of the target audience. This early information from focus groups is used by designers to develop the intervention strategy that incorporates factors deemed important or desirable by the target audience. A second wave of focus groups is often held to "pilot-test" one or more intervention strategies prior to the financial decision to invest in best choice (Brown, 1992).

EXAMPLE 6: DISCOVERING WHAT CUSTOMERS
CONSIDER WHEN DECIDING

Focus groups have provided beneficial insights on proposed housing development projects. A Massachusetts developer listened to critiques of his planned project and found features that were liked and disliked by potential customers. Early identification of the disappointing features allowed the developer to modify the plans to avoid the potentially negative features. In other situations, the focus groups uncover positive features that were not initially identified by the builders. One of the developers commented:

The focus groups told us that was the best part of the design [the layout with buildings clusters in groups with mini-courtyards], yet we had never emphasized it in our advertising. Now we do. (Hanafin, 1989, p. 45)

EXAMPLE 7: IDENTIFYING TRENDS

Focus groups can be helpful in spotting trends—especially emerging trends that may take 3 to 4 years to show up in quantitative studies. *Marketing News* staff writer Cyndee Miller (1991) interviewed Judith Langer on the forecasting capability of focus groups. Langer relates:

People will tell you what's going on before it's in a survey or shows up in a set of numbers. Focus group participants in the early '80s, for example, made a lot of jokes about parents not being able to get their grown up kids out of the house, and that turned out to be a major trend of the last decade. (p. 2)

Focus Groups During a Program

Focus groups can be conducted during a program or experience such as in customer surveys, formative evaluations, or recruiting new clientele for existing programs. Consider these examples of how others have used focus groups while a program or activity was underway.

EXAMPLE 8: UNDERSTANDING THE STIGMA OF MENTAL ILLNESS

Focus groups have been useful in helping to understand the public perception of mental illness. A county department of mental health used focus group research to plan a program to reduce the stigma of mental illness. In addition, the researchers sought to find out the conditions by which local residents would approve of a local facility to treat mentally ill patients. The study revealed that interpersonal channels of communication were more effective in addressing the stigma than were the more formal, mass media approaches. As a result, small neighborhood meetings in area churches, women associations, and civic centers were held and led by individuals who have had personal experiences with mentally ill patients (Grunig, 1990).

EXAMPLE 9: RECRUITING NEW MEMBERS

In an effort to reach the "unchurched," a metropolitan church conducted focus groups with people not now attending religious services. Insights from the focus groups prompted the church leaders to drop the denominational name from the church title. Baby boomers, a target audience for the church, lacked the institutional loyalty and instead were swayed more by the quality of church programs. As a result of the focus group research, the church made changes in its name and marketing strategy to attract new participants. In this situation the strategy proved to be very successful. Later reports indicated that the changes were so successful that the church had to position parking attendants on the church roof with walkie-talkies to direct the Sunday morning traffic (Anderson, 1986).

EXAMPLE 10: ASSESSING CUSTOMER RELATIONS

Focus groups have been helpful to a California hospital in improving customer relations. The billing process was a source of frustration to both the hospital and its customers. Bills that weren't understood tended to be unpaid. The billing process was designed with the hospital in mind and was not necessarily intended to be easily read and understood. As a result of these findings, the hospital was able to modify the billing process and train hospital staff to better respond to patient concerns (Bernstein, Harris, & Meloy, 1989).

Focus Groups After a Program Ends

Focus groups can be helpful after a program or experience has been conducted. This might occur in assessments of programs, summative evaluations, or program postmortems to discover what went wrong. Here are examples of such uses.

EXAMPLE 11: SUMMATIVE EVALUATION OF A FUND-RAISING DRIVE

Syracuse University recently launched a $100 million fund drive. The key aspect of the drive was a film depicting science and research efforts. The film was shown in over two dozen focus groups of alumni with surprising results to university officials. Alumni simply did not like the film and instead were more attracted to supporting undergraduate humanistic education (Bennett, 1986).

EXAMPLE 12: FOLLOW-UP TO A MAIL-OUT SURVEY

University researchers used focus groups as a follow up to a mail-out survey of farmers in northwestern Minnesota. In the first phase of the study, over 400 randomly selected farmers participated in a mail-out survey in an attempt to identify major problems of commercial farmers. Once problems were identified, 27 farmers were invited to share interpretations of the data in three focus group discussions. The focus groups provided rich insights relating to marketing, farm decision making, and stress. The farmers in the discussions were sophisticated learners who had clear notions of what they wanted to learn. Interaction with other farmers with similar backgrounds was highly valued in educational programs, and farmers were not tolerant of instructors who had limited background in the subject area (Mueller & Anderson, 1985).

EXAMPLE 13: UNDERSTANDING AN ORGANIZATION'S IMAGE

The Minnesota Zoo had been in operation for nearly a decade and zoo officials were concerned about the image they had been conveying to the public. A series of focus groups revealed that entertainment was the most powerful incentive for attendance, as contrasted to education and economic value. In addition, the focus groups identified areas needing improvement such as food service and viewing distance from animals (Cook, 1986).

EXAMPLE 14: ASSESSMENT OF QUALITY

Focus group interviews can be beneficial in studies of quality. The term *quality* can be seen in a number of ways and organizations can make a critical mistake if they assume they know the specifications of quality. One of the appealing tenets in the TQM (Total Quality Management) movement is placing attention on how the customers define quality. Although the perceptions of professionals who deliver the services are important, it is the customer, client, or user who is the ultimate recipient. Focus groups have proven beneficial in gaining a better understanding of the customer.

Focus groups proved to be important in the landmark study by Valarie Zeithaml, A. Parasuraman, and Leonard Berry (1990). In their effort to measure service quality, they began with focus groups and later incorporated the concepts into closed-ended surveys. One of the contributions of focus groups was that

[they] unambiguously supported the notion that the key to ensuring good service quality is meeting or exceeding what customers expect from the service. (p. 18)

EXAMPLE 15: FEEDBACK TO ADMINISTRATORS

Focus groups with pharmacy students have been found to be a helpful feedback tool for university administrators in the School of Pharmacy at the University of North Carolina. They held focus groups to uncover the nature and extent of problems encountered by students. Diamond and Gagnon (1985) concluded that "focus group techniques are both useful and valid for assessing student problems within undergraduate pharmacy curriculum" (p. 54).

Qualitative and Quantitative Research Procedures

Research is often categorized as *qualitative* or *quantitative*. The former concentrates on words and observations to express reality and attempts to describe people in natural situations. In contrast, the quantitative approach grows out of a strong academic tradition that places considerable trust in numbers that represent opinions or concepts. I have discovered through experience that information users regularly have a limited understanding of quantitative procedures and vague perceptions of qualitative techniques. As a result, I have found it helpful to provide these individuals with a brief overview of each procedure by the use of an example.

Here is an example that highlights the use of qualitative and quantitative methods. The first approach was quantitative. The purpose of the study was to determine whether or not volunteers were satisfied with their position. All 150 volunteers were invited to complete a short questionnaire containing one key question: How satisfied are you with your volunteer position?

[ ] 5. Very Satisfied
[ ] 4. Satisfied
[ ] 3. Neither Satisfied nor Dissatisfied
[ ] 2. Dissatisfied
[ ] 1. Very Dissatisfied

The analysis revealed an average score of 4.1, which would indicate that overall the workers were satisfied. When the results were separated by work responsibilities, it was discovered that those who had served as a volunteer for over 3 years had a lower level of satisfaction. The experienced volunteers had an average score of 1.7, which indicated a cause for concern. The survey was helpful because it provided a composite score for all volunteers and highlighted a specific group that needed greater attention.

The second approach was qualitative. The qualitative approach was to ask participants how they felt about their volunteer position. They then used their own words as opposed to the response categories used in the quantitative questionnaire. A qualitative survey involving all volunteers would take too much time and resources, so instead 48 people were randomly selected to participate in four focus group interviews. The theme of the focus group was volunteering, and people were invited to share their views and reasons for satisfaction or dissatisfaction. Volunteers expressed their opinions in various ways, but a theme emerged. The critical factor was access to printed materials used by volunteers in their teaching. In the past year the organization decided to save money by cutting the printing budget and restricted the amount of printed materials available to these volunteers. Those who were used to having easy access to printed materials now found themselves with fewer educational tools. As a result the experienced volunteers were dissatisfied.

In the qualitative example there were no percentages, but the researcher obtained an explanation of why there was dissatisfaction. The percentage of respondents indicating satisfaction versus dissatisfaction was helpful information, but in this example the qualitative results provided decision makers with the critical information for correcting the problem. Typically, qualitative research will provide in-depth information into fewer cases whereas quantitative procedures will allow for more breadth of information across a larger number of cases.

In some situations, quantitative data can be carefully obtained using well-designed questionnaires and can incorporate elaborate analysis but still be dead wrong. In his classic study in 1934, Richard LaPiere surveyed the attitudes of hotel owners in providing lodging for Chinese travelers in the United States. Overwhelmingly, the innkeepers indicated that they would not provide lodging; however, in actual practice, 54 of the 55 hotels actually had provided lodging to Chinese travelers in the previous year. In this situation, the quantitative study of attitudes provided a measurement of what the innkeeper thought he would do, but in fact, the qualitative observations of the researcher proved to be far more accurate indicators of actual behavior.

Quantitative measurements are quantitatively accurate; qualitative evaluations are always subject to the errors of human judgment. Yet it would seem far more worthwhile to make a shrewd guess regarding that which is essential than to accurately measure that which is likely to prove quite irrelevant. (LaPiere, 1934, p. 237)

Qualitative data are typically welcomed by decision makers because the results are presented in a concrete and understandable manner. Unfortunately, quantitative data have a complexity that is met with suspicion. Alkin, Daillak, and White (1979) contend that "it is a simple fact that many people are uncomfortable in dealing with quantitative data" (p. 237). Carol Weiss (1976, p. 226) suggests that there is good reason for the discomfort. Social scientists have aided and abetted the communication obstacles with methodological, technical, and statistical "jargon that litters their prose." As a result, Weiss relates, the decision maker "has to either accept or reject the researcher's interpretation of the data on faith." It may well be that discomfort with and lack of faith in quantitative data explain why decision makers find qualitative data to be more useful than other research (Van de Vall, Bolas, & Kang, 1976).

Increasingly, researchers are recognizing the benefits of combining qualitative and quantitative procedures, resulting in greater methodological mixes that strengthen the research design. Focus groups can be used in four different ways in relation to quantitative methods.

First, focus groups can precede quantitative procedures. When used in this way, the focus group interview can help the researcher learn the vocabulary and discover the thinking pattern of the target audience. In addition, focus groups can provide clues as to special problems that might develop in the quantitative phase. For example, the questionnaire might have an illogical sequence of questions that confuses respondents, omits important response choices, or simply fails to ask critical questions. Qualitative procedures such as focus groups or individual interviews enable the researcher to get in tune with the respondent and discover how that person sees reality. These insights can then be used to develop more efficient follow-up quantitative procedures such as telephone or mail-out surveys. The quantitative studies then enable the researcher to make inferences about the larger population.

Second, focus groups can be used at the same time as quantitative procedures. At times the researcher may wish to use triangulation: two or more different research methods to address the same issue to confirm findings and to obtain both breadth and depth of information.

Third, focus groups can follow quantitative procedures. Questionnaires typically yield a sizable amount of data, and focused interviews can provide insights about the meaning and interpretation of the results. In addition, the follow-up focus groups can suggest action strategies for problems addressed in the questionnaire. Focus groups have been particularly helpful when used after quantitative needs-assessment surveys. Needs assessment surveys can be vexing to researchers because quantitative procedures alone are often incomplete. Needs assessment surveys often only provide a portion of the desired information and omit critical factors. Furthermore, needs-assessment surveys tend to identify concerns that already have achieved some visibility within the community as opposed to the less visible concerns that lie below the surface. Some of these visible needs may have already been addressed by existing organizations or institutions, and by the time the survey is completed, the needs may have already been met.

Fourth, focus groups can be used alone, independent of other procedures. They are helpful when insights, perceptions, and explanations are more important than actual numbers.

Focus groups can be used before a quantitative study, during a quantitative study, after a quantitative study, or independent of other methodological procedures. The decision to use a methodological mix is often made in the planning stages at the beginning of the study. In some situations, however, the researcher may consider incorporating a quantitative study after conducting focus group interviews, especially in situations in which focus groups have revealed unexpected results that need further confirmation.

The Validity of Focus Group Results

The nub of qualitative research—and its claim to validity—lies in the intense involvement between researcher and subject. Because the moderator can challenge and probe for the most truthful responses, supporters claim, qualitative research can yield a more in-depth analysis than that produced by formal quantitative methods. (Mariampolski, 1984, p. 21)

Are focus group results valid? How much confidence can one have in focus group results? Researchers frequently encounter questions such as these from lay groups or from decision makers. I have found through experience, painful at times, that these questions can present special problems for researchers. Researchers typically have spent some time thinking about this issue and are tempted to respond using research jargon and concepts that are confusing to lay audiences. I have found it helpful to explain *validity* in the following manner: *Focus groups are valid if they are used carefully for a problem that is suitable for focus group inquiry.* If the researcher deviates from the established procedures of focus group interviews addressed earlier in this chapter, the issue of validity should be raised. Also, if the problem does not lend itself to focus groups, then focus groups are an invalid procedure. In short, focus groups are very much like other social science measurement procedures in which validity depends not only on the procedures used but also on context.

Validity is the degree to which the procedure really measures what it proposes to measure. For example, if you conducted focus groups to gain perceptions on a potential program, did the focus group procedure really provide perceptions on this program or were the results artificially developed by the interactions of group participants?

The cynic can argue that nothing is valid. Measurements or assessments of the human condition can be distorted intentionally or unintentionally. People are not always truthful, and sometimes they give answers that seem best for the situation. Other times people hold back important information because of apprehensions or social pressure. Experts who work with small groups testify about the unpredictable nature of groups, and that group leaders or moderators can skillfully or unwittingly lead groups into decisions or consensus.

Others have an optimistic faith in measurement procedures and assume that if a procedure has been developed by leading experts then it must be valid. Social scientists typically go to considerable effort to ensure that they are really measuring what they propose to measure. They will pilot test the procedures under varying conditions, develop a protocol to administer the test, and at times build in questions that check on the truthfulness of the respondent.

I recommend that decision makers consider the middle ground—have some faith in all procedures but also retain skepticism. Indeed, all data should be regarded with a healthy skepticism whether it is obtained from official documents, personal interviews, questionnaires, standard-ized tests, opinion polls, or focused interviews.

Validity can be assessed in several ways. The most basic level is *face validity*: Do the results look valid? Another type of validity is the degree to which the results are confirmed by future behaviors, experiences, or events: *predictive* or *convergent validity*.

Typically, focus groups have high face validity, which is due in large part to the believability of comments from participants. People open up in focus groups and share insights that may not be available from individual interviews, questionnaires, or other data sources. Fred Reynolds and Deborah Johnson (1978) reported on a comparison of focus group discussions with a large scale mail-out survey. The two studies were both nationwide in scope—a mail survey of 2,000 females with a 90% response rate compared to a series of 20 focus groups in 10 cities. When these two market research studies were compared, there was a 97% level of agreement, and in the area of discrepancy the focus group results proved to have greater predictive validity when compared to later sales data.

The decision maker, when confronted with focus group results, may find explanations that seem infinitely reasonable, explanations that have come directly from the clients and not from secondhand summaries. If anything, the face validity of focus groups may be too high. Focus group results seem so believable that decision makers may have the tendency to rush out and implement the resulting recommendations without adequate skepticism.

Generalizing Focus Group Results

Researchers have tended to describe focus group results as explor-atory, illuminating, and not suitable for projection to a population. Some researchers have even included a disclaimer to that effect in the focus group report, in part to temper the decision maker's urge to rush off and implement the findings. The warnings are well intended, but often do more to confuse the decision maker regarding the degree of trust to place in focus group results. Consider the following conversation:

A Conversation With a Decision Maker

Decision Maker Hold it a minute, professor. I like what I hear about focus groups but there's something I just don't understand. You've told me that focus groups will give me information that is exploratory, illuminating, and enlightening. I'm the person that makes the decisions. I need to know if focus group results are good enough for me to use for making decisions. I mean, those people with the numbers tell me about some kind of margin of error, which tells me something about how confident I can be that their numbers are right. You don't give me a margin of error. You tell me I can't project to the whole group—I think you call it "infer to the population"—with this focus group stuff. Well if your focus group stuff doesn't represent the population, who does it represent and why should I use it?

Professor In all research we make assumptions. We do it when we use numbers and we also do it with focus group interviews. When we do quantitative research in social sciences—things like mail-out surveys—we make a number of assumptions and sometimes the researchers do not clearly label these as assumptions. For example, sometimes we assume that the person who was sent the survey really did in fact fill it out. Sometimes these surveys are filled out by a co-worker or another member of the family. We regularly make assumptions about the nature of the questions we ask. We assume that the respondent really understands the question, interprets the questions in the same way that the researcher does, and then provides us with an honest answer. The researcher also assumes that he or she knows enough about the reality of the respondent to construct meaningful questions. Then, depending on the type of analysis, we make assumptions about the nature of the numbers (nominal, ordinal, interval, ratio), and about those not responding—regarding the degree of similarity to those who did respond. In some statistical procedures we assume that the responses are normally distributed or that variables are related in linear manner as well as other things about the population. So you see, lots of things can influence the degree of confidence we have in the data.

Decision Maker All right professor, what about the assumptions in focus group interviewing?

Professor Well, the same is true of focus group interviews. Only here the assumptions are a bit more obvious and apparent. We've selected a small number of people—often less than 50 people and sometimes as few as 15 or 20 out of a much larger population. One of the greatest advantages of focus groups—or qualitative methods in general—is that they give us information in depth. The respondent can provide additional background information about the circumstances of the answer. Furthermore, the researcher is in a better position to know if the respondent really understood the questions by examining the answers to follow-up questions. Although you gain in depth from focus group interviews, you also lose in breadth of information when compared to most quantitative procedures. There is a risk in using focus group data to generalize to a population because the sample is not necessarily intended to be reflective of the entire population. But the same is true of using quantitative data to generalize. In a perfect survey our statistics would allow us to generalize, but we might have asked foolish questions to begin with; when you make inferences on bad data, you don't improve the quality of your decision.

Decision Maker Well, can I generalize or not with focus group results?

Professor My suggestion is to make cautious generalizations. If you're making really big decisions where the consequences of error are major, then by all means use a multiple set of methods. If the different methodological procedures lead you to the same conclusions, then you can move with greater confidence. At times you might have more confidence in a small qualitative sample of a carefully executed research study than with large quantitative samples with complex statistical procedures. Your goal in focus group research is to understand reality. Because of the inductive nature of focus group research, greater attention is directed to discovering the manner and way in which respondents perceived the problem. As a result, the researcher has a clearer fix on how the issue is understood by respondents. If the focus group research has been carefully conducted and appropriately analyzed, then the user should be able to make generalizations to other respondents who possess similar characteristics.

Decision Maker OK, now who can I generalize about?

Professor That's exactly the right question. When we speak of generalizing we need to consider the nature of that generalization. Who are you talking about? You don't select a sample of seniors citizens and then generalize to people of all ages. Likewise, you don't select a sample of program users and generalize to nonusers. Now, it could be true that in both of these areas the groups are similar, but you just don't know that because you've not included other groups in your sampling strategy.

Decision Maker Thanks, now tell me more about focus groups.

Advantages of Focus Group Interviews

The focus group interview offers several advantages. First, it is a socially oriented research procedure. People are social creatures who interact with others. They are influenced by the comments of others and make decisions after listening to the advice and counsel of people around them. Focus groups place people in natural, real-life situations as opposed to the controlled experimental situations typical of quantitative studies. Also, the one-to-one interviews are not able to capture the dynamic nature of this group interaction. Inhibitions often are relaxed in group situations, and the more natural environment prompts increased candor by respondents. Morgan and Spanish (1984) elaborate:

In essence, the strengths of focus groups come from a compromise between the strengths found in other qualitative methods. Like participant observation, they allow access to a process that qualitative researchers are often centrally interested in: interaction. Like in-depth interviewing, they allow access to the content that we are often interested in: the attitudes and experiences of our informants. As a compromise, focus groups are neither as strong as participant observation on the naturalistic observation of interaction, nor as strong as interviewing on the direct probing of informant knowledge, but they do a better job of combining these two goals than either of the other two techniques. We believe this is a useful combination, and one which, for some types of research questions, may represent the best of both worlds. (p. 260)

The second advantage of focus group discussions is that the format allows the moderator to probe. This flexibility to explore unanticipated issues is not possible within the more structured questioning sequences typical of mail-out surveys.

A third advantage is that focus group discussions have high face validity, as discussed earlier. The technique is easily understood and the results seem believable to those using the information. Results are not presented in complicated statistical charts but rather in lay terminology embellished with quotations from group participants.

A fourth advantage is that focus group discussions can be relatively low cost. The key word in the previous sentence is *relatively*. A series of focus groups costing $15,000 hardly seems cheap to the nonprofit agency. However, this study may be cheap when compared to a $30,000 mail-out study. Furthermore, nonprofit agencies can often tap internal resources and volunteers to substantially reduce the cost. Alan Andreason (1983) recommends focus groups as a cost-conscious form of market research that does not require "big bucks":

> Another low-cost approach is the commissioning of focus group interviews of 8 to 12 members of the target audience at a time. Although the results are not strictly projectable to the larger market because the groups are not randomly selected, these results do cut the cost of interviewing by a quarter or a half. Interviewers can sometimes develop richer data in the relaxed, chatty format of the focus group. (p. 75)

A fifth advantage is that focus groups can provide speedy results. In emergency situations skilled moderators have been able to conduct three to four discussions, analyze the results, and prepare a report in less than a week. When compared to other means of obtaining information about behaviors and attitudes, the focus group method has a considerable advantage.

A sixth advantage is that focus groups enable the researcher to increase the sample size of qualitative studies. Qualitative studies typically have limited sample sizes because of the time and cost constraints of individual interviewing. Focus groups enable the researcher to increase the sample size without dramatic increases in the time required of the interviewer.

Limitations of Focus Group Interviews

All techniques for gathering information have limitations, and focus group interviews are no exception. It is important to be aware of these limitations in deciding whether to use this technique. Among the limitations are the following:

First, the researcher has less control in the group interview as compared to the individual interview. The focus group interview allows the participants to influence and interact with each other, and, as a result, group members are able to influence the course of the discussion. This sharing of group control results in some inefficiencies such as detours in the discussion, and the raising of irrelevant issues, thus requiring the interviewer to keep the discussion focused.

Second, data are more difficult to analyze. Group interaction provides a social environment, and comments must be interpreted within that context. Care is needed to avoid lifting comments out of context and out of sequence or coming to premature conclusions. Occasionally participants will modify or even reverse their positions after interacting with others.

Third, the technique requires carefully trained interviewers. At times, an untrained moderator can achieve remarkable results, but it is far better to influence the odds by using skilled interviewers. The open-ended questioning, the use of techniques such as pauses and probes, and knowing when and how to move into new topic areas require a degree of expertise typically not possessed by untrained interviewers.

Fourth, groups can vary considerably. Each focus group tends to have unique characteristics. One group can be lethargic, boring, and dull; the next selected in an identical manner might be exciting, energetic, and invigorating. Because of the differences in groups, it is recommended to include enough groups to balance the idiosyncrasies of individual sessions.

Fifth, groups are difficult to assemble. The focus group requires that people take time to come to a designated place at a prescribed time to share their perceptions with others.

Sixth, the discussion must be conducted in an environment conducive to conversation. These factors often present logistical problems and may require participant incentives to participate. By contrast, an individual interview can be held in a location and at a time most convenient to the interviewee.

Summary

Focus groups are special creatures in the kingdom of groups. In terms of appearances, focus groups look very much like other kinds of group experiences. On closer inspection, however, focus groups have a distinctive cluster of characteristics:

1. Focus groups involve homogeneous people in a social interaction in a series of discussions.
2. The purpose of focus groups is to collect qualitative data from a focused discussion.
3. Focus groups are a qualitative approach to gathering information.

Focus groups have been found useful prior to, during, and after programs, events, or experiences. They have been helpful in assessing needs, developing plans, recruiting new clientele, finding out customer decision processes, testing new programs and ideas, improving existing programs, and generating information for constructing questionnaires.

Focus groups are valid if they are used carefully for a problem that is suitable for focus group inquiry.

Focus groups offer several advantages, including these: The technique is a socially oriented research method capturing real-life data in a social environment, possessing flexibility, high face validity, relatively low cost, potentially speedy results, and a capacity to increase the size of a qualitative study.

Focus groups have limitations that affect the quality of the results. Limitations include these: Focus groups afford the researcher less control than individual interviews, produce data that are difficult to analyze, require special skills of moderators, result in troublesome differences among groups, are based on groups that may be difficult to assemble, and must be in a conducive environment.

The kingdom of groups has many creatures and some of them look very much alike. The focus group is one of those experiences that resembles other group situations we may have experienced. In some respects that is exactly what the focus group intends to do, to achieve a naturalness in which people feel free to talk and share insights and observations. The way to identify the focus group is to examine the purpose and the process of the group experience, as reviewed in Chapter 1, and then consider the degree of fit with the characteristics included in this chapter.

PART II

The Process of Conducting Focus Groups

The process of conducting a focus group study consists of three phases: planning the study, conducting the interviews, and analyzing and reporting. Within each of these phases there are steps that require consideration and action.

The planning phase is critical for successful focus group interviews. In this phase, the researcher gives consideration to the purpose of the study as well as the users of the information. The researcher then develops a plan that will guide the remainder of the research process. This planning phase begins in Chapter 3 and is continued in Chapter 4 as the researcher develops the questions and in Chapter 5 as the focus group participants are selected.

The conducting phase consists of moderating the focus groups (Chapter 6).

The analysis/reporting phase is the final aspect of the focus group process. The data are analyzed (Chapters 7 and 8) and the results are reported (Chapter 9).

3

Planning the Focus Group

Once upon a time there was an adventurous little field mouse who lived in a large forest. The field mouse had rarely wandered far from home, but on one sunny summer day the urges for fame and fortune were too great to resist. Besides, he thought, "I need to see the world." In spite of warnings from mama and papa, the little field mouse took the coins from his piggy bank, put them in his knapsack, and set off to seek fame and fortune. After a short while the field mouse met an eagle.

"Where are you going?" asked the eagle.

"I'm off to seek fame and fortune," said the field mouse.

"Well," said the eagle, "for two coins I'll sell you this feather that will speed you through the forest."

"Great," said the field mouse as he gave the coins to the eagle.

Soon the field mouse came across a squirrel.

"Where ya headed?" inquired the squirrel.

"I plan to see the world and make my fortune," replied the little field mouse.

"Well, in that case you'll want to get there as quickly as possible. I have these special acorns that will give you extra energy and help you get there faster. Ya got any coins?" asked the squirrel.

"Sure," said the little field mouse, and he swapped two coins for two acorns and hurried on his way, until he was stopped by a wolf.

"You seem to be in a big rush," said the wolf. "Where ya goin'?"

"I'm off to seek my fortune and I'm goin' as fast as I can," replied the field mouse.

"There's a shortcut that will get you there immediately," said the wolf with a toothy grin. "Just go right through that hole over there," and the little field mouse dashed into the wolf's den, never to be seen again.

The moral of this tale is that if you don't know where you're headed, you're likely to end up somewhere else—and it could cost you more than a few coins.

Planning seems so simple yet it can be the most complex part of the focus group process. We often speak in admiration of the planning process and yet our actual behavior suggests less enthusiastic adherence to the practice of planning. Have you ever met anyone who was really against planning? Likely not. You might as well be against motherhood and apple pie! In a similar vein, we are skeptical of people who are overly enthusiastic about planning.

Successful planning requires that we commit our thoughts to paper and invite others to provide corrective feedback, it forces us to go beyond our individual experiences and seek the insight of colleagues. Successful planning keeps promises reasonable, time lines efficient, and budgets balanced. The planning stage involves consideration of the purpose, users, and target audience and matching all of these to the available resources in a written plan.

Think of the plan as a small investment in time and energy that is intended to prevent costly mistakes. The plan keeps the study on target and enables the researcher to arrive at the intended destination within time and budget guidelines.

Determine the Purpose

Planning begins by reflecting on the purpose of the study and is followed by organizing those thoughts in a logical, sequential manner. At times the need for the study might originate from someone relatively unfamiliar with focus group interviews. For example, a director of an educational organization might wish to reach new clientele; a curriculum coordinator might want to test out new programs; or a coordinator of county human services may want to discover perceptions of the organization. When the idea of the study is handed down to a research unit in a bureaucratic organization there is often need for additional clarity and precision on the nature of the problem and what information is being requested. Failure to clarify the problem can result in a sizable investment of time and resources that misses the mark. To avoid this wasted time, the researcher should begin by writing down as precisely as possible a description of the problem at hand and the purposes of the study. This step is of considerable value both to beginning researchers and to experts. This background information should include a discussion of the following questions:

- Why such a study should be conducted?
- What kinds of information will be produced?
- What types of information are of particular importance?
- How will this information be used?
- Who wants the information?

It is beneficial to respond to these questions in writing in order to share the ideas with others and receive feedback from the expected users of the study. The first goal is to achieve agreement on the nature of the problem and the types of information needed to address the problem. Organizational politics, incomplete disclosure, and hidden agendas are among the obstacles encountered in achieving agreement, therefore, open and written communication by the researcher is often essential for further progress.

Determine the Research Procedures, or "Should I Do Focus Groups?"

Research procedures are supposed to be identified in a systematic and careful manner after consideration of alternatives, intended audiences, and available resources. Sometimes the impression is given that researcher preferences should be set aside and the decision made without regard of researcher interests or capabilities. But human preferences and experiences should be acknowledged and have a role in the decision of research methodology. The carpenter selects tools that are appropriate to the task at hand, and so too the researcher selects research methods that fit the specifications of the problem. To carry the analogy a step farther, the carpenter—operating under the instructions of a designer or architect—may have differing levels of skills and familiarity with various tools. Some tasks can be performed by one of several different tools and the carpenter makes the decision based on several factors: availability, past experience, expertise, and so on.

Although this careful process is our goal, in actual practice research procedures are often identified using different protocol. We often think about it in questions such as these:

- What kind of research methodology is the client asking for?
- To what degree is the client aware of alternative methodological choices?
- To what degree is the client committed to one methodological choice?
- Has the client been unduly impressed by one particular method in the past?
- What kinds of information have been deemed most credible by this audience?
- Which methodological procedures can I, the researcher, conduct with quality?
- If I use a methodological mix of procedures, what is the rationale for each item in the mix?

Up to this point, the research procedures have not yet been identified, and this process of determining the purpose is essential no matter what methods are used for obtaining information. Now should be the time the researcher begins to think about the benefits of alternative information sources such as surveys, observation, individual interviews, focus groups, or a combination of several procedures. Before launching a focus group study it may be helpful to review the advantages and disadvantages of focus groups presented in Chapter 2 as well as to consider the following suggestions.

When to Use Focus Group Interviews

Focus group interviews should be considered when the following circumstances are present:

- Insights are needed in exploratory or preliminary studies. This could occur at the beginning of a larger scale research effort or when the study has a limited scope or limited resources. The goal might be to gain reactions to areas needing improvement or general guidelines on how an intervention might operate.
- There is a communication or understanding gap between groups or categories of people. This gap has a tendency to occur between groups who have power and others who do not. Professional groups (medical, educational, scientific, technical, business, legal) are facing a crisis due to communication gaps caused by language and logic. Professionals have developed

unique ways of thinking that are substantially different from the very people they are trying to reach.

- The purpose is to uncover factors relating to complex behavior or motivation. Focus groups can provide insight into complicated topics where opinions or attitudes are conditional or where the area of concern relates to multifaceted behavior or motivation.
- The researcher desires ideas to emerge from the group. Focus groups possess the capacity to become more than the sum of their participants, to exhibit a synergy that individuals alone can not achieve.
- The researcher needs additional information to prepare for a large-scale study. Focus groups have provided researchers with valuable insights into conducting complicated and often quantifiable investigations.
- The clients or intended audience place high value on capturing the open-ended comments of the target audience.

When Not to Use Focus Group Interviews

Focus group interviews should NOT be considered when the following circumstances are present:

- The environment is emotionally charged and more information of any type is likely to intensify the conflict. This is likely to occur in situations in which the issues are polarized, trust has deteriorated, and the participants are in a confrontational attitude.
- The researcher has lost control over critical aspects of the study. When control is relinquished to other individuals or groups the study is prone to manipulation and bias. The researcher should maintain control over such critical aspects as participant selection, question development, and analysis protocol.
- Statistical projections are needed. Focus groups do not involve sufficient numbers of participants nor does the sampling strategy lend itself to statistical projections.
- Other methodologies can produce either better quality information or more economical information of the same quality.
- The researcher cannot ensure the confidentiality of sensitive information.

Conversations With the Decision Makers

Those who use the focus group results to make decisions may not know what information is essential. You've probably heard it before: "I don't know what I'm looking for, but I'll know it when I see it." These experiences occur with regularity and the researcher needs to probe the issue a little deeper or risk missing the mark. In these situations a helpful strategy is to ask the decision maker to describe the end result or how the results will be used. Occasionally the client can envision characteristics of the final result, and if these are described, the researcher can then design a process to collect this information. A variation of the strategy is to ask the decision makers to think out loud about how they will make decisions regarding the program. Listen for the type and nature of evidence they feel they need as they ponder the program's future.

Focus group information is sought for a variety of reasons. In some situations, the information might be used for a specific and defined decision at a designated point in time. In other situations, the information might merely provide interested parties with insights on the nature of the program and participants. At times, the information is sought because of tradition or a perceived expectation from others in the environment. As a result, the researcher must inquire about the "why" of the study and then become an active listener. It may be beneficial to ask the question of why the information is needed in several different ways. For example: "Tell me about the background of the proposed study." "What prompted you to consider the study?" "Who is interested in the study results?" "What might those individuals do with the study results?" This pattern of questioning can enable the researcher to get a better picture of the information needs of intended users and thereby keep the study on target.

Determine Whom to Study

The researcher should consider the purpose of the study and think about who can provide the information. Be as specific as possible in this endeavor. For example, suppose decision makers were interested in how clients perceive current programs. On the surface this question appears straightforward, but it may be complex and require more thought. Are the decision makers interested in current clientele, past clientele, or potential clientele? Are clientele with certain demographic characteristics more critical than others? Precise definition of the clientele may be essential to undertake the study.

Nonprofit organizations may have a variety of educational or service-related programs. Some of the programs may be more intensive, visible, or popular than others. The researcher should give thought to both the diversity of people who participate in programs as well as their exposure to the variety of program opportunities. Nonprofit and service organizations typically have three categories of people who are of special importance: advisory/decision groups, employees, and clients or donors. Each of these three audiences could represent an area of study with focus group interviews.

   I. Advisory/Decision Groups: The organizational decision makers
     A. Decision-making boards with budgetary authority
     B. Advisory committees in subject or programmatic areas
  II. Employees
     A. Employees who deliver programs and services
     B. Support staff who perform clerical and related functions
     C. Volunteers
     D. Administrators and managers
 III. Customers or Clients
     A. Clients who use the program: Limited, moderate or heavy users
     B. Potential clients who are not currently using the programs or services
     C. Past clients

In addition, consideration should be given to the more traditional ways of dividing people into categories. Factors such as geographic location, age, gender, income, participation characteristics, family size, and employment status are all helpful ways to identify who should participate in focus groups. The decision of whom to involve must be related to the purpose of the study. These demographic factors will be important in determining who should be invited to the focus group interviews.

Listen to Your Target Audience

Seek out and visit with several people who have the characteristics of your target audience. These interviews could be individual or group. Perhaps share a meal with them and ask their advice on how to undertake the study. These are people who are connected, trusted, and may have offered valuable advice in the past. Describe the basic features of the study and ask questions such as these:

- How do I locate the participants?
- How are people in this general category alike or different? If I want to assemble people who feel like each other, what advice do you have for me?

- What incentives are needed, if any?
- Where would be the best place to hold the discussion?
- What would be some good questions to ask?
- What kind of person should moderate?

Listen attentively and avoid making commitments or promises about the nature of the study. After listening to their advice and that of your research colleagues, you are ready to put the plan on paper.

Selecting the Focus Group Location

Focus group interviews have been successfully conducted in a variety of locations, such as restaurants, hotel rooms, private homes, public buildings, and so on. A primary consideration is that the location is easy to find. Private homes may be difficult for other participants to locate, but they do offer a relaxed informal environment. Private homes are acceptable if they are easy for participants to find and if directions are clearly provided in the letter of invitation. The room should be free from outside distractions. Meeting places that have visual or audio distractions should be avoided. If at all possible the moderator should "scout out" the location in advance and watch for factors that could interrupt or interfere with the group session. For example, tape recording is nearly impossible in some locations because of background music or the hum of ventilation systems. Attempt to eliminate visual distractions to the participants. Some rooms have large windows and are close to open doors and hallways where the traffic flow causes constant interruption.

The environment for the focus group should be neutral. At times, the location of the session will influence the type of responses provided by participants. Effort is sometimes made initially to conceal the identity of those sponsoring the group interview to avoid advance bias and participant self-selection. Therefore, a meeting room in the sponsoring organization is probably not a wise choice. Police conference rooms, courthouse meeting rooms, and church basements have potential to evoke inhibitions or reactions among participants.

The room should have chairs that can be arranged with participants facing each other. Tables are often desirable because they enable participants to lean forward and be less self-conscious about their bodies. Eye contact among all participants is vital and having participants equally spaced around a table is preferred.

Market research firms regularly use specially designed rooms with oval tables, built in microphones, and a one-way mirror behind the moderator. Behind the mirror is a special viewing room for clients where they can observe and listen to the proceedings. Market research firms differ in terms of how much attention they give to the one-way mirror. In some situations, it is pointed out to the participants and described as a way for the clients to hear consumer comments. In other situations, the mirror is not mentioned, and at times the mirror is constructed to appear unobtrusive. In some circumstances the session is also videotaped from behind the one-way mirror.

I have shied away from these room arrangements because of limited availability in many communities as well as the secretive image of one-way mirrors. I have avoided videotaping the groups, but for a different reason. Videotaping is obtrusive and usually not worth the effort. I have found that it may change the environment and affect participant spontaneity. Videotaping usually requires several cameras plus camera operators who attempt to swing cameras quickly to follow the flowing conversation. The fuss and fury of videotaping make the focus group appear more like a circus than a discussion.

Develop a Plan and Estimate Resources Needed

The researcher should begin by writing a description of the problem and a plan of action. This plan should include the procedures that will be followed, whether a task force will be involved, a time line, and a proposed budget. The value of the written plan is threefold. First, it forces the researcher to think through the steps in a logical manner. Ideas that seem to make sense in our heads sometimes have easily identifiable shortcomings when placed on paper. Second, the written plan allows more effective feedback from decision makers. Written plans can be circulated, distributed, and discussed more readily than our invisible thoughts. Third, it ensures that adequate resources and time are available to obtain needed information.

The plan should be shared with colleagues, particularly those who have assisted in developing the program. It is also helpful to share it with colleagues or professionals familiar with focus group interviewing procedures. When others are asked to review the plan, they should be requested to identify aspects that are illogical, impractical, or unclear. Feedback that spots these problems early in the planning is most helpful and should

Time Allocation for Activities to Be Completed							
Week 1	Week 2	Week 3	Week 4	Week 5	Week 6	Week 7	Week 8
Develop Plan	Develop Questions Identify Participants Recruit	1st FG 2nd FG 3rd FG 4th FG <----Analysis---->		Draft Report	Review Draft	Final Draft	Oral Report

Figure 3.1 Chronological Plan

be encouraged. It may be of value to also share these plans with those who are making decisions on the program. These decision makers could be invited to comment on whether critical information is overlooked.

The effective plan should contain information on the chronological sequence of events, due dates, costs involved, and decision points at which the plan may be modified or abridged. Consideration should be given to developing both a *chronological plan* and a *fiscal plan* for the project.

A chronological plan should contain the following elements: dates, steps, persons responsible, people assisting, and comments (see Figure 3.1). The chronological plan presents a timetable of the sequence of steps as well as identifies the tasks to be completed by various individuals. Administrators have regularly criticized evaluators and researchers for not respecting the time requirements of decision making. At some point a decision will be made, regardless of whether or not the results are available. The chronological plan provides decision makers

RESOURCES NEEDED FOR FOCUS GROUP STUDY				
Task	Person Responsible	Days Needed	Budget	Comments
Planning	Dick Jerry	1.5 .5		
Develop questions	Dick Jerry Task force of 4 (.2 X 4)	2.0 .5 .8		Dick leads brainstorming with task force
Identify participant characteristics	Dick	.5		
Feedback on plan & pilot test with task force	Dick Task force of 4 (.2 X 4)	.5 .8		
Obtain list of potential participants	Dick 4 office managers (.2 X 4)	.5 .8		List obtained from county offices
Recruitment	Secretary (2 calls, 1 letter) Dick supervises	8.0 .5	$200	Phone
Focus groups (4)	Dick moderates Jerry assists	3.0 3.0	$200 $200 $160	Room Refreshments Travel
Type transcripts	Secretary	6.0	$50	Supplies
Analyze	Dick Jerry	5.0 1.0		
Type draft report	Secretary	1.0	$20 $20	Supplies Copies
Review draft	Task force (.2 X 4)	.8		
Revision	Dick Secretary	.5 .5		
Printing	Secretary	.2	$200	Printing
Present report	Dick	1.0		
TOTALS: Time: Dick = 15.0 days, Jerry = 5.0 days, Task force = 2.4 days, Sect. = 15.7 days, Office manager = .8 days. Budget: $1,050				

Figure 3.2 Fiscal Plan

with a timetable for information—a timetable that must be prepared in advance and then respected by both the researcher and the decision maker.

The fiscal plan is a project budget summary that complements the chronological plan and provides additional insights as to the amount of time, effort, and expenses that will be required (see Figure 3.2). It is often helpful to consider both the high and low estimates of all needed resources. The planning worksheet at the end of Chapter 13 may prove helpful in estimating the time and cost requirements of a focus group interview study.

Summary

In the focus group plan, the written description of purpose comes first. This is followed by identification of the questions or issues to be studied and the target audience that will provide the answers. The written plan is a roadmap to achieving a successful design. Writing assists in organizing and allows other partners to provide helpful feedback. Focus groups require resources, time, and money. Sound conceptualization and planning ensures appropriate questions and allocation of adequate resources.

4

Asking Questions in a Focus Group

The mother thought her daughter should have a comprehensive checkup before starting kindergarten. To be on the safe side, she made an appointment with an eminent psychologist to examine the youngster for any possible abnormal tendencies. Among the questions, the man of science asked: "Are you a boy or a girl?" "A boy," the little girl answered. Somewhat startled, the psychologist tried again. "When you grow up, are you going to be a woman or a man?" "A man," the little girl answered. On the way home, the mother asked, "Why did you make such strange replies to what the psychologist asked you?" In a serious tone of voice, the little girl replied, "Since he asked such silly questions, I thought he wanted silly answers!"

Quality answers are directly related to quality questions. Forethought must be given to developing questions for a focus group. Questions are the heart of the focus group interview. They may appear to be spontaneous, but they have been carefully selected and phrased in advance to elicit the maximum amount of information. We tend to be too casual about asking questions. We're exposed to questions every day and perhaps it is this continuous exposure that has dulled our senses to the importance of asking quality questions. In order to understand the features of a quality question we must explore some of the dynamics of communication as well as the human cognitive process.

The series of questions used in a focused interview or questioning route look deceptively simple. Typically, a focused interview will include about a dozen questions. If these questions were asked in an individual interview, the respondent could probably tell you everything he or she knows about the subject in just a few minutes. However, when these questions are placed in a group environment the discussion can last for several hours. Part of the reason is in the nature of the questions and the cognitive processes of humans. As participants answer questions, the responses spark new ideas or connections from other participants. Answers provide mental cues that unlock perceptions of other participants—cues that are necessary in order to explore the range of perceptions.

Types of Focus Group Questions

The focus group goes through several different types of questions, each of which serves a distinct purpose. These are the categories of questions:

Opening Question. This is the round robin question that everyone answers at the beginning of the focus group. It is designed to be answered rather quickly (within 10-20 seconds) and to identify characteristics that the participants have in common. Usually it is preferable for these questions to be factual as opposed to attitude- or opinion-based questions.

Introductory Questions. These are the questions that introduce the general topic of discussion and/or provide participants an opportunity to reflect on past experiences and their connection with the overall topic. Usually these questions are not critical to the analysis and are intended to foster conversation and interaction among the participants.

Transition Questions. These questions move the conversation into the key questions that drive the study. The transition questions help the participants envision the topic in a broader scope. They serve as the logical link between the introductory questions and the key questions. During these transition questions, the participants are becoming aware of how others view the topic.

Key Questions. These questions drive the study. Typically, there are two to five questions in this category. These are usually the first questions to be developed and also the ones that require the greatest attention in the subsequent analysis.

Ending Questions. These questions bring closure to the discussion, enable participants to reflect back on previous comments, and are critical to analysis. These questions can be of three types:

All Things Considered Question. This question is used to have the participants state their final position on critical areas of concern. It allows the participant to consider all the comments shared in the discussion and then identify which aspects are most important, most in need of action, and so on. Also, individuals may have shared several different points of view that were mutually inconsistent and this question allows them to clarify their positions at the conclusion of the discussion. Often this question is asked in a round-robin manner. Examples include: "Suppose you had one minute to talk to the governor on the topic of merit pay. What would you say?" or "Of all the needs that were discussed, which one is most important to you?"

Summary Question. The summary question is asked after the moderator or assistant moderator has given a short oral summary (2 to 3 minutes) of the key questions and big ideas that emerged from the discussion. After the summary the participants are asked, "Is this an adequate summary?" This question has a critical role to play in analysis. (This will be discussed in greater depth in Chapters 6 and 8.)

Final Question. This is a standardized question asked at the end of the focus group. Following the summary question, the moderator gives a short overview of the purpose of the study. This overview may be slightly longer and more descriptive than what was said in the advance letters or oral introduction to the focus group. Following this overview the moderator asks the final question: "Have we missed anything?" For this question to work effectively there must be sufficient time remaining at the conclusion of the focus group. It is best to have about 10 minutes remaining before the promised adjournment time. This questions is of particular importance at the beginning of a series of focus groups as insurance that the questioning route is logical and complete.

Topic Guide Versus Questioning Route

An issue to be considered is whether to use a *topic guide* format as opposed to developing the actual questions in sentence format. The topic guide is a list of topics or issues that are pursued in the focus group. This list consists of words or phrases that remind the moderator of the topic of interest. The questioning route, however, is a sequence of questions in complete sentences. Each approach has advantages. The questioning route

- takes longer to prepare in order to achieve the exact content desired by the sponsor.
- produces more efficient analysis because it eliminates subtle differences in language that may alter the intent.
- is preferred when different moderators may be used on the same project.
- ensures that the question is exactly what the sponsor intended.

The topic guide

- may seem more spontaneous to the participants because the moderator can incorporate the participants' colloquialisms or jargon into the question.
- works best when the same moderator conducts all focus groups because the individual styles in asking questions can alter the nature of the question.
- works best with veteran moderators who are aware of how slight differences in asking questions can affect the analysis of results.

The topic guide approach further assumes that the moderator is skillful in spontaneously phrasing the topic into a coherent, single-dimension question presented in a complete sentence. This may take some effort and practice on the part of beginning moderators and as a result the questioning route is advised until mastery is achieved. Appendix 4A includes an example of a focus group questioning route; Appendix 4B has the questions converted into a topic guide.

The Art of Asking Questions

Asking quality questions is not easy; it requires forethought, concentration, and some background knowledge. Consider the following characteristics of good questions for focus groups.

Focus Group Interviews Use Open-Ended Questions

The questions are the "stimulus" for the respondent. This stimulus can be of two varieties—structured or free. If the stimulus is free, as in an open-ended question, it allows the respondent the opportunity to structure an answer in any of several dimensions. Merton (1990/1956) describes this type of question as "one which does not fix attention on any specific aspect of the stimulus situation or of the response; it is, so to speak, a blank page to be filled in by the interviewee" (p. 15).

The answer is not implied and the type or manner of response is not suggested. Individuals are encouraged to respond based on their specific situation. The major advantage of the open-ended question is that it reveals what is on the interviewee's mind as opposed to what the interviewer suspects is on the interviewee's mind. Toward the end of the group interview it may be productive to limit the types of responses and bring greater focus to the answers by shifting to close-ended questions. Consider the following examples of open-ended questions:

- "What did you think of the program?"
- "How did you feel about the conference?"
- "Where do you get new information?"
- "What do you like best about the proposed program?"

It is possible to add structure to the stimulus question by delimiting or bounding the question and yet allowing respondents to select their own way of answering. For example:

- "What did you think of the part of the program that described new farming techniques?"
- "How did you feel about Dr. Jones's presentation at the conference?"
- "Where do you get new information on parenting skills?"
- "What do you like best about how the new program is promoted?"

Some questions are deceptive and appear to be open-ended but are really close-ended questions in disguise. Questions that include words such as *satisfied*, *to what extent*, or *how much* imply answers that fall within a specified range, such as *very satisfied*, *to a great extent*, or *a great deal*. These questions are usually preferred toward the latter parts of the focused interview as the moderator narrows the range of inquiry.

Bounding the questions in this manner may also be helpful to the moderator in an effort to regain control of a rambling discussion or in situations where the topic requires more specific insights to the topic of discussion.

Focus Group Interviews Avoid Dichotomous Questions

Dichotomous questions are those that can be answered with a simple "yes" or "no" response. These questions are often asked in social situations, and part of our socialization is the ability to sense what the question really means and answer accordingly. "Did you have a nice day?" "Do you feel OK?" "It's a nice party, isn't it?" or "Do you work at the university?" can be answered literally with a "yes" or "no" or expanded on.

It is interesting to note that children, and particularly teenagers, answer questions literally, especially questions from parents. Consider the conversation described by Patton (1990):

> (Teenager returns home from a date.)
> Do you know that you're late?
> Yeah.
> Did you have a good time?
> Yeah.
> Did you go to a movie?
> Yeah.
> Was it a good movie?
> Yeah, it was okay.
> So, it was worth seeing?
> Yeah, it was worth seeing.
> I've heard a lot about it. Do you think I would like it?
> I don't know. Maybe.
> Anything else you'd like to tell me about your evening?
> No, I guess that's it.
> (Teenager goes upstairs to bed. One parent turns to the other and says: It sure is hard to get him to talk to us. I guess he's at that age where kids just don't want to tell their parents anything.) (pp. 297-298)

Dichotomous questions seem appealing because they are so simple, easy to ask, and familiar in social situations. However, researchers should use them with caution. In focus group interviews, the yes-no questions usually do not evoke the desired group discussion. They also tend to elicit ambiguous responses, which can in turn restrict the clarity of the discussion.

"Why" Is Rarely Asked in a Focus Group

"Why" questions imply a rational answer, one developed by thought and reflection. A great many decisions are made by impulse, by habit or tradition, or generally in a nonrational manner. When asked why, respondents provide quick answers that seem rational or appropriate to the situation. Moreover, the "why" question has a sharpness or pointedness to it that reminds one of interrogations. This sharpness sets off defensive barriers and the respondent tends to take a position on the socially acceptable side of controversial issues.

If the researcher decides to use a "why" question, it should be specific. Paul Lazarfeld (1986) has referred to this as the *principle of specification*. Lazarfeld's principle of specification is that "why" questions typically can be answered on two levels. When asked why, the respondent may respond on (1) the basis of *influences* that prompted the action or (2) the basis of certain desirable *attributes*.

Lazarfeld's model can then be used to examine the responses to a seemingly simple question: "Why did you go to the zoo?"

Influence Answer: "Because my kids really wanted to go."
Attribute Answer: "Because I wanted to see the new aquarium."

What seems like a straightforward and simple question can really be answered on several dimensions. The first answer describes an influence and the second answer relates to a feature or attribute of the zoo. The preferred strategy is to break the "why" question down into different questions, for example:

Influence: "What prompted (influenced, caused, made) you to go to the zoo?"
Attribute: "What features of the zoo do you particularly like?"

A less directive approach is to ask people "what" or "how" they feel about the object of discussion. Often people are able to describe the feelings they had when they considered using a particular product or program. In addition, they may be able to describe the anticipated consequences from using the product or program. Grossman offers a succinct summary of the limits of "Why?":

In short, people can tell you what they fear and how this fear developed, which, in effect, tells you why they feel as they do. But, when they're asked "Why?" directly, it frequently creates difficulties. (Grossman, 1979, p. 10)

Uncued Questions First, Cued Questions Second

The moderator often faces a dilemma in the questioning route. In some questions the moderator is seeking new ideas, approaches, or examples from the participant. If examples are provided by the moderator it can limit or restrict the thinking of the participants. A better approach is to begin by asking the question without providing a cue— the *uncued question*. The uncued question is open-ended but it is also so all-encompassing that participants may have difficulty in providing lengthy commentary. Typically, the responses will be based on most recent or most vivid experiences or impressions. The rule of thumb is to ask the question in an uncued manner first and then follow up with cues to prompt additional discussion. After the topics have been discussed in a general way, the moderator then might offer some cues and ask for comments. If the moderator does not offer cues and a certain topic is not mentioned, then it is impossible to determine if it was an oversight or if it was just not of importance. Only by offering cues can the moderator determine the difference. The cues themselves require some thought. They are developed by the moderator in advance of the focus group. The cues should be limited in number yet also reasonably exhaustive. They should be general enough to allow for a variety of comments and yet specific enough to prompt ideas and thoughts.

Let's try an example. In a community needs assessment the participants might be asked to identify what is needed by local residents. The moderator might expect that the initial comments from individuals would come from those who have given this topic previous thought or who have had relevant recent or vivid experiences. These most recent or vivid experiences are like first impressions in that they have a tendency to be unstable and change as the discussion ensues. After a while the discussion will lag and then the moderator might offer cues. The moderator might hold up a list of categories as cues to the participants and then ask: "Here is a list of topics that might help us think of needs within the community. It includes: family, transportation, health, safety, recreation, youth, seniors. After looking at this list, are there any additional needs that come to mind?" If the cues are given first it may limit the range and diversity of comments.

In this type of question it may also be helpful to include an "all things considered" question, described earlier. In this question, the participants are asked to identify the one factor (need, concern, etc.) that they consider to be the most important (critical, necessary to address, etc.).

Responses to this question greatly aid the analysis. An analysis error sometimes made in focus groups is to assume that what is frequently mentioned is of greater importance. A far less risky approach is to include a specific question to allow the participants to comment on what they consider to be most important.

Focus Group Questions Can Use Standardized Strategies

Two styles of questioning have proved to be beneficial in a number of focus group studies. These are *sentence completion* and *conceptual mapping.*

Sentence Completion. With sentence completion the moderator invites participants to complete one or more sentences (questions). These questions are designed to elicit information on motivation and feelings regarding a desirable or undesirable behavior. Suppose our target audience is men with high cholesterol who have used diet and exercise to lower their cholesterol. The purpose of the study is to uncover strategies that promote exercise and desirable diets. The moderator might hand out a set of completion questions and give the participants several minutes to record their answers. For example:

1. When I first found out that my cholesterol was high I felt . . .
2. Now, as I think about changing my diet, what really helped me was . . .
3. What got in the way was . . .
4. I was surprised that . . .

After participants have had an opportunity to jot down their comments they are asked to share what they have written and talk about it. Usually the moderator takes one question at a time and asks participants to share their comments for each question.

The benefit of this type of question is that it allows participants a few moments to collect their thoughts and then respond based on their personal experiences. This exercise has the benefit of allowing all participants to provide information and involving the quieter group members. It also minimizes the "me-too" tendency, because each person completes the exercise privately before sharing with the group.

Conceptual Mapping. The second standardized strategy is the conceptual mapping exercise. Suppose that decision makers sought to discover how their service agency was seen by potential customers. One way would be to incorporate into the focus group a process called conceptual mapping. This exercise allows participants to describe the agency in relation to similar organizations using each participant's classification system.

The exercise begins when participants are given a small grid with six boxes and asked to list all organizations that perform similar services on the grid, grouping the ones that they consider to be similar into the same boxes. They need not use all six boxes and if more are needed they can be added (see Figure 4.1).

The moderator gives the participants about 5 minutes to complete the exercise. When all are finished, the moderator asks the participants, one at a time, to share their results. While the participant is describing his or her map, the moderator might reproduce it on a flip chart for all to see. The moderator asks each participant for the reasons the categories were created. When all have shared results the moderator can pursue greater discussion of the commonalities and differences between various cells. In essence, the participants develop a classification system that describes similar or different items based on categories developed by the respondents. An individual might categorize the choices in a variety of ways: by cost, convenience, size of operation, availability, or a host of other means. The greater insight comes from the discussion as the moderator listens to the rationale for the classification.

This conceptual mapping strategy makes a critical assumption. It assumes that participants are sufficiently familiar with the choices to be able to recall what they are and also to be able to identify differences among the alternatives. If the topic is specific and tangible—such as toothpaste, breakfast cereals, or automobiles—then the participants can often launch right into the exercise. In other cases the topic may be abstract relating to "programs," "opportunities," or organizations that have multiple functions. In these cases the moderator might begin the exercise by listing on a flip chart all possible choices that the participants can think of before the choices are classified. If some are unfamiliar with the choices the moderator might invite brief descriptions.

Focus Group Questions Are Carefully Prepared

Good focus group questions require effort and systematic development. The best questions rarely come like a bolt of lightning out of the sky. Quality questions require reflection and feedback from others.

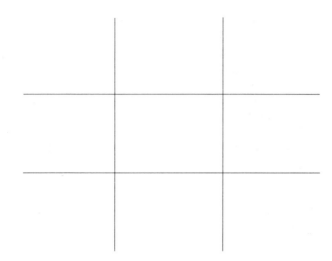

Figure 4.1. Conceptual Mapping Grid

Researchers shouldn't expect perfect questions in the early drafts, but they should instead allow ample time to explore phrasing and words that achieve clarity, precision, and brevity.

The first step is to identify potential questions. The researcher begins by thinking about the problem or area of concern and listing all questions that are of interest to the users. Brainstorming sessions with information users or colleagues can be helpful in obtaining a range of possible questions and variations in phrasing. The brainstorming should begin by being as exhaustive as possible and include all questions of interest, even if they appear to be only variations of each other. When the list is complete and no further suggestions can be made, the critical questions can be identified. These are the questions that capture the intent of the study.

Focus Group Questions Are Clear

Quality focus group questions must be clear. Clarity doesn't mean short sentences and single-syllable words. Clarity has several attributes, including: length, unidimensionality, and wording. The length of the question is of some concern because lengthy questions tend to be redundant or add complicating factors that can be confusing to respondents. The risk of the longer question is that the participant's attention is directed to a phrase within the question and thus the response is to just one aspect as opposed to the overall intent. Generally, clarity is reduced as the length of the question increases. Sometimes, however, in focus groups the moderator must ask a question that provides a longer statement of needed background information before the question is asked. This background is often essential before the participant can respond to the question.

Questions should be limited to a single dimension. Inadvertently, moderators might include words that they think are synonyms but to the participants they are seen as different concepts. For example: "To what extent or in what ways was the program useful and practical?" For some "useful" and "practical" may be very different concepts. Other times moderators might sometimes add a second sentence or phrase that supposedly amplifies the question but in fact confuses the respondents because it introduces a second dimension. For example: "What is most important to you, that is, which topic should be acted on first?" Once again, the moderator assumed that what was important should be acted on first, but this may not be the view of the participants.

The words must be understandable to the participants. Professionals are sometimes held captive by their language and inadvertently use technical terms or jargon that is confusing. Consequently, the words should be reviewed by those similar to your target audience. I vividly remember a focus group question that bombed out the first time it was used. It seemed so clear to the adult educators who were developing the questions, but the participants felt differently. When the question was asked, "What was the most significant learning experience you've had in the past year?" the first person responded, "I have no idea what you are talking about." The second person asked, "What is a significant learning experience?" The rest of the group were convinced that the moderator was an alien from another planet. Earlier, the adult educators loved the question because this was the type of topic that they regularly think about, but to noneducators it just made no sense.

Another aspect of wording is that the same words can have multiple meanings. Although this attribute may be a problem in a close-ended survey, in the focus group it is often an asset to discover the meaning participants ascribe to these words. Consider the question: "What's hard about working for this organization?" The word *hard* could have a variety of meanings. When participants mention that they see certain words in a different way, the moderator can invite the participants to suggest different meanings and to indicate the one they favor. Because this strategy is time-consuming it should be used sparingly.

The Art of Focusing Questions

Focus group interviewing is more than asking questions in a group; it involves asking well-thought-out questions in a focused environment. Consider these features when focusing the questions.

Focus Begins With Consistent and Sufficient Background Information

Provide consistent background information to each participant about the purpose of the study in order to minimize tacit assumptions. In all interview situations, respondents make assumptions about the nature of the questions and then answer accordingly. These tacit assumptions are vexing because the respondent may be providing an answer based on faulty assumptions. Paul Lazarfeld (1986/1934) provides an illustration of tacit assumption from a detective story of G. K. Chesterton's:

> Have you ever noticed this—that people never answer what you say? They answer what you mean—or what they think you mean. Suppose one lady says to another in a country house, "Is anybody staying with you?" the lady doesn't answer "Yes; the butler, the three footmen, the parlourmaid, and so on," though the parlourmaid may be in the room, or the butler behind her chair. She says "There is *nobody* staying with us," meaning nobody of the sort you mean. But suppose a doctor inquiring into an epidemic asks, "Who is staying in the house?" then the lady will remember the butler, the parlourmaid, and the rest. All language is used like that; you never get a question answered literally, even when you get it answered truly. (Chesterton, 1951, p. 58)

All information given in preparation for the discussion helps develop the tacit knowledge of participants. Focus group participants usually want to know the purpose of the session. They may wonder why the session is being held, who the sponsor is, or how the information is going to be used. These topics might be discussed during the invitation phase or at the beginning of the focus group. This information provides clues to respondents about how or in what manner they might respond. Care must be taken in all advance communication to ensure consistency and sufficient generality regarding the purposes of the discussion.

Focus Questions Are Presented in a Context

It is vital to establish the context of the question so that participants are mentally ready to respond. This is accomplished through introductory comments by the interviewer and also through the first few questions in the group interview. Often verbal cues are helpful to guide the interviewee back to the original situation, event, or experience. By using past tense and requesting the participants to "think back," the interviewer places individuals back in the original environment as opposed to the immediate interviewing situation. There is a tendency for participants to respond to the more immediate interviewing experience—the here and now—unless they are requested to shift themselves to another time frame. This focus on the past increases the reliability of the responses because it asks about specific past experiences as opposed to current intentions or future possibilities. The question asks what the person has actually done as opposed to what might be done in the future. The shift is from what might be, or ought to be, to what has been. In addition, this time shift cues the respondent to speak from actual experiences as opposed to wishes and intentions.

The context is also influenced by activities and exercises introduced by the moderator. Occasionally handouts, surveys, or background materials may be given to participants during the focus group. This typically occurs about midway through the focus group when participants are asked to review the materials, respond to the brief surveys, or offer their impressions of the handouts. This strategy has several benefits. It focuses attention on a specific topic, changes the participants' role from passive to active, and provides cues that help participants collect their thoughts.

The Special Problem of Money. Focus group studies that seek information about money have been vexing and require special attention to establish the context. Questions about salary or prices of products have been predictably unreliable—in focus group studies as well as in other forms of questioning. Money is so tied to symbolism that people have difficulty separating its financial role from the images it creates in our minds. Salary is often linked to our ego or our image of ourself. Furthermore, human beings are not necessarily rational in decision making about money. The importance of money can fluctuate depending on our present state of mind, what we have available, and what the current alternatives are. When prices of products or services are asked in focus groups it is wise to be wary when interpreting what is said. George Leaming (1991) suggests, "When it comes to prices, what people say is almost always different from what they do" (p. 16). Pricing discussions, by their nature, are artificial. The most reliable way to determine price, according to Leaming, is to use test markets. What we spend will be a function of what we have available to spend at the time of purchase. Asking the question outside of this context inherently makes the answer unreliable. Focus groups, says Leaming, are most appropriate after the test marketing results are in as a way to understand buyer reaction to price.

Several years ago the U.S. General Accounting Office was investigating the consequence of low salary for federal law enforcement officers. At the time of the study, federal officers had salaries that many considered to be noncompetitive with county and municipal law enforcement employees. The concern was the degree to which low salaries influenced morale. Focus groups were to be conducted with federal officers and considerable attention was taken to place the issue of salary into the larger work context. Premature questions about salary were avoided and discussion began with the factors that lead up to first becoming a law enforcement officer. Questions proceeded to the current positive and negative factors about employment. If salary was mentioned by one of the participants as either a positive or negative factor, then the moderator would encourage more discussion. In this case, salary needed to be placed into the larger context of overall working conditions.

Focus Questions Are Focused

Arrange questions in a focused sequence that seems logical to participants. The most common procedure is to go from general to specific— that is, beginning with general overview questions that funnel into more specific questions of critical interest. Avoid hitting the participants with a specific question without first establishing the context created by the more general questions.

For example, suppose that a series of focus group interviews will be held with young people. The purpose is to determine their perceptions of youth organizations and eventually to identify an effective means of advertising a particular organization. It would be premature to begin with questions on advertising the organization. Instead, the moderator might ask the participants to describe their favorite youth organization or to describe what they like about youth clubs. Later in the discussion, the moderator might narrow the topic to focus on the specific youth organization under investigation. Perhaps toward the end of the discussion, the moderator might solicit participants' opinions on several different approaches that are being considered for advertising the youth group.

An actual illustration of the general-to-specific technique of focusing questions comes from Hawaii. In an effort to gain insights as to how consumers use Kona coffee, the moderator began with questions about gourmet foods, then asked about gourmet beverages. When one of the participants suggested Kona coffee, the moderator then encouraged discussion of how and when this type of coffee was used.

Serendipitous Questions

Occasionally in the flow of a focus group interview the moderator or assistant moderator will discover a question that might be useful to the study. The question may never have occurred to the research team prior to the discussion, but the idea is cued by comments or perceptions of participants. These serendipitous questions can be beneficial. Often it is best to hold back on them until the end of the discussion, because they may take the discussion off on a quite different trail of unknown consequences. Also, throughout the focus group the moderator must monitor the time remaining—without noticeably looking at the clock or watch. Unanticipated questions inserted in the middle of the discussion can take precious minutes in a potentially unproductive route. Therefore, it is best to use the final 5 to 10 minutes for serendipitous questions.

Pilot Testing the Focus Group Interview

Focus group interviews cannot be pilot tested in the manner used in mail-out or telephone surveys. In questionnaires, a small number of people is typically selected out of the intended audience and asked to complete the survey. In focus groups, the pilot testing must take into consideration not only the nature of the questions but the characteristics of the audience, the interactions between participants, and the moderator procedures. The pilot testing can be accomplished in several steps, beginning with having experts review the questioning route and potential probes. It is preferable that these experts have had experience with focus groups, but at a minimum they should be familiar with the purpose of the study and also be familiar with the type of participants involved in the study. In this initial pilot test, attention is placed on the logical and sequential flow of questions and on the ability of probes to elicit the information desired.

A second pilot test is to invite selected representatives of your target audience to comment on your questions as well as other aspects of the study. You might consult with people who meet the specifications or who are intimately familiar with the people who are to be invited to the focus group. I've found it helpful to invite several individuals or a small group to lunch to discuss the research project. Over lunch, I'll give a short overview of the research project, recruitment strategy, and incentives and read the questions. This procedure can provide some valuable clues on fine-tuning the questions as well as making adjustments to critical logistical factors in the study. Furthermore, it provides an opportunity to gain a beginning sense of the type of comments that might be expected. These individuals will have had considerable exposure to the focus group study as a result of this pilot test and consequently they should not be invited to later focus group interviews.

The third pilot test procedure is actually the first focus group interview. After the first focus group the moderator should reflect once again on the wording and sequencing of the questions. Consideration should also be given to the room arrangement, the composition of the participants, and the moderator procedures used to encourage (but not direct) the participant responses.

If major changes are made in the questions or moderator procedures, then the results of the first discussion are set aside and not used in later analysis. If, however, there are no major changes, the first "pilot" discussion is included in later analysis.

A final procedure that can be used in pilot testing is to seek comments from participants at the conclusion of the focus group. This is the "final question" discussed earlier that provides a brief description of the study and then asks the participants, "Have we missed anything?" This final question, although helpful for all the focus groups in the study, is usually particularly helpful in the first few interviews.

Summary

Much of the success of the focus group depends on the quality of the questions. Quality questions require forethought and planning. Successful focus groups begin with well-thought-out questions that are appropriately sequenced. Open-ended questions allow the respondent to determine the nature of the answer. Dichotomous questions and "why" questions are to be avoided. Interviews are focused by providing participants with consistent and sufficient background information and by presenting the questions in a context.

APPENDIX 4A

Focus Group Questioning Route for Youth Focus Groups

INTRODUCTORY QUESTION: Tell us your name and one thing you enjoy doing (hobby, activity, etc.).

1. What are the most serious problems facing families and teenagers in this community?

2. A number of concerns have been mentioned. Think about teens using alcohol, tobacco, and other drugs. How do these problems compare to the others already mentioned?

3. In your community, what is acceptable use of alcohol?

   A. By adults

   B. By young people under 21

   C. If there is a difference, why?

4. Tell us about the circumstances when teens drink. When and where is it most likely to occur?

5. How do you think the alcohol is obtained?

6. What are some characteristics of people your age who never use, occasionally use, or regularly use alcohol?

7. Let's talk about what can be done to prevent people your age from using alcohol or other drugs [Feel free to mention cigarettes, chewing tobacco, and drugs you think are used in your community]. Let's start with parents.

   A. What do you think parents could do that would help prevent their kids from using alcohol or other drugs?

   B. What are the best ways for parents to communicate with their kids about alcohol and other drug use issues?

8. What about other people your age? What can they say or do to prevent other young people from using alcohol or other drugs?

9. Who are the other groups or individuals who could influence teenagers' decisions about use of alcohol or other drugs and what could they do?

[After they have answered, hand out the *list of groups*.]

This is a list of some of the groups that might have some influence on teens, decisions about using alcohol or other drugs. As I read through this list, please feel free to comment on what you think any of these groups might be able to do.

School personnel

Coaches

Employers

Religious leaders

Police

Youth leaders (4-H, scouts, etc.)

Other

10. What are the things in our lives that can make it easier for us to be healthy and independent in the future?

[After they have answered, hand out the *list of activities*.]

In addition, how could the following things influence you?

Activities:

Sports	Hobbies
Music	Church
Social	Other

Community service opportunities

Supportive family

Parents who set and enforce rules

Other supportive adults

Educational and/or vocational goals

Job opportunities

Spiritual or religious beliefs

11. Are there any of these you would like to see more of in your community?

12. Let's summarize the key points of our discussion.

[The assistant moderator will give a brief 2-minute summary of the responses to questions 6, 7, 8, 9, & 10.]

Does this summary sound complete? Do you have any changes or additions?

13. The goal is to reduce alcohol and other drug abuse among youth and families in our county. Have we missed anything?

14. What advice do you have for us?

APPENDIX 4B

Focus Group Topic Guide
for Youth Focus Groups

I. Introduction: Your name and one thing you enjoy doing.

II. Community Concerns

    1. Most serious problems facing families and teenagers?

    2. How do alcohol, tobacco, and other drugs compare?

    3. In your community, what is acceptable use of alcohol?

        A. By adults

        B. By young people under 21

        C. If there is a difference, why?

III. Alcohol Use

    4. When and where do teens drink?

    5. How do you think alcohol is obtained?

    6. Characteristics of youth who

        A. Never use alcohol?

        B. Occasionally use alcohol?

        C. Regularly use alcohol?

IV. Prevention Strategies

    7A. What can parents do?

    7B. Parent communication strategies

    8. What can young people do?

    9. Who influences teens about alcohol or other drugs?

[After they have answered, hand out the *list of groups*.]

CUES: Hand out list

       School personnel

        Coaches

        Employers

        Religious leaders

        Police

        Youth leaders (4-H, scouts, etc.)

        Other

    10. What makes it easier to be healthy and independent?

[After they have answered, hand out the *list of activities*.]

CUES:

        Activities:

Sports	Hobbies
Music	Church
Social	Other

        Community service opportunities

        Supportive family

        Parents who set and enforce rules

        Other supportive adults

        Educational and/or vocational goals

        Job opportunities

        Spiritual or religious beliefs

    11. What would you like more of?

V. Summary and Conclusion

    12. Summary of questions 6, 7, 8, 9, & 10.

    13. Have we missed anything?

    14. What advice do you have for us?

5

Participants in a Focus Group

Of all the elements of focus group interviewing, the most overlooked and underestimated aspect is the recruitment of the right people. Careful preparation, trained moderators, and quality questions are important, but these are of limited value if the right people don't attend. Too often public sector organizations and institutions underestimate the importance of careful recruitment of participants. Who should be invited? How many people should participate? How should participants be identified? What can be done to ensure that invited participants actually attend? How many groups should be conducted?

When public and nonprofit organizations sponsor focus groups, they operate within an environment different from that of private-based market research firms. The public and nonprofit organizations must operate within their traditional constraints, rules, and budgets. A topic that has minimal importance in the private sector, such as paying participants to attend, can be of major philosophical importance for religious, educational, or public service agencies.

Nonprofit organizations can have difficulty when they use the same procedure to recruit focus group participants that they use to recruit volunteers. These organizations sometimes assume that getting volunteers is one of their strengths. After all, they reason, people come to meetings now, so why can't we use our traditional means of soliciting and advertising for focus group participants? The answer is NO! The old methods may be suitable for meetings, events, or activities, but they lack the deliberate features that ensure that the right people will attend.

Employees in public organizations may feel that their traditions and values require them to conduct meetings open to the public. In some instances decision makers may seek to allow anyone and everyone to participate in the focus groups. In some respects these session resemble public hearings, to which citizens come to ventilate or to watch others as they share their wrath. Focus groups are not open public meetings because this defeats critical characteristics that are essential for the focus group to work, such as having homogeneous participants, a permissive environment, and a limited number of people.

To illustrate the difficulties that can occur, consider the story of a Midwestern community. The city council was concerned about building a new fire station. The old station needed major improvements. Estimates for repairs were greater than the cost to build a new station. For a new station to be built the city needed to pass a bond issue, a task that has been difficult for many municipalities in the past few years. Twice before, the city council had placed the bond issue on the ballot, and twice the referendum was defeated. To avoid an embarrassing third defeat the officials commissioned a research firm to study the possibility of a favorable vote. The research firm conducted what they called "focus groups" within the municipality. The public was invited to attend any or all of the discussions held in various places in the community. Announcements were made on cable TV, posters were placed in public buildings and on bulletin boards in grocery stores and pharmacies, and special ads were placed in newspapers. Naturally, the attendance varied and the discussions were more like a town meeting. The research firm indicated that the results suggested that the vote would now be favorable, and the city council decided to move ahead with the election. The city council sent advance publicity to residents supporting the new fire station bonding election. This publicity emphasized that local elected officials had "listened" to the residents and the council had responded by asking for the election. The election results were a disappointment to the elected officials. The bonding bill was resoundingly defeated. In hindsight, the city council discovered the opponents to the fire stations were largely composed of senior citizens who were quite concerned about increased property taxes. The seniors had greater difficulty in getting to the meetings and instead just saved their energy until the day of the election.

The "focus groups" were attended by supporters of the fire station. Residents who were against the bill just ignored the meetings but showed up for the election. In this situation the lack of careful procedures for selecting respondents produced embarrassing and erroneous results. Furthermore, generalizations or projections to a population based on limited focus group interviews are risky.

The first ingredient in successful recruitment is to realize that special efforts must be made. In working with focus groups most nonprofits might as well forget about their traditional means for recruitment and substitute a systematic and deliberate process. Conventional methods such as newsletters, form letter invitations, or announcements at meetings yield disappointing results. If the organization is truly interested in getting quality information, then these inefficient methods should be set aside, because they will not be effective in getting the correct number of the right people to attend.

The Purpose Drives the Study

To decide who should be invited to the group interview, think first about the purpose of the study. Usually the purpose is to make statements about what people think—specifically people who have certain things in common. This purpose should guide the invitation decision. The statement of purpose may require some additional refinement and clarification to ensure the audience is precisely defined. It is vital to identify the target group as precisely as possible, and this then becomes the unit of analysis. For example, the researcher might have initially identified community residents but later, after some thought, restricted the audience to unmarried residents between the ages of 18 and 40. In other situations, the key unit of analysis might be stated in broad terms such as homemakers, teenagers, or residents of a geographic area.

The purpose of the study gives us clues as to the degree of specification needed in the target audience and is the first of three ingredients that influence the decision. The second includes everything you currently know about your target audience and groups that are close to your target. Is the target audience distinctive, identifiable, and reasonable to locate? Is the target audience sufficiently different from other groups in terms of values, opinions, and lifestyle? Can other categories be clustered with your target audience? This information about the environment of the group and the community will help you make decisions about the normal and natural groupings of people.

The third, and perhaps the most controlling, factor that influences the degree of specification is the research budget. Simply put, how many different groups can you afford to conduct? Or another way of asking the question is this: How much are you willing to invest in this study? If the budget is restricted and only three focus groups can be conducted, you will need to decide where you can get the most meaningful information.

Caution is needed when the focus group participants represent diverse categories of people. It is a fallacy to assume that any one individual can "represent" their neighborhood, race, gender, or culture. Each person speaks for himself or herself. When asked, however, these individuals may attempt to offer insights about the opinions of the entire group and the degree of accuracy may vary greatly. If you want to capture the opinions of a certain group of people then you'll need to conduct a sufficient number of focus groups with that particular category of people. Diverse focus group are not sufficiently sensitive to pick up trends of subcategories of people.

Let's suppose that a religious group wanting to reach new members decided to use focus groups to discover those features that would prompt attendance. The religious group would need to decide what type of members it is seeking to attract—teenagers, young families, single parent families, seniors, residents living within a geographic area, and so on. Background information should be sought on the target audience using whatever means are available to the religious group. This background data could involve census information, secondary data in the public domain, or even individual interviews with experts. If several different audiences are sought, then it is advisable to conduct a series of focus groups with each audience category: teens, single parent families, and so on. A strategic decision is needed regarding the research budget. What is the worth of this information? With X resources, one audience category might be investigated, but 2X resources are needed to include two audiences, 3X for three audiences, and so on.

The Composition of the Group

The focus group is characterized by homogeneity but with sufficient variation among participants to allow for contrasting opinions. Most commonly, homogeneity is sought in terms of occupation, past use of a program or service, educational level, age, gender, education, or family characteristics. The guiding principle is the degree to which these factors will influence sharing within the group discussion. Some mixes of participants do not work well because of limited understanding of other lifestyles and situations. For example, care must be exercised in mixing individuals from different life stages and styles—young working women with homemakers in their 60s who have not been employed outside of the home—unless the topic clearly cuts across these life stages and styles. Unfortunately, it doesn't work well to divide the group up into thirds with equal numbers from three contrasting groups and expect the discussion to be a forum of differing points of view. A more workable strategy is either to conduct a separate series of focus groups with each segment or to target the most important group if resources are limited.

At times, it is unwise to mix gender in focus groups, particularly if the topic of discussion is experienced differently by each sex. Men may have a tendency to speak more frequently and with more authority when in groups with women—sometimes called the "peacock effect"—and consequently this can be an irritant to the women in the group. Myril Axelrod (1975, p. 5) recommends against mixing sexes in a focus group because "men tend to 'perform' for the women and vice versa."

A related topic is the involvement of both husband and wife in the same focus group discussion. I have found that there is a tendency for one spouse to remain silent and defer to the talkative spouse. Even if the silent spouse disagrees, it appears that he or she is reluctant to comment even when such comments are solicited from the moderator. As a result, I have found that a focus group composed of four married couples turns out to be a discussion of four people with four rather silent partners.

The Size of a Focus Group

The traditionally recommended size of the focus group has ranged from 6 to 12 participants. The prevailing norm within marketing research is still in the range of 10 to 12 people; however, when dealing with complex topics or with knowledgeable participants, this size is still too large. The ideal size of a focus group typically falls between 6 and 9 participants. Focus groups with more than 12 participants are not recommended for most situations because they limit each person's opportunity to share insights and observations. In addition, group dynamics change when participants want but are not able to describe their experiences. For example, if people do not have an opportunity to share experiences in the total group, they may lean over to the next person to whisper their concerns. This phenomenon is a signal that the group is too large. Small focus groups, or "mini-focus groups," with 4 to 6 participants are becoming increasingly popular because the smaller groups are easier to recruit and host and more comfortable for participants. The disadvantage of the mini-focus group is that it limits the total range of experiences simply because the group is smaller. Four people will have had fewer total experiences than a dozen.

Often the nature of the questioning route and participant characteristics yield clues as to the ideal size. Focus groups with specialized audiences in which the intent is to get more in-depth insights are usually best accomplished by smaller groups. Also, smaller groups are preferable when the participants have a great deal to share about the topic or have had intense or lengthy experiences with the topic of discussion. In other discussions in which the researcher wants to discover the range of perceptions in more general terms, larger groups are preferable.

General Selection Rules

I will begin with rules of thumb for guiding the selection of participants for focus group interviews. These rules are then woven into several specific strategies for identifying participants. First, I offer these general rules to guide the selection process:

Set Exact Specifications. As precisely as possible, identify the characteristics of the people you want in the group. Be cautious when making selections on nonobservable factors such as attitudes, opinions, or values. Use these nonobservable factors only if you have nonbiased empirical data with which to make your decisions.

Maintain Control of the Selection Process. The researcher should maintain control of the selection process. At times, it is advisable or even necessary to let others make decisions on the selection process or to carry out strategies used for selection. For example, suppose the U.S. Postal Service wanted to conduct focus groups with experienced mail sorters and clerks in five major cities. Line supervisors would have to be consulted because of the impact on work floor productivity when workers are absent. These supervisors must be aware of and approve the release of the employees. Because of budget limitations the researcher may not be able to make advance site visits to conduct the employee screening and make final decisions about participation. In these cases, the researcher would have to depend on the local site supervisors to ensure that there are a sufficient number of participants who are correctly screened and able to leave the work floor during the focus group interview. Unless precise instructions are developed for selection and recruitment, there is a risk that those attending will not be typical of the employee category.

Use the Resources of the Sponsoring Organization in Recruiting. A strategy that has been beneficial in public and nonprofit organizations is to use the skills and strengths of the organization to recruit participants, using carefully laid out protocol developed by the researcher. Suppose a college wanted to conduct focus groups with alumni to discover the ways alumni preferred to be informed about developments at the school. Also suppose that the budget is tight and the college could conduct focus groups with additional categories of alumni if the recruiting could be conducted by the alumni office. The researcher might want to use the resources of the alumni office—the class lists by year with demographic data to screen the participants; the clerical staff to make the telephone contacts; the name of the school and the alumni office to establish credibility and legitimacy. Although all of these tasks could be done by a research firm, the costs would likely be greater. However, the researcher must be explicit in laying out the steps needed for selection, giving instructions about how to make the telephone request and preparing the official letter of request.

Beware of Bias. An often overlooked problem with focus group interviewing is *selection bias.* Selection bias can develop in subtle ways and seriously erode the quality of the study. Here are some examples:

- Beware of participants picked from memory. Memory is fallible, limited, and selective. Those names that can be readily recalled may differ in substantial ways from the available study population.
- Beware of participants picked because they've expressed concern about the topic. The conscientious supervisor or local influential inquires about the purpose of the study and after it is explained, several names quickly come to mind. These names may include those who have expressed concern, anger, or frustration with the topic. The supervisor assumes that the study would be improved if the researchers received this input and also show the employees that the supervisor took their concerns seriously

enough to suggest they be included in the group discussion. Similar problems can emerge when selection is based on nominations from local residents or influentials. Once again the names that first come to mind to these knowledgeable local residents may be considerably different from a cross-section of residents.

- Beware of participants picked because they are clones of the supervisor doing the selection. It is our human tendency to assume that those who think like we do are insightful, intelligent, and perceptive. Their logic and vocabulary is familiar and values are similar. The supervisor, with the best of intentions, unwittingly selects those with similar characteristics.

- Beware of participants who are nonproductive. In certain situations, the supervisor may not be interested in releasing the most productive employees to attend a focus group. If someone has to go the focus group interview and the pressure is on the work crew, it's tempting to send the dead wood. Although it may not be your intent, you may inadvertently assemble the disinterested employees or those who are tuned out to the organization.

Randomization Is Useful. Randomization helps ensure a nonbiased cross section, essentially giving everyone in the pool an equal chance of selection. Randomization is an effective strategy to minimize the selection bias described above. However, randomization works only if your pool of prospective participants meet your selection criteria.

Balance Cost and Quality. Locating participants can involve considerable cost. Lower cost alternatives should be considered. Several factors can result in higher recruitment costs: too many selection screens, selection screens based on attitudes or opinions, participants who are hesitant to participate, topics that seem trivial or frivolous, the sponsor's image, interview locations or times that are inconvenient, just to name a few. In virtually all situations, there are multiple options for recruitment— each of which will have differing costs, efficiency, and quality of result. Quality refers to the ability to locate the right people—those targeted for the study. At times, compromises are needed, such as finding alternative locations or dropping some selection screens. Creative alternatives can sometimes be found through collegial brainstorming.

Nonusers Can Be Difficult to Locate. Organizations sometimes seek views of nonusers but find that recruiting is quite difficult. Typically, there are no reliable lists of nonusers. In some ubiquitous services, such as Cooperative Extension, it is regularly found that residents do not consider themselves to be users—but in fact, they have made use of information provided by that agency. In other situations, an individual may use services of an agency infrequently and the screening questions may need to specify a time period for use or a frequency of use. Generally, nonusers are harder to find, often because reliable screening questions are cumbersome and in some situations the participants are just not aware of their use.

Users May Differ in Ways That Can Affect the Study. When organizations, either public or private, seek insight from their users they often discover that these users differ in frequency or intensity of use. Whether your organization provides social services, information, or consumer products, some will use your products more often or more in depth than will others. For example, in a study, church members were categorized in two ways: by how frequently they attended church services as well as how much money they contributed annually to the church. Financial contributions are an imprecise measure of intensity, but in this study the intent was to determine the level of financial support for a new building project—and financial support was essential if the addition was to be feasible.

No Selection Process Is Perfect. We make the best choices we can with the knowledge we have available at the time. Selection involves trade-offs and is limited by our human capacities. We may overlook certain aspects of the problem and inadvertently neglect individuals with unique points of view. A test of the selection process is whether you are able to successfully defend the selection process to colleagues and clients. Trade-offs constantly occur and require weighing a possibility of bias or perception of bias against costs.

Selection Strategies

Several specific strategies are regularly used for identifying participants for focus group interviews.

The List. Usually the preferred choice is an existing list because it is fast and economical. This could include existing lists of clients, members, employees, or those who use services of the organization. Whenever possible, attempt to obtain more than the name, phone number, and address. In some situations the organization may have a database of customers' sociodemographic characteristics or employees' years of experience, age, and educational level. These additional demographics may be of use in screening participants. The quality of the list needs to be considered, because some of these pre-existing lists are well maintained and revised regularly to reflect address changes, but other lists contain substantial errors.

An alternative strategy is to contact other organizations or groups for names. Once the audience has been targeted and the necessary characteristics for individual selection have been determined, the researcher might investigate if existing groups in the community have members with these characteristics. Some groups will be reluctant to release names or will have formal restrictions on releasing member lists. Cooperation is more likely if the researcher explains that there is no selling, that volunteers can decline to participate, and that participants will receive a gift. In some situations in the nonprofit environment, a contribution to the group treasury, tactfully offered, can be a reflection of the value placed on assistance in obtaining names of volunteers.

Piggyback Focus Groups. Piggyback focus groups can be effective when you add focus group interviews to another event, meeting, or occasion. The participants are gathered for another purpose and the focus group is held during free time, during a meal, or after hours so as not to interrupt the primary purpose of the gathering. This strategy works well with professional associations or special interest associations, especially when national representation is desired.

On Location. Increasingly, focus groups are being held on location—at the place where the participants come for recreation, shopping, or other purposes. A key success factor is the ability to observe and intercept participants as they pass through a gate, turnstile, or hallway, ask several screening questions, and then offer an invitation to the focus group. The focus group is held soon after recruitment in a convenient location. Care must be exercised in using this method so that those selected have the requisite characteristics of your target audience. This is the method of choice when the purpose of the study relates to their attendance. For example, a nature center, zoo, or recreational center might intercept a random assortment of people passing through the gate and invite them to a special discussion. The incentive for participation might be free tickets for another visit.

A state department of natural resources wanted to learn more about visitors at the state parks. Park employees were trained to conduct regular focus groups with park visitors. At designated times when a vehicle entered the park, the park employee offered a special invitation: "We'd like to invite one adult from your party to join us in an hour discussion at 7:00 pm tonight. We will be talking about the park and we would like your suggestions. If someone is willing to join our discussion we'll give you a free bundle of firewood."

Nominations. An effective strategy in community studies is to ask neutral parties for names. These neutral parties are often people who have an opportunity to get to know a number of other people such as local merchants, clergy, or influentials, but in some cases they might be local residents selected at random. The first step is to identify the specifications for participants and then use multiple sources for a nomination list. Only a few names are sought from each source to ensure an adequate mix of participants. Names are then randomly selected from this nomination list for the invitation to the focus group. For example: If you wanted to find senior citizens who live within a community who own cars you might seek nominations from local service stations, other senior citizens, or merchants who do business with seniors. If you wanted to find parents from the community who have at least one child in high school you might ask school staff, park and recreation staff, clergy, or perhaps randomly selected teens. In these studies it is often advantageous to have the identification of focus group participants conducted by local residents who are trusted and have roots in the community. Also beneficial when seeking nominations for names is to be able to briefly describe the study in terms of how the results will benefit the participants or the community.

Snowball Samples. A variation of the nomination strategy is the snowball sample, in which you ask those who have already passed through the selection screen for their suggestions for participants. The logic is that those who have the targeted characteristics are likely to know of others who also have these same features. A key factor, however, is that the study have obvious benefit to the community or individual; if this is not possible, then another type of incentive to participation must be used. This snowball sampling could be used at two different times. When making initial contact with the potential participants you might ask if they know of others who meet the qualifications, or you might ask at the conclusion of the focus group.

Screening/Selection Services. These services are located in most metropolitan areas around the country and are regularly used by commercial market research firms. These agencies usually have an existing database of potential focus group participants categorized by sociodemographic characteristics. In addition, they are often able to supplement their existing lists with telephone screening if and when needed. These agencies are often listed in the "Market Research" section of the telephone book.

Random Telephone Screening. A popular means of recruiting focus group participants, especially by commercial market research firms, is random telephone screening. The procedure typically begins by random selection of names from a telephone directory. A series of screening questions is used to determine if those called meet the criteria established for the focus group.

Telephone screening is most efficient when searching for participants with fairly common characteristics. As the number of screens increases, the efficiency of this procedure will decrease. For example, in an effort to reach working homemakers, it was necessary to call 50 households in order to identify 25 working homemakers. However, only 10 of these were able and willing to participate in a focus group interview at the designated time. If the screen would have been more restrictive, for example, working homemakers with children between the ages of 5 to 10, then the efficiency of the calling procedure would decrease.

The efficiency of the telephone screening procedures is also affected by the skills of the interviewer. Friendly and sincere calls that convey interest and enthusiasm are most effective. Several years ago I had an opportunity to work cooperatively with a market research company in helping a community nonprofit organization. The nonprofit organization had employed several college students and used a predetermined interviewing script for calling. The students were finding that people did pass through the screens but then often declined the invitation to attend the discussion. The percentage of invitations accepted dramatically increased when a professional moderator began making the phone calls. The professional conveyed a sense of confidence, friendliness, and sincerity that had been developed after years of experience. Since invitations over the phone are often regarded with suspicion, those making the invitations require considerable communication skill.

Ads in Newspapers and on Bulletin Boards. A recruitment strategy that is used by some marketing agencies is media ads. For example: "Bought a new car lately? If so, call Debbie at 765-4321." Or "Participants wanted for a marketing study on lawnmowers. If you have purchased a new lawnmower in the past year you may qualify. Receive $20 for participating in a discussion. Call 987-6543 for more information." Or an ad placed on the apartment bulletin board: "Wanted, apartment residents who recycle cans, glass, and paper to participate in a market research study. No sales. $25 if you qualify. Call 876-5432 for more information." These ads can be effective in certain situations but the primary draw is often the financial incentive for participation. As a result, there is a slight risk that those motivated by the $25 incentive are different in some critical respects from those who do not call.

The process of identification and recruitment for focus groups is considerably easier when begun with names, phone numbers, and background information about these potential participants. Existing directories, membership lists, or organizational records can be consulted to identify potential candidates. More effort is needed when membership lists or organizational records are unavailable.

Sampling Procedures for Focus Groups

When researchers approach focus group interviewing they carry with them many of the traditions, wisdom, and procedures that were intended for experimental and quantifiable studies. Some of these procedures readily transfer, but others do not. The issue of sampling procedures requires some special thought when planning focus group interviews.

Most researchers have "cut their teeth" on randomization and because these procedures have served them well in some arenas they may assume that the same procedures are also appropriate for qualitative studies in general and focus group interviews in particular. Randomization essentially removes the bias in selection—that is, all participants possess an equivalent chance to be involved in the study. Random selection is particularly appropriate when inferences are made to a larger population because of the assumption that opinions, attitudes, or whatever being studied will be normally distributed within that population. Therefore, a random sample of sufficient size will be an adequate substitute for surveying the entire population.

It is important to keep in mind that the intent of focus groups is not to infer but to understand, not to generalize but to determine the range, not to make statements about the population but to provide insights about how people perceive a situation. As a result, focus groups require a flexible research design, and although a degree of randomization may be used, it is not the primary factor in selection.

The driving force in participant selection is the purpose of the study. Once again, researchers must focus on why the study is being conducted and about whom statements will be made. Although the purpose dictates the nature of the selection, the process is also tempered by practical concerns and the credibility of the study. With all sampling strategies the researcher must be concerned about the degree to which that strategy could lead to distortions in the data. The researcher should anticipate questions about the means of selection and provide the rationale for those decisions.

When randomization is used in focus groups, it is often for the purpose of elimination of selection bias inherent in some forms of personal recruitment. Typically, lists provide more names than needed and either a systematic or random sampling procedure should be used in picking the actual names. In a *systematic sample*, each *n*th number is picked to be in the selection pool. For example, if 10 names are needed from a list of 200, every 20th person on the list is selected. The *random sample* consists of drawing names or ID numbers out of the hat or using a random number table to select from the list of 200 people.

The Danger of Existing Groups

At times, the focus group interview is used with groups that are already established, such as employee work groups, boards of directors, or professional colleagues. People within these groups may have formal or informal ways of relating to each other that can influence their responses. Superior-subordinate relationships among participants can inhibit discussion. The focus group technique works well when all participants are on an equal basis, but if supervisors, bosses, or even a friend of the boss is in the group, the results might be affected. In addition, there might be a reluctance to express negative observations in front of co-workers, especially if supervisors are present. Focus groups should be conducted without the presence of supervisors; if necessary, a special group session can be conducted for supervisors. Furthermore, it is critical to assure confidentiality and to remind them that their names will not be attached to any report.

Another concern about existing groups are the pre-established lines of communication among colleagues or people who are close friends. Because communications are so sophisticated in these settings it makes analysis almost impossible. The raise of an eyebrow, the tone of voice, teasing of colleagues, or humor may have one interpretation to the analyst but quite another to the participants themselves. The focus group process might work rather well with the group eagerly sharing information, but the problem lies in interpretation of the results.

Number of Groups Needed

When compared to quantitative survey methods, the number of different individuals and groups involved in a focus group study is surprisingly small. A helpful rule of thumb is to continue conducting interviews until little new information is provided—or when you have reached theoretical saturation. *Theoretical saturation* is a concept coming from grounded theory, which was described by Glaser and Strauss (1967). With theoretical saturation, one samples until each category of investigation is saturated. Strauss and Corbin (1990) describe it as a situation that occurs when

(1) no new or relevant data seem to emerge regarding a category; (2) the category development is dense, insofar as all of the paradigm elements are accounted for, along with variation and process; (3) the relationships between categories are well established and validated. (p. 188)

In focus group interviews typically, the first two groups with a particular audience segment provide a considerable amount of new information, but by the third or fourth session a fair amount has already been covered. If this occurs, there is limited value in continuing with additional group discussions with that particular audience segment. The suggested rule of thumb is to evaluate after the third group. If new insights are provided in the third group, then conduct additional groups as needed.

The recommendation of three focus groups is conditioned by the nature of the study, the diversity of the participants' exposure to the topic of discussion, and differences that reflect social, ethnic, or geographic diversity. In some situations it is highly advisable to go beyond three focus groups. More groups are advisable when participants are heterogeneous or when statewide or national level insights are wanted. Fewer groups will be needed if the study is intended to provide helpful insights about an easily reversible program decision. For example, occasionally focus groups are conducted to determine how a new program will be received. If the new program involves a slight realignment of staff time and does not require an additional investment for staff or buildings, fewer groups are probably appropriate. However, if focus groups are intended to assist decision makers in making major decisions that are hard to reverse (e.g., new buildings, hiring more staff), then more focus groups would be warranted.

The topic of the focus group interview might relate to a narrow category of people with similar backgrounds who have had the same level of exposure to the program. Consequently, fewer focus groups would be needed. In other circumstances, the people may be exposed to differing levels of the program, and each category of participant may have different perceptions. This diversity of exposure to the issue of investigation would favor increasing the number of focus groups.

Getting People to Attend the Focus Group

A number of years ago my colleagues and I began conducting focus groups for nonprofit organizations. Some of these early experiences with focus groups were disastrous because so few people showed up for the discussion. Invitations were extended in the same way that we had traditionally invited people to other types of meetings, seminars, or workshops. As we analyzed what had gone wrong we discovered several major flaws in our traditional invitations. Our invitations were not personalized, we had no follow-up to the original invitation, we were requesting people to take time to attend a discussion on a seemingly insignificant topic, we were unaware of the seasonal time demands on some audiences, we did not build on existing social and organizational relationships, and, finally, we did not offer incentives.

Invitations to focus groups should be personalized. Each participant should feel that they are needed at the interview. Staff members who make telephone invitations should receive special training to extend warm and sincere requests for participants—without sounding like the invitation is being read. The invitation should stress that the potential participant has special experiences or insights that would be of value in the study. Form letters prepared on copy machines are not personal. They should be replaced by individual letters on letterhead stationary.

Systematic notification procedures provide the necessary follow-up on invitations. This involves a series of sequential activities, including the following:

First, establish meeting times for the group interviews that don't conflict with existing community activities or functions. Some people have time schedules that change on a regular and predictable basis. Farmers, tax consultants, certain small businesspeople, and teachers are but a few examples. Focus groups are best conducted during their slack or off season. For example, I have avoided conducting focus groups with Minnesota farmers from mid April to early August, and again from early September to late October. On a related note, care should be taken to avoid dates that conflict with popular sporting events (local or college teams, the World Series, Monday Night Football, etc.), national events (political conventions, elections, etc.), or periods of high television viewing (rating weeks, beginning of fall network shows, etc.).

Second, contact potential participants via phone (or in person) approximately 10 to 14 days before the focus group session. If you are contacting professionals or others with busy schedules you may need to make this contact a month or more in advance. Usually it is best to slightly overrecruit at this initial stage, often between 10% and 25% depending on the topic and incentive. Overrecruiting is usually not necessary if employees are released from work responsibilities to attend the focus group.

Third, send a personalized invitation just after the phone or in-person invitation. For many groups, this is one week before the session. The letter is sent on official letterhead with a personal salutation, an inside address, and the signature of the sender. It provides additional details about the session, location, and topic of discussion. An example of such a letter is included in Appendix 5B.

Fourth, phone each person the day before the focus group to remind them of the session and inquire about their intent to attend. This "dentist" style phone call serves two purposes. It reinforces the importance of the group ("This must be an important session because you've invited me three times!") and it reminds participants who might have forgotten about the session.

People are more likely to take time to attend a focus group interview if they believe the study is important. Importance is conveyed in several ways, one is by providing information about the study and the anticipated benefits or consequences of the study. The invitation must build a convincing case that the study has benefit or value to certain specific parties. It could mean providing a rationale of why the study is important, linking it to another major event or activity, or indicating how the results will be used. However, additional actions, such as incentives are often needed to convey importance.

Incentives to Participation

Incentives are needed because participation in a focus group requires time and effort. Typically, the prospective participant must reserve time on a busy schedule. For some individuals whose lives are unpredictable or who are subject to the wishes of others, this can be a promise of considerable magnitude. Furthermore, this prospective participant typically incurs expenses to participate that could involve child care, travel, and meals. Finally, the prospective participant will spend time in the focus group itself. This level of individual contribution exceeds that needed for other forms of information gathering. The mail-out survey and the telephone interview are conducted in the participant's home or office and no travel is necessary. With the mail-out survey, and to a lesser extent the telephone interview, the participants have some choice as to when they will respond. Furthermore, it is the rare survey or telephone interview that will last for 2 hours. Individual interviews come closest to the focus group in terms of the investment the participant must make. However, with individual interviews the participant is a partner in setting the time of the interview and the location is often convenient, such as within the home or office of the interviewee.

Focus groups are unique from other information gathering processes in terms of the investment that must be made by the individual. It is therefore no surprise that a tradition has been established to compensate people for their investment of effort. From a practical aspect, it would be near to impossible to conduct focus groups in a number of situations without attention to incentives.

The incentive is not a reward, and not really an honorarium or salary. It is an incentive! It serves as a stimulus to attend the session. The primary function of the incentive is to get the participants to show up for the focus group—and to show up on time. The motivational influence of the incentive hasn't worked if the participants are surprised when they receive it. Imagine yourself coming home from a hard day's work. You are tired and hungry and the day really hasn't gone that well. You are looking forward to a relaxing evening at home. But, you promised someone a couple of weeks ago that you would go to a focus group tonight. Now the incentive kicks in. You recall what was promised if you attend and you decide that it will be worth the effort to participate in the focus group. Another way in which the incentive works is as an encouragement to hold open the time of the scheduled focus group. Some people will receive a number of last-minute requests for the same time period. The incentive serves to protect the promised time slot from being preempted. The third function of the incentive is to communicate to the participants that the focus group is important.

By far the most common type of incentive is money. Money has several advantages in that it is immediately recognized and understood by the participants, it is portable, most people like it, it fits into small spaces, and, most important, it works. When considering money several principles apply. Immediate payment in cash is preferred. The promise of a check in the mail within a few weeks will be a disappointment to some. The amount of the payment can and should vary—but not within the same focus group. Each person within a particular group, and sometimes within the total study, should receive the same payment. Researchers don't want to create the impression that some people's opinions are worth more than others. When considering the amount of payment the researcher should be mindful of the workable range (see Figure 5.1). At the lower end of the range the researcher risks insulting the participants with a payment that is too small. Although each person will vary, often promises of payments in the range of $10 to $15 may be too low and be a detriment to the project. When time and travel are considered, it may be below minimum wage and just not enough to be taken seriously. At the upper end of the range the researcher will find that the study can quickly get too expensive and the participants may feel awkward receiving what they perceive to be an excessive payment—especially from a public or nonprofit organization.

Generally, as the payment approaches the ceiling the time needed to recruit is reduced. In some studies it may be more efficient to pay more for incentives and thereby reduce the recruitment time. At the time of this writing, amounts of $20 to $50 have been found to be an efficient

CEILING   Amounts above this level are less efficient. Maximum efficiency in promoting attendance is achieved as the ceiling is approached.

WORKABLE
RANGE OF
PAYMENT

FLOOR   This is the minimum amount to promote attendance and yet avoid insulting participants. When payments go below this amount the participants may feel slighted at being paid too little for their time and inconvenience.

Figure 5.1. Range of Payment for Focus Group Participants

range for public and nonprofit studies. As the amount approaches $50 an interesting phenomenon begins to occur. If the participant has a last-minute conflict, he or she is more likely to call the moderator and offer to send a replacement. When working with elite categories of focus group participants, the amounts may need to be adjusted upward. Focus groups with engineers, physicians, attorneys, upper management, and similar categories may require amounts in the $50 to $100+ range.

When asked why they participate in focus groups, 66% of those surveyed indicated compensation as the main motivator, based on a study by Rodgers Marketing Research in Canton, Ohio. However, other factors can be considered as well. The topic, previous participation in focus groups, and interest in participating all contribute to the likelihood that focus group participants will attend ("Study: Money Not the Only Motivation," 1991, p. 17).

Money is not the only incentive and in some cases it can be inappropriate or illegal. Employees released from work to attend the focus group are already being compensated and financial incentives are usually deemed inappropriate, if not illegal.

The incentive is symbolic and other symbols may be worthy substitutes. Food, which can range from light snacks to a full-fledged meal, can be effective in some circumstances. Gifts also can work well but they must be adequately described in advance to avoid confusion when they are presented. Sometimes gifts can be of limited financial value but have significant emotional or psychological value.

Several years ago a researcher was sending out a burdensome survey to private forest landowners. Because the survey was lengthy the research team was concerned that the respondents would not reply. As a result, considerable discussion was given to an incentive to participate. A number of items were suggested and rejected. Finally one of the team members had a clever idea. "Up at the Forestry School we have a garbage can full of tree seeds. But these are not just any seeds. Back a number of years ago during the Bicentennial we were experimenting with hybrid spruce trees. We interbred red, white, and blue spruce and the result was called the 'All American Spruce.' The problem was that the new tree did not possess the desirable features we wanted and as a result we did not commercially market the tree. Nevertheless, we have lots of seed from a new variety of tree and we could put this seed in small envelopes along with a note describing the development. Maybe the forest owners would consider it interesting." The comment was a considerable understatement. Inadvertently we discovered that we had given the forest owners an object of major value. It reinforced their values and could not be obtained elsewhere at any cost. The respondents wrote back and asked for more seeds. They put the packets on their coffee tables and told their friends about it. Some even framed the seeds. The seeds were about to be dumped out by the researchers, but to those receiving the seeds it was a gift beyond value.

A positive, upbeat invitation, the opportunity to share opinions, meals, or refreshments, and tangible gifts are all helpful incentives for potential participants. So is a convenient and easy-to-find meeting location. It is also helpful if participants know they will be involved in an important research project in which their opinions will be of particular value. A number of people have a natural curiosity and an interest in sharing their opinions. They feel honored when they are asked to provide opinions. Finally, people are more likely to attend a focus group if the invitation builds on some existing community, social, or personal relationship. Thus, an invitation might mention the connection between the study and a local organization.

The researcher should also consider the barriers to participation, those factors that would prevent people from attending. Start by making attendance easy and comfortable. Consider the barriers that might inhibit participation—child care, starting time, distance. Each of these barriers should be removed.

Identification of the Sponsor

Who's sponsoring the study? This is one of the first questions asked by some people when they receive a telephone invitation to participate in a group discussion. When a market research firm offers invitations to a focus group interview, they will use their agency name and letterhead but will not reveal the specific client or product being tested. They will describe it as a type or category of product, such as soft drinks, farm pesticides, or automobiles. Care is taken to avoid naming the specific product so that participants will not come with presuppositions. Often the client wants to determine how their product, service, or organization is positioned in relation to the competition. If the participants know the sponsor of the study they may be biased. Also, excessive background information encourages participants to offer solutions to the client's problem as opposed to the intended purpose—that of identifying the nature of the problem. Also, too much advance information may prompt some participants to "research" the topic, discuss it with others in advance, or rehearse their opinions. These activities have a tendency to cause respondents to act like experts and trap them into a point of view that they feel they need to defend. Furthermore, knowing the name of the product might bias comments in the group discussion. It is often best to anticipate that people will inquire who is sponsoring the study and to have a generic response that provides an answer without influencing later responses. At the end of the focus group session the participants can be provided more specific information on the sponsorship and purpose of the study.

Nonprofit organizations conducting their own focus groups should give special thought to how they will respond to questions about the sponsorship of the study. Premature revelation of the sponsor can bias later responses, and yet the answer must be truthful. Truthful responses need not be all-inclusive, and it may be sufficient to describe the sponsor as a subunit of the organization or a higher level in the same organization. For example, community education might be described as a study sponsored by the school district. A human services department may be identified as county or state government.

Summary

Effective focus groups require the right participants. Homogeneity is the guiding principle of focus groups, and the researcher must determine the nature of that homogeneity based on the purpose of the study. Participants can be recruited in a variety of ways, including lists or directories, cooperating organizations or individuals, telephone screening, or "on location" at an event or activity. Care should be exercised when conducting focused interviews with existing groups or organizations.

People often ask how many focus group sessions should be conducted. There is no universal answer, but the helpful rule of thumb is to initially plan three sessions and then modify the number as needed. If nothing new emerges from the third session, then additional groups may be unneeded. If new insights and opinions continue to develop at the third session, then more interviews should be added. When the same themes repeat, it is time to stop interviewing and write the report. Incentives and systematic invitation procedures help guarantee attendance. People are often skeptical of attending meetings where the purpose or sponsor is unknown. Respect the cautious attitude of potential participants by providing sincere, sensitive, and upbeat encouragement.

APPENDIX 5A

Telephone Screening Questionnaire: Working Women Between 25 and 49 in Fairview County

Interviewee Name _____ Date _____
Address _____ Phone ( )_____
Hello, my name is _____ , and I'm calling for Northern Research in Minneapolis. We are conducting a short survey in Fairview County and I would like to talk to a woman in the household who works outside the home. Is that person available?

[IF AVAILABLE THEN CONTINUE. IF NOT, THEN TERMINATE]
Northern Research is conducting a study on informal education in Fairview County and I would like to ask you a few questions. The questions will take less than 2 minutes. Is it OK to begin?

1. Do you live in Fairview County?
   ( ) Yes [CONTINUE]
   ( ) No [TERMINATE]
2. Are you employed full time or part time outside the home?
   ( ) Full time [CONTINUE]
   ( ) Part time [TERMINATE]
3. In what age category do you belong?
   ( ) Under 25 [TERMINATE]
   ( ) 25-34 [RECRUIT AT LEAST 8]
   ( ) 35-49 [RECRUIT AT LEAST 8]
   ( ) 50 or over [TERMINATE]

[PARTICIPANT RECRUITMENT]

Ms. _____, Northern Research is sponsoring a meeting with working women in Fairview County to discuss informal education. We know that working women are busy and yet they get new information and education from a variety of sources. We would like you to join a group of other working women as we discuss this topic. This is not a sales meeting, but strictly a research project. It will be held on Thursday evening, December 3rd, at the Riverside Restaurant in Conover. We would like you to be our guest for dinner, which will begin at 7:00 p.m. The meeting will be over at 9:30 p.m. Will you be able to attend?

( ) Yes [CONFIRM NAME AND ADDRESS]

( ) No [THANK AND TERMINATE]

[IF YES]

I will be sending you a letter in a few days confirming this meeting. If you need any help with directions or if you need to cancel, please call our office at _____ . Thank you and good-bye.

APPENDIX 5B

Sample Letter of Invitation
to Focus Group

[OFFICIAL LETTERHEAD]

[Date]

[Name and address of participant]

Thank you for accepting our invitation to attend the discussion at the Riverside Restaurant in Conover on Thursday, December 3rd. The Riverside Restaurant is on Highway 42 on the north side of town. The street address is 2345 Highway 42. We would like you to be our guest for dinner, which will begin at 7:00 p.m. The meeting will follow the meal and conclude by 9:30 p.m.

Since we are talking to a limited number of people, the success and quality of our discussion is based on the cooperation of the people who attend. Because you have accepted our invitation, your attendance at the session is anticipated and will aid in making the research project a success.

The discussion you will be attending will be a forum of women in the community who are employed outside of the home. We will be discussing educational opportunities and we would like to get your opinions on this subject. This is strictly a research project, and no sales or solicitations will be made. At the conclusion of the session we will be giving you $20.00 to cover your expenses in attending. Child care will be provided.

If for some reason you find you are not able to attend, please call us to let us know as soon as possible. Our phone number is (612) 555-1234.

We look forward to seeing you on December 3.

Sincerely,

Richard Krueger
Forum Moderator

6

Moderating Skills

Interviewing looks deceptively simple but requires mental discipline, preparation, and group interaction skills. Much of the success of the focused interview depends on good questions asked of the right respondents, but another ingredient is essential—a skillful moderator.

Throughout this chapter I purposely choose to describe the interviewer's role by using the term *moderator*. This term highlights a specific function of the interviewer—that of moderating or guiding the discussion. The term *interviewer* tends to convey a more limited impression of two-way communication between an interviewer and an interviewee. By contrast, the focus group affords the opportunity for multiple interactions not only between the interviewer and the respondent but among all participants in the group. The focus group is not a collection of simultaneous individual interviews but rather a group discussion where the conversation flows because of the nurturing of the moderator.

Selecting the Right Moderator

When selecting a moderator, it is important to look for certain personal characteristics that have relevance for focus group leaders. These attributes have a direct bearing on the nature of the group interaction and thereby affect the quality of discussion. The moderator should be comfortable and familiar with group processes. Previous experience in working with groups or training in group dynamics is helpful. Amy Andrews (1977) expands on this requirement:

> Since half of the moderator's function is to stimulate and guide the group, a knowledge of group dynamics would seem to be an important criterion for selection. For example, the moderator must know how to deal with a quiet, passive group, an overly exuberant group, an outspoken group member, a group member who is unqualified, a group which consistently goes off on a tangent, a group which appears to be giving inconsistent responses, a group which does not understand the question, a group which misses the point completely, a group which is inarticulate, a hostile group or group member, a nervous, tense group discussing a sensitive subject, etc. (p. 128)

The moderator exercises a mild, unobtrusive control over the group. As the discussion proceeds, irrelevant topics may be introduced by participants and the moderator carefully and subtly guides the conversation back on target. Part of the skill of moderating is the ability of the moderator to make these transitions and yet maintain group enthusiasm and interest for the topic. The moderator also must have a sense of timing—timing for the mood of the group and the appropriateness of discussion alternatives. Like the actor who takes too many bows, the moderator also must know when to wrap up the questioning and move on to the next issue, but not prematurely.

The moderator should possess a curiosity about the topic and the participants. Indifference, apathy, and cynicism are quickly spotted by participants and severely curtail the conversation. Furthermore, this curiosity may result in follow-up questions and probes that uncover new avenues or connections that shed new insight on the topic of study.

Respect for participants may be one of the most important factors affecting the quality of focus group results. The moderator must truly believe that the participants have wisdom no matter what their level of education, experience, or background. Indeed, they may have limited knowledge, hold opposing values to that of the researchers, or have fuzzy logic, but still the moderator listens attentively with sensitivity. Often after the fourth or fifth group the moderator will have heard the topic discussed in a variety of ways and many of the concerns and key ideas have been said several times. At this point the information is old stuff to the moderator, but it still deserves the respect and active listening that was present the first time it was heard. Lack of respect quickly telegraphs to the participants and essentially shuts down meaningful communication. The moderator must truly believe that the participants have wisdom and insight that need to be uncovered.

The moderator must have adequate background knowledge on the topic of discussion to place all comments in perspective and follow up on critical areas of concern. Some moderators are able to use naïveté to an advantage by prompting participants to amplify their comments, but if used in excess it can become tiresome and inhibit complicated responses. Naïveté is a two-edged sword. In some circumstances it elicits considerable new information that may have been assumed—sometimes incorrectly—by the moderator. Furthermore, it can produce eloquent statements that place the topic of discussion into a larger context. Unfortunately, this same tactic can become infuriating to knowledgeable participants who feel the moderator has not yet earned the right to ask questions or if they feel the moderator is just "playing dumb."

The moderator must be able to communicate clearly and precisely both in writing and orally. Complicated questions reflecting fuzzy thinking are confusing. Sometimes in an effort to be helpful, the moderator asks the question in several ways. The moderator may assume that this strategy helps the participant, but in fact it can do just the opposite. If the questions are perceived as different from each other then the respondent may become confused with the intent of the inquiry.

Moderating requires self-discipline. Focus groups have been jeopardized because novice moderators could not hold back their personal opinions. Internal researchers and others who have a personal commitment to the topic of inquiry need to be particularly careful to suspend their personal views and seek out the perceptions of the group participants. It's hard to listen to people with limited knowledge, who offer half-truths and then criticize a program near and dear to your heart. Harder yet is to smile and say thank you after they've commented. Professional focus group moderators have a distinct advantage in this respect because of their emotional detachment from the topic of the study.

Participants must feel comfortable with the moderator and that the moderator is the appropriate person to ask the questions and that the answers can be openly offered and discussed. There are few absolutes about the physical characteristics of the moderator because much depends on the situation and the past experiences of the participants. It is more than having the participants comfortable with the moderator's dress and appearance. Consideration should be given to factors such as: gender, race, age, socioeconomic characteristics, and technical knowledge. Each of these characteristics, depending on the circumstances, has the potential for inhibiting communication, especially when there is a perceived power differential between the moderator and the participants.

For example, recently an AIDS researcher was planning to conduct focus group interviews with prostitutes who were also intravenous drug users. The topic was on the use of condoms and sterilized needles in AIDS prevention. This situation presented difficulties to the researchers, who understood little of the culture or environment of the target audience. The best strategy in situations such as this may be to enlist the help of someone who understands the culture in moderating the focus groups.

The moderator is not neutral—no matter how hard he or she may try. The moderator is a person, a member of a racial group, an age category, and a gender, and any one of these may be the decisive factor that inhibits or prompts openness within the group. A valuable asset of many nonprofit and public institutions is the ability to recruit volunteer moderators who are not researchers but who possess the critical characteristics essential for success. (This is discussed in greater length in Chapter 10.)

The decision on what kind of moderator to select requires some thought and reflection. Although researchers may have some advice on these characteristics, it may be best to seek the counsel of several potential participants about this and other design factors necessary for a successful focus group.

Finally, a friendly manner and a sense of humor are valuable assets. Just a smile from the moderator can put the group at ease. Smiles typically connote warmth, caring, and empathy and as such are powerful factors in promoting conversation. Humor is a powerful bonding agent, particularly when it is spontaneous and not at anyone's expense. Excessive efforts at humor can fall flat, be misinterpreted, and be counterproductive. However, if someone says something funny, don't hold back your laugh.

The Moderator and Assistant Moderator

Consider using a moderator team: a moderator and an assistant moderator. With this team approach each individual has certain tasks to perform. The moderator is primarily concerned with directing the discussion, keeping the conversation flowing, and taking a few notes. The notes of the moderator are not so much to capture the total interview but rather to identify a few key ideas or future questions that need to be asked. The assistant, however, takes comprehensive notes, operates the tape recorder, handles the environmental conditions and logistics (refreshments, lighting, seating, etc.), and responds to unexpected interruptions. In addition, the assistant notes the participants' body language throughout the discussion. Occasionally the assistant will ask additional questions or probe the response of a participant in more depth near the end of the discussion. The assistant is also extremely helpful in performing the postmeeting analysis of the session.

The assistant moderator is not usually used in private sector market research projects unless as an apprentice in training. This limited use of assistant moderators is due to additional labor costs. I have found assistant moderators well worth the investment. A second set of eyes and ears increases both the total accumulation of information and the validity of the analysis. Furthermore, an assistant provides a means for dealing with interruptions such as latecomers, background noises, or switching tapes.

Public and nonprofit organizations have a potential advantage in the use of assistant moderators. Within many organizations there are individuals that are willing to "sit in" on the focus group out of curiosity or concern and help with assigned functions. In some circumstances these individuals may have background characteristics similar to that of the participants and as a result they may offer valuable assistance in analysis. Care must be taken to ensure that the newly recruited assistant moderator understands the roles and responsibilities and doesn't inadvertently upstage the focus group. This can be solved by explicitly outlining the purpose and rules of the session. An example of assistant moderator rules are included in Appendix 6B.

Moderator Roles

Occasionally the moderator will choose to take on a specific role in the focus group interview. This role or style is selected because it creates an ambience that influences how the participants share information. Each moderator often has a preferred style and it is unknown how successfully one can shift from one preferred role to another. It has been my observation that those who are successful with a particular role should generally stay consistent within that approach. The guiding principle for beginning moderators is to build on your existing strengths. The commonly used roles are:

The Seeker of Wisdom. This moderator is out to obtain understanding, insight, and wisdom. This moderator assumes that the participants have that wisdom and if asked the right questions, they will share it. This moderator may have considerable knowledge or expertise in the topic of discussion.

The Enlightened Novice. This moderator is bright but lacks knowledge (or gives the impression of lacking knowledge) in the area of expertise possessed by the participants. This person will appear to have less knowledge on the topic of discussion than others in the room. The strategy is to get participants to break their assumption that the moderator has adequate background knowledge and therefore the participants need to explain more about the topic and causes. Caution is needed with some elite audiences who may be insulted by the dumb questions of novices. (A variation of the enlightened novice is the dumb novice, which is not recommended. This moderator has done no homework and does not understand the topic or the participants. As a result the focus group experience is an insult to the participants.)

The Expert Consultant. This moderator is clearly an expert in the topic of discussion and functions more like a consultant to the client. This moderator is sought out by the client not just because of his or her ability to lead the focus group but because they are truly experts in the topic of study. They have worked closely with the client and have learned to think like the client by anticipating concerns and questions. This role is regularly used in the market research sector with consumer products.

The Challenger. This moderator is more combative and challenges participants to explain, amplify, and justify their ideas and actions. Occasionally the challenger will even pit one participant against another who seems to have opposite views. Challengers need good timing and effective group skills to avoid alienating the participants. Successful challengers surface opposing points of view that may remain undisclosed with other strategies.

The Referee. The referee role provides balance within the group when there are opposing points of view. In a number of situations, this role is quickly assumed by the moderator who discovers the group has become polarized. The referee gets both sides to describe their views in detail and ensures fairness and respect for all participants. The guiding principle is fair play. Each person deserves an opportunity to talk and is expected to listen and respond to the opinions and views of others.

The Writer. The writer spends a considerable amount of time standing up and writing on a flip chart. Questions may have previously been written on the top of the chart and the writer records the comments on the paper. When the chart is filled the writer will tear it off and tape it on the wall for later review. This strategy has several advantages: participants see what is being recorded and can focus their attention on the specific question at hand, and it allows for seemingly immediate correction. The disadvantage is that this moderator-writer needs to stand (a superior position creating a leader-type role) and participants need to wait, or feel they need to wait, for the moderator to finish writing before contributing additional thoughts. As a result, this discussion can miss some of the spontaneity and synergy that characterize other moderator strategies.

The Team—Discussion Leader and Technical Expert. The team has two individuals with differing areas of expertise but who work well together. The moderator guides the group discussion but is assisted by a technical expert who is able to answer complex technical questions in a nonbiased manner. The technical assistant can sit at the table, often opposite the moderator, or slightly back from the circle. The technical assistant may also carry out many of the same functions of the assistant described above.

The Therapist. The therapist is often seeking information on psychological motivation or why we think the way we do. This moderator will press participants on some aspects of their behavior or past actions by asking follow-up questions such as "Why is that?" or "Why did you do that?" or "How did you feel?" Participant comments that may go unnoticed or are ignored by other moderators are seized by the therapist as a clue to greater insight and understanding.

Mental Preparation

Moderators must be mentally alert and free from distractions, anxieties, or pressures that would limit their ability to think quickly. Moderating a group discussion requires concentration and careful listening. Therefore, they should plan their schedule to minimize the risk of unexpected pressures that would limit their ability to concentrate. Moderators must be able to give their full attention to the group.

Novice moderators must discipline themselves to listen and not talk. A number of people have never learned how to keep silent. Effective moderating in a focus group demands that the moderator avoid expressing personal points of view. When the moderator has controlled the urge to speak, the next task is in focusing complete attention on the group conversation. One can practice this discipline of listening in small group situations and then attempting to remember the points and views expressed by various individuals.

The moderator should be completely familiar with the questioning route and at times the questioning route might be memorized. Typically, the key questions will be limited to about two to five questions, with possible subpoints within each question. The moderator will have a list of questions but will use it only as a reminder of upcoming questions. A mastery of all questions is valuable because the sequence of questions is sometimes modified during the interview. Glancing at the questioning route to remember the next question is tolerable, but reading the question (and taking the eyes off the participants) destroys the spontaneous flow of the discussion.

Another aspect of mental preparation is the discipline of listening and thinking simultaneously. It is not enough to be an empty vessel, listening and absorbing the comments of participants. Judith Langer (1979) offers a series of questions that pass through the moderator's mind while the discussion is in process:

- What else do I need to ask to understand this respondent's statement--what it means, why he/she feels that way, etc.?
- Am I hearing everything I need to know to understand the problem and answer the objectives of the research? Is there a question not on the topic guide [questioning route] that I should ask?
- How much time do I have left? Will I be able to cover everything when just one section of the topic guide could take the full two hours?
- What does all this mean anyway? What am I learning about consumer feelings, beliefs, and behavior? What ideas does this suggest about solving the particular marketing problem?
- How do I get beyond the intellectualizing to respondents' real feelings? I want to reach the level of unanalyzed impressions and emotions—what

goes through people's minds before it becomes censored. The issue is, "What do you feel?" not "What is your opinion?" (p. 10)

The moderator must have a past-present-future time perspective throughout the discussion. Moderators must remember what has already been discussed, what is currently taking place, what the next topic of discussion will be, and finally, what will it all mean when it is concluded.

Without doubt, the moderating process is hard work and fatiguing. Because of the mental and emotional discipline required, it is advisable not to conduct more than two focus groups on the same day.

Purposeful Small Talk and Pre-Session Strategy

Small talk is essential just prior to beginning the group discussion and moderators must be able to casually and comfortably talk about issues of minor importance. When participants arrive for a focus group session they are greeted by the moderator or assistant and made to feel comfortable. The participants may be asked to fill out a short registration form that asks questions about demographic characteristics, particularly those characteristics you may not want to discuss within the group. The hosting role should be similar to that of greeting guests in your home. Emphasis is on creating a friendly, warm, and comfortable environment. Before the participants sit down there is a period of brief, sociable small talk, coupled with refreshments.

The function of small talk is to create a warm and friendly environment and put the participants at ease. But, purposefully avoid the key issues to be discussed later in the session. Participants may want to express their points of view only once during the session, and if they explain their perceptions in the informal part of the meeting, they may be reluctant to repeat the observations. Purposeful small talk avoids the focused issue and instead concentrates on common human experiences such as weather, children, or sports. Avoid controversial topics (e.g., religion, politics, or sensitive local issues) and topics that highlight differences within the group (e.g., income, education, political influence).

Because participants arrive at different times, the small talk maintains the warm and friendly environment until a sufficient number of participants are present to begin the session. In most situations this small talk period will last only 5 to 10 minutes, and the two-person moderating team should plan their welcoming strategy in advance.

Often one person (either moderator or assistant moderator) meets the participants at the door and brings them into the social gathering while the other person on the team visits with the group.

During this period, the moderator and assistant are observing participant interaction and noting individuals who tend to dominate the group, are excessively shy, or consider themselves as experts. Individuals who talk a lot may later dominate the conversation and should be seated at the moderator's side if at all possible. Then, if necessary, the moderator can turn slightly away from the domineering individuals, thereby giving a nonverbal and diplomatic signal for others to talk. Shy and quiet participants are best placed immediately across from the moderator to facilitate maximum eye contact. The moderator might expect that about 40% of the participants are eager and open to sharing insights and that another 40% are more introspective and willing to talk if the situation presents itself. The remaining 20% are apprehensive about the experience and rarely share (Kelleher, 1982).

This strategic positioning of participants is achieved in the following manner. The moderating team will have a list of participants who are expected to attend the discussion and will prepare "name tents" to place on the table in front of group members. Name tents can easily be made from 5 × 8 cards, folded in the middle, with first names printed. Last names are unnecessary. Name tents are preferred because they are larger and more legible than name tags. The moderator will "drop" the name tents around the table in a seemingly random manner. In fact, the moderator arranges the cards using observations from the informal pre-session, quickly checking perceptions with the assistant moderator and then placing the name tents.

Snacks and Meals

Food can help the focus group. Eating together tends to promote conversation and communication within the group. Most focus group use a variety of snacks such as cookies or pastries, but full meals also can be effective. Snacks and light refreshments are typically placed on a table to the side of the room and are enjoyed at the beginning of the focus group during the pre-session small talk. Full meals require additional planning. If they are conducted in restaurants, then advance arrangements are needed to ensure speedy service. Meals can be catered or delivered (e.g., pizza, box lunches) when the focus group is outside of a restaurant. Thought should be given to when the meal is served. Traditional protocol was that the meal should occur before the focus group as a way for the participants to get to know each other. Unfortunately, this can prove to be awkward as the moderator makes efforts to avoid the central topic of discussion. An alternative strategy is to provide the meal after the focus group, during which time the moderator continues to listen for relevant comments concerning the study. At times, it is in this relaxed environment that the participants, who now have more complete knowledge of the study purpose, offer comments or suggestions that are most beneficial.

Problems and Headaches

Special problems can greatly affect the focus group interview. For example, alcohol and focus groups do not mix, either for participants or moderators. If a meal is served prior to the focus group session, be certain to inform the server that drinks will not be ordered and they should not be solicited. Participants who arrive under the influence should be politely but firmly informed that their assistance will not be needed in the group interview. It is prudent to give them the financial incentive or gift if one was promised. An alternative strategy works well if the moderator has doubts about the ability of the participant. In these cases, the moderator might give the participant a set of the focus group questions and ask him or her to respond to these in writing. "We are asking some people to answer these questions in writing. We would like you to use the next room (even a lobby will do) and complete the questions. When you are finished you can leave them on the table. Thank you for coming." This way, if the participant is sober enough to respond effectively, his or her comments can be considered. This same strategy can be used for other unwanted or unneeded participants. Due to overrecruiting, the researcher might occasionally find that she or he needs to turn away participants. When this occurs, the participant receives whatever incentive was promised and then might be requested to respond to the questions in writing.

Another special problem is small children. Young children running in the room or babies crying can completely upstage the discussion, at least from the moderator's perspective. Ideally, this problem is anticipated and solved in advance. When young parents are the target audience, the moderator should expect the problem and arrange for child care services. If it happens unexpectedly, quick thinking and tactful concern on the part of the moderator can alleviate embarrassment and achieve a solution. The moderator might make a quick assessment of the child's activity level and then decide on the potential for interruptions. If the child is reasonably passive, the moderator might decide to take a risk and include the parent in the discussion. At times, the assistant moderator might function as a baby-sitter and take the child into another room. Puzzles, crayons, and coloring books could provide some temporary relief, but not for the entire 90-minute discussion.

At times, people will show up unexpectedly at the focus group. It could be a spouse, a family member, a friend who provided transportation, someone who thought it was a public meeting, or someone in a position of authority who is interested in the study. Quick thinking and diplomacy may be needed to preserve the quality of the focus group. The first rule of thumb is to not let visitors determine what they will do or where they will sit. Seek out anyone who doesn't belong in the group and chat with them in the pre-session of the focus group. Then make a decision. Sometimes a visitor might be allowed to participate in the discussion or to sit in the room, often along the side. Other times, a visitor is invited to wait in the lounge or another place while the focus group is taking place.

Recording the Group Discussion

Focus group sessions are typically recorded in two ways: by a tape recorder and by written notes taken by the assistant moderator and to a lesser extent by the moderator. Written notes are essential. Typically, the moderator will take brief notes and the assistant will attempt to capture complete statements of the participants—especially those comments that may be quotable. The note taking should not interfere with the spontaneous nature of the group interview, and the moderator will only be able to capture brief comments by participants. If the group has to wait until the moderator finishes taking notes, the discussion will hardly be comfortable or free-flowing.

The note taking should be done in such a manner that notes are complete and usable if the tape recorder stops working. Tape recorders shouldn't be completely trusted. Murphy's Law dictates that the most insightful comment will be lost when the tape is being switched or when background noise drowns out voices on the tape. At times, the moderator and assistant moderator may get so involved in the discussion that they both forget to monitor the tape recorder.

Tape recorders are invaluable for focus group interviews. The tape recording equipment and remote microphone are set up before the meeting begins and in plain sight of participants. Hidden recorders and microphones are unwise, because they create a secretive atmosphere and inhibit conversation if discovered. The importance of the recorder is mentioned at the beginning of the group discussion and it is introduced as a tool to help capture everyone's comments. Therefore, participants are encouraged to speak one at a time to avoid garbling the tape.

Care is needed to avoid excessive attention to the tape recording. Occasionally a novice moderator will comment at length about the tape recording: that the comments are confidential, that no names will be used in the report, that the participants should share their honest opinions. Inadvertently, the moderator creates an environment that restricts the free flow of information. Best to mention that recording is taking place and move to the next topic. In some situations, the tape recording is perceived as symbolic of careful listening.

Recently, a large school system conducted focus groups on merit pay of teachers—a sensitive topic to most teachers. In the planning phase concern was expressed about the wisdom of tape recording and whether it would inhibit conversation. The decision was made to try it and then, if necessary, turn off the recording equipment. When the teachers arrived in the room, one of the first comments was that "finally the school administration was taking the opinions of teachers seriously." The moderator asked the teacher to comment further. The reply, "Well, you're tape recording our comments! All along the school administrators said they were listening and we knew they weren't because they didn't record, take notes, or anything. Now it looks like they are serious about listening to our observations." Indeed, throughout that and future focus groups, when topics of concern were addressed the teachers would lean toward the microphone in the center of the table and talk more slowly so that there comments would be clearly understood.

Tape recording group conversations is difficult. Recorders are prone to pick up background noise, tapping of pencils, and the hum of the ventilation system instead of the softly spoken comments of participants. Built-in microphones on cassette recorders tend to have limited sensitivity. Instead, an omni-directional remote microphone is placed in the center of the table. Moderators have had considerable success with pressure-sensitive microphones that pick up sound vibrations from the table. Occasionally moderators use two microphones placed at different ends of the table, each connected to a recorder. Immediately before the group interview, the moderator should test the recording equipment to be sure that all comments in the room will be captured, even if spoken in quiet tones. In addition, the moderator may want to fast forward and rewind new tapes to ensure they do not stick or jam. The C-90 tapes are preferable; C-60 tapes are too short and C-120 tapes are prone to break and jam. The C-90 tape provides 90 minutes of recording time, 45 minutes per side.

Beginning the Focus Group Discussion

The first few moments in focus group discussion are critical. In a brief time the moderator must create a thoughtful, permissive atmosphere, provide the ground rules, and set the tone of the discussion. Much of the success of group interviewing can be attributed to this 2 to 4 minute introduction. Excessive formality and rigidity can stifle the interaction among participants. By contrast, too much informality and humor can cause problems in that participants might not take the discussion seriously. Veteran moderators testify that groups are unpredictable: one group may be exciting and free-flowing and another group might be restrained, cautious, and reserved. Differences among groups are typical and should be expected; however, the moderator should introduce the group discussion in a consistent manner.

The recommended pattern for introducing the group discussion includes these stages:

1. The welcome
2. The overview of the topic
3. The ground rules
4. The first question

Here is an example of a typical introduction:

> Good evening and welcome to our session tonight. Thank you for taking the time to join our discussion of airplane travel. My name is Dick Krueger and I represent the Happy Traveler Research Agency. Assisting me is Jerry Migler, also from the Happy Traveler Agency. We want to find out more about how

public employees feel about airplane travel. We have invited people who work in different governmental agencies to share their perceptions and ideas.

You were selected because you have certain things in common that are of particular interest to us. You are all government employees who work here in the metropolitan area and you have all traveled by air at least four times in the past year. We are particularly interested in your views because other employees may have similar views.

Tonight we will be discussing your experiences and your opinions about airline travel. There are no right or wrong answers but rather differing points of view. Please feel free to share your point of view even if it differs from what others have said.

Before we begin, let me share some ground rules. This is strictly a research project and there are no sales involved. Please speak up—only one person should talk at a time. We're tape recording the session because we don't want to miss any of your comments. If several are talking at the same time, the tape will get garbled and we'll miss your comments. We will be on a first name basis tonight, and in our later reports no names will be attached to comments. You may be assured of complete confidentiality. Keep in mind that we're just as interested in negative comments as positive comments, and at times the negative comments are the most helpful.

Our session will last about an hour and a half. Let's begin. We've placed name cards on the table in front of you to help us remember each other's names. Let's find out some more about each other by going around the room one at a time. Tell us your name and the last place that you traveled to by air.

The first question is designed to engage all participants one at a time in the group discussion. It "breaks the ice" and gets each participant to talk. After the participant has once said something, it becomes easier to speak again. In addition, the first question underscores the common characteristics of the participants and that they all have some basis for sharing information. This first question must be the type that can be answered in about 15-20 seconds, and as a result will often consist of descriptive information. Furthermore, this first question cannot demand excessive reflection or long-past memories.

It is risky to ask the participants if they have questions before proceeding with the conversation. Unfortunately, these early participant questions may preempt the discussion and place the moderator in a defensive position. When confronted by questions such as "Who really wants this information? Are you really going to use what we tell you? Can we see copies of the report? the moderator will often appear apologetic and uncertain of the study. Instead, don't invite questions at the beginning and if someone does ask a question the moderator will need to decide if he or she wants to answer it at that moment or postpone the answer to later in the discussion.

Anticipate the Flow of the Discussion

Group discussions are unpredictable and the topics of discussion might flow precisely as planned or they might take leaps and detours. Moderators are advised to anticipate the various directions the discussion might take and to be able to recognize beneficial topics of discussion as opposed to dead ends. For example, in focus groups relating to community organizations I have found that the discussion can lead to an evaluation of agency professionals—a topic that is usually not the purpose of the study. In these cases it became helpful to include a comment in the introduction about the scope of the study: "We are more interested in your opinions about programs, building facilities, and activities sponsored by various organizations and less concerned about the people who deliver those services." Often a "mock discussion" with colleagues familiar with the participants will help identify some of the varieties of responses. One of the hallmarks of a skillful moderator is flexibility in modifying the questioning route at the last minute and yet obtaining the needed information.

. Give License to Expressing Differing Points of View

Participants may need to be reminded a second time of the value of differing points of view. The introduction provides the first suggestion that all points of view—positive and negative—are needed and wanted. A second reminder is helpful if the moderator senses that participants are simply "echoing" the same concept. After several echoes on the same idea the moderator might ask: "Does anyone see it differently?" or "Are there any other points of view?"

Two Essential Techniques: The Pause and the Probe

Moderators of group discussions should be familiar with two essential techniques: the 5-second pause and the probe. Both techniques are easy to use and helpful in soliciting additional information from group participants. The 5-second pause is most often used after a participant comment. This short pause often prompts additional points of view or agreement with the previously mentioned position. There is a tendency for novice moderators to talk too much, to dominate the discussion with questions, and to move too quickly from one topic to another. Often the short pause will elicit additional points of view, especially when coupled with eye contact from the moderator. The 5-second pause can be practiced on family, friends, and co-workers with interesting results. Advance practice allows the moderator to become familiar with this technique, so it can be used comfortably in group interviews.

The second essential technique is the probe, the request for additional information. In most conversations and group discussions, there is a tendency for people to make vague comments that could have multiple meanings or to say "I agree." When this occurs, the probe is an effective technique to elicit additional information. Typically, probing involves such comments as these:

- "Would you explain further?"
- "Would you give me an example of what you mean?"
- "Would you say more?"
- "Is there anything else?"
- "Please describe what you mean."
- "I don't understand."

It is usually best to use the probe early in the interview to communicate the importance of precision in responses, and then use it sparingly in later discussion. For example, if a participant indicates agreement by saying, "I agree," then the moderator should follow up with: "Tell us more," or "What experiences have you had that make you feel that way?" A few probes used in this way underscore the impression that more detailed answers are needed and wanted. Excessive probing, however, can be extremely time-consuming and unnecessary.

Responding to Participant Comments

Moderators should be attentive to how they respond to comments from participants—both verbal and nonverbal. Often these moderator responses are unconscious habits from past social interactions. Self-discipline and practice are needed to overcome habits such as head nodding and short verbal responses.

Head Nodding. Some moderators will nod their head as comments are being made. Head nodding at times can be helpful if used sparingly and consciously, such as in eliciting additional comments (a single nod to a person who seeks to talk) from participants. Unfortunately, it is often an unconscious response that signals agreement and, as a result, tends to elicit additional comments of the same type. Less often used is the negative nod, with the head going side to side, which tends to signal to the participant that the comment is not needed, not wanted, or wrong. As a rule of thumb, beginning moderators should try to restrict head nodding.

Short Verbal Responses. In many social interactions we have become conditioned to provide short verbal responses that signal approval or acceptance. Many of these are acceptable within the focus group environment, such as "OK," "Yes," or "Uh huh," but others should be avoided if they communicate indications of accuracy or agreement. Responses to avoid include "Correct," "That's good," or "Excellent," because they imply judgments about the quality of the comment.

Aspiring moderators should be encouraged to monitor their normal social interactions and become comfortable with "value neutral" gestures and comments. Practice focus group sessions and coaching from others can also prove helpful.

The Expert, the Dominant Talker, the Shy Participant, and the Rambler

One of the exciting aspects of focus group discussions is that it brings together a variety of people with differing backgrounds and characteristics. Sometimes, however, individual characteristics can present special problems for the moderator. These four types of participants—the expert, the dominant talker, the shy participant, and the rambler—regularly participate in focus groups, and each type presents special problems.

Self-appointed "experts" can present special problems in focus groups. What they say and how they say it can inhibit others in the group. Participants often defer to others who are perceived to have more education, affluence, or political/social influence. Some people consider themselves experts because they have had considerable experience with the topic under discussion, because they hold positions of influence in the community, or because they have previously participated in this type of session. Often the best way of handling experts is to underscore that everyone is an expert and all participants have important perceptions that need to be expressed. In addition, the introductory question should avoid responses that would identify participants' levels of education, affluence, or social/political influence.

Dominant talkers sometimes consider themselves to be experts. Often dominant talkers are spotted in presession small talk. As indicated earlier in this chapter, attempt to seat the dominant individual beside the moderator in order to exercise control by the use of body language. When this strategy does not work, then the more frontal tactic of verbally shifting attention is required. For example: "Thank you, John. Are there others who wish to comment on the question?" or "Does anyone feel differently?" or "That's one point of view. Does anyone have another point of view?" Other nonverbal techniques also can be used such as avoiding eye contact with the talker and appearing bored with the comments. Most important, be tactful and kind because harsh and critical comments may curtail spontaneity from others in the group.

Shy respondents tend to say little and speak with soft voices. It seems that these participants think first and then speak. Others will think and speak at the same time: "I don't know what I think until I say it." These reluctant participants often have much to share but extra effort is required to get these individuals to elaborate their views and to feel that their comments are wanted and appreciated. If possible, the moderator should place shy respondents directly across the table to maximize eye contact. Eye contact often provides sufficient encouragement to speak, and if all else fails, the moderator can call on them.

Rambling respondents use a lot of words and usually never get to the point, if they have a point. These individuals are comfortable with talking and seem to feel an obligation to say something. Unfortunately, the rambling respondent can drone on and on and eat up precious discussion time. As a rule of thumb I usually discontinue eye contact with the rambler after about 20-30 seconds. The assistant moderator should do likewise. Look at your papers, look at the other participants, turn your body away from the speaker, look bored, look at your watch, but don't look at the rambler. As soon as the rambler stops or pauses, the moderator should be ready to fire away with the next question or repeat the current question being discussed. In the remainder of the discussion, the moderating team should limit eye contact with the rambling participant.

Be Ready for the Unexpected

One should prepare for the unexpected by thinking about the possible things that can go wrong. Here are some of the things that might go wrong and possible courses of action:

1. Nobody shows up. Review your letter of invitation to be certain you are at the right location on the correct date. Telephone a few of the participants to see if they are coming and if they have received the invitation. Always take a list of invited participants with their phone numbers to the discussion location.

2. Only a few attend. Conduct the session anyway, but after the meeting check to be certain that all people received the written letter of invitation and telephone reminder.

3. The meeting place is inadequate. Improvise, but attempt to spot this in advance. Arrive at the interview location well in advance of the participants, especially if it is a location that you have not used before.

4. The group doesn't want to talk. Consider calling on individuals or going around the group answering a specific question. Use pauses and probes. Consider revising the questions to add more interest.

5. The group gets so involved that they don't want to leave. A delightful problem that does occasionally occur. Stay a while and listen to the conversation if your time permits. Formally adjourn the meeting, pack up, and leave.

6. Hazardous weather occurs just hours before the meeting. Phone each person to let them know if the session has been canceled.

7. The early questions take too much time, leaving little time to ask the final questions. Pace the questions and monitor the clock during the interview to allow enough time for the final questions. Often the last questions are the most focused and revealing. Before the interview, pretend that you've only asked half of the questions and 5 minutes remain. Consider how you would ask the remaining questions.

Concluding the Focus Group

The moderator has several options for closing the focus group. Perhaps the most common procedure is simply to thank the group for participating, provide them with the gift or cash if promised, and wish them a safe journey home. A far better alternative is for the assistant moderator or the moderator to summarize briefly the main points of view and ask if this perception is accurate. This task of summarization is often helpful to the moderator in the subsequent analysis process. It is the first opportunity the research team has to pull together a summary of the overall group discussion. When presenting the brief summary, the researchers should watch the body language of the participants for signs of agreement, hesitation, or confusion. When the 2- to 3-minute summary is completed, the moderator invites comments, amendments, or corrections.

An additional tactic for closure is asking the "final question" that was described in Chapter 4. The moderator provides an overview of the study and then asks the participants, "Have we missed anything?" A variation of this strategy is useful if participants are reluctant to talk because of sensitivity to the recording equipment. The variation is to turn off the recording equipment, indicate that the discussion is now completed, thank them for their assistance, and then ask, "Do you think we've missed anything in the discussion?" This closure may uncover some avenues of thought that were not anticipated.

Summary

There is a lot to think about in preparing to moderate a focus group interview. The logistics and equipment should be checked out in advance and then crossed off a worry list. The most frequent danger of novice moderators is that they worry about too many things just before the group session and consequently begin the discussion with high anxiety. The best advice for beginning moderators is to practice asking questions, worry several days before the focus group, and then relax just before the discussion.

A characteristic of focus group interviews is that participants will often compensate for the awkward questions of the moderator and provide enlightening answers. It's hard to predict in advance how a focus group session will go. Groups vary greatly and flexibility is essential. Ask the unexpected questions that emerge from the discussion, but avoid major detours in the questioning route. Consider the various strategies for bringing closure to the discussion. Throughout the discussion the moderating team should remember that they are visitors in the world of the participants, and for a brief time they are sharing the reality of the participants' environment. The permissive moderator allows the discussion to flow and topics may be introduced in a different sequence from that originally anticipated.

APPENDIX 6A

Checklist for Focus Group Interviews

Advance Notice
——Contact participants by phone 1-2 weeks before the session.
——Send each participant a letter of invitation.
——Give the participants a reminder phone call prior to the session.
——Slightly overrecruit the number of participants.

Questions
——The introductory question should be answered quickly and not identify status.
——Questions should flow in a logical sequence.
——Key questions should focus on the critical issues of concern.
——Consider probe or follow-up questions.
——Limit the use of "why" questions.
——Use "think back" questions as needed.
——Provide a summary of the discussion and invite comments.

Logistics
——The room should be satisfactory (size, tables, comfort, etc.).
——The moderator should arrive early to make necessary changes.
——Background noise should not interfere with the tape recording.
——Have name tags and/or name tents for participants.
——A remote microphone should be placed on the table.
——Bring extra tapes, batteries, and extension cords.
——Plan topics for small talk conversation.
——Seat experts and loud participants next to the moderator.

——Seat shy and quiet participants directly across from the moderator.

——When having a meal, limit selections and stress fast service.

——Bring enough copies of handouts and/or visual aids.

Moderator Skills

——Be well rested and alert for the focus group session.

——Practice the introduction without referring to notes.

——Ask questions with minimal reference to notes.

——Be careful to avoid head nodding.

——Avoid comments that signal approval, such as "Excellent," "Great," "Wonderful."

——Avoid giving personal opinions.

Immediately After the Session

——Prepare a brief written summary of key points as soon as possible.

——Check to see if the tape recorder captured the comments.

APPENDIX 6B

Rules for Assistant Moderators

1. Take responsibility for all equipment. Ensure that it works and is complete.

- Tape recorder
- Microphone
- Extension cords (power and microphone)
- Blank tapes
- Name tents or name tags
- Honorariums
- Marking pens
- Refreshments
- Duct tape to hold down the cords
- Spare batteries
- Visuals or handouts

2. Take responsibility for refreshments. Obtain the refreshments and set them up in the room.

3. Arrange the room. Rearrange chairs and table so everyone can see each other. Be attentive to background noises that would affect the audio recording.

4. Set up the equipment and verify that it is working properly.

5. Welcome participants as they arrive.

6. Sit in the designated location. Sit outside the circle, opposite the moderator, and close to the door. If someone arrives after the session begins, meet the person at the door, take him or her outside the room, and give him or her a short briefing as to what has happened and the current topic of discussion. Then bring the late participant into the room and show him or her where to sit.

7. Take notes throughout the discussion. Be attentive to the following areas of concern:

- *Well said quotes.* Capture word for word as much of the statement as possible. Listen for sentences or phrases that are particularly enlightening or eloquently express a particular point of view. Place quotation marks around the statement or phrase and indicate the name of the speaker. Place your opinions, thoughts, or ideas in parentheses to keep them separate from participant comments. If a question occurs to you that you would like to ask at the end of the discussion, write it down in a circle or box.

- *Note the nonverbal activity.* Watch for head nods, physical excitement, eye contact between participants, or other clues that would indicate level of agreement, support, or interest.
- *Make a sketch of the seating arrangement.*

8. Monitor recording equipment. Occasionally glance at the tape recorder to see if the reels are moving. Turn over the tape or insert another tape when appropriate. Attempt to do this as smoothly as possible without drawing attention to the recording equipment. Label the cassette tapes. Indicate date, location, and number of each tape.

9. Do not participate in the discussion! You talk only if invited by the moderator. Control your nonverbal actions no matter how strongly you feel about an issue.

10. Ask questions when invited. At the end of the discussion, the moderator will invite you to ask questions of amplification or clarification.

11. Give an oral summary. At the end of the discussion, the moderator or assistant should provide a brief summary (about 3 minutes) of responses to the important questions. Invite participants to offer additions or corrections to the summary.

12. Hand out the honorariums and thank the participants.

13. Debrief the session with the moderator. Following the focus group, participate in the debriefing with the moderator.

14. Read and provide feedback on the analysis.

7

Principles of Analyzing
Focus Group Results

It's best to begin the study of the process of analyzing focus group results with an overview of the principles of focus group analysis. These principles guide the researcher's actions and help determine specific decisions that are needed. No part of the focus group interview is as ill-structured as analysis. Analysis is based on a number of assumptions, which exert considerable influence on the process of analysis. This chapter addresses the principles that guide focus group analysis. The analysis process grows out of these principles and is discussed in the following chapter.

The principles of focus group analysis have roots in many sources, but two deserve special mention. Each source has contributed greatly and each, by itself, has limits. The challenge is to develop strategies that use the best of each tradition. One major contributor has been the field of academically oriented qualitative research. This source has contributed to the systematic procedures that constitute rigorous analysis. Up to now, many of these academic contributions have been confined to the analysis of one-to-one interviews as opposed to the more dynamic interaction that occurs within a focus group interview. From these academic roots we have gained systematic and verifiable procedures that add rigor to the analysis. A second source of assistance with the focus group analysis has been marketing research. Here we learn respect for practicality as well as appreciation of results that are understandable and applicable to the clients. Among the principles that guide analysis are the following.

Analysis Must Be Systematic

Systematic analysis has two dimensions. The first, which is described in this section, is the manner by which data are gathered and handled. The second includes specific processes used by the analyst and is presented in detail in Chapter 8. Both dimensions require that the analyst follow a prescribed, sequential process. The process used, however, could vary from one study to another, and different processes are possible. The process itself is one that is deliberate and planned and not capricious, arbitrary, or spontaneous. Systematic analysis procedures help ensure that results will be as error-free as possible.

Our society has gotten more complex in many ways. As our human processes become more complex, we institute systematic protocol to avoid making mistakes or overlooking critical factors. Consider the difference between getting in your car and driving off and the process used by a pilot in preparing for takeoff in a jet airliner. Even though the pilot has flown hundreds of times and can remember each step in the takeoff sequence, the takeoff procedures are still religiously followed—in part because of the complexity and in part because one step overlooked can influence the operation of the aircraft. Focus group analysis is also complex and subject to human frailties. The systematic protocol reminds the analyst of upcoming steps but it also communicates to the user of the study that the analyst is attempting to minimize human errors. In focus group interviews there are several systematic steps that have proven beneficial in data collection.

Systematic Steps in Data Gathering

1. Sequencing Questions to Allow Maximum Insight. Occasionally moderators prematurely launch into the key questions. A more systematic process is to allow participants to become familiar with the topic, giving each individual a chance to recollect personal opinions and to listen to the opinions of others in the group. This is then followed by key questions relating to the core topic of interest and then later followed with the opportunity for final summary questions by each participant.

2. Capturing and Handling Data. Most often focus groups are electronically recorded with additional notes taken by the moderator and assistant moderator. Lack of notes or lack of electronic recordings greatly impedes the ability to reconstruct critical parts of the focus group.

3. Coding Data. As the researcher comes across an idea or phenomenon a label is attached. When the idea or phenomenon reappears the label is once again attached. In focus groups this process consists of codes placed in the margin of the transcript, or if a computer is used a section of text is marked and assigned the designated code. Later, the researcher may want to selectively retrieve and review information pertaining to certain codes, combinations of codes, or related situations. This information can then be assembled differently from the original version. This process, which is called *axial coding*, allows the researcher to fracture the data and to reassemble it in new ways. (For a more complete discussion of coding see Strauss and Corbin, 1990, pp. 61-74, 96-115.)

4. Participant Verification. This step ensures that the researcher has adequately understood the intent of participants. This can occur in several ways, such as including an opportunity for an individual summary statement on critical questions, or a chance to respond to the moderator's (or assistant moderator's) summary of key points while still in the focus group, or a post-focus group verification of the written report.

5. Debriefing Between Moderator and Assistant Moderator. This occurs immediately after the focus group interview. This debriefing captures the first impressions and then highlights and contrasts findings from earlier focus groups.

6. Sharing of Preliminary and Later Reports. The individual(s) writing the report should share draft copies with other members of the research team for review, verification, and comment. In some situations the analyst shares the first draft with the research team and the second draft with focus group participants. Participants who have not attended other focus group sessions will be able to comment only on a portion of the report. In essence, this process of member checking enables focus group participants to verify the analyst's description of constructs (see Guba & Lincoln, 1989, pp. 238-240).

Systematic analysis processes force the researcher to examine and challenge his or her assumptions. These assumptions are made throughout the research process, building on past experiences, and are intended to make analysis protocol more efficient. Care is needed however, because even experts make unfounded assumptions. Stephen Covey (1989) shares this account made by Frank Koch in *Proceedings*, the magazine of the Naval Institute:

> Two battleships assigned to the training squadron had been at sea on maneuvers in heavy weather for several days. I was serving on the lead battleship and was on watch on the bridge as night fell. The visibility was poor with patchy fog, so the captain remained on the bridge keeping an eye on all activities.
>
> Shortly after dark, the lookout on the wing of the bridge reported, "Light, bearing on the starboard bow."
>
> "Is it steady or moving astern?" the captain called out.
>
> Lookout replied, "Steady, captain," which meant we were on a dangerous collision course with that ship.
>
> The captain then called to the signalman, "Signal that ship: We are on a collision course, advise you change course 20 degrees."
>
> Back came a signal, "Advisable for you to change course 20 degrees."
>
> The captain said, "Send: I'm a captain, change course 20 degrees."
>
> "I'm a seaman second class," came the reply. "You had better change course 20 degrees."
>
> By that time the captain was furious. He spat out, "Send: I'm a battleship. Change course 20 degrees."
>
> Back came the flashing light, "I'm a lighthouse."
>
> We changed course. (p. 33)

Analysis Must Be Verifiable

The analysis must also be verifiable—a process that would permit another researcher to arrive at similar conclusions using available documents and raw data. As humans, we often need to make quick decisions based on fragmentary information. Unfortunately, the fragment that we select may not be the one that is relevant to the situation. There is also a tendency to selectively see or hear only those comments that confirm a particular point of view and to avoid dealing with information that causes us dissonance. Our training, our background, and our experiences influence what we notice and what we attend to.

Two scientists had not seen each other since they were undergraduates at the university—15 years earlier. They were good friends but their careers lead them to different parts of the world. One had become a herpetologist and traveled around the world studying snakes. Her friend became an ornithologist, and she conducted most of her research studying birds in the Amazon rain forest. Eventually their paths would cross again. The snake expert had to travel to the Amazon en route to her next assignment and took the opportunity to visit her old friend. While they were visiting, they decided to walk together through a portion of rain forest. When they finished, the bird expert was excited because in 1 hour she had seen 18 varieties of birds, but she apologized to her friend for the lack of snakes. "What do you mean?" said her friend. "While we were walking, I saw 12 varieties of snakes."

Researchers must continually be careful to avoid the trap of selective perception. Verification in analysis is a critical safeguard. In order for analysis to be verifiable there must be sufficient data to constitute a trail of evidence. The data stream begins with field notes and recordings taken during the focus group, continues with the oral summary (verification) of key points during the focus group, goes into the debriefing with the moderator team immediately following the focus group, and also includes the electronic recording with the possibility of a transcript of the interview.

Analysis Must Be Focused

Focus group research produces a phenomenal amount of data, so much so that novice analysts are regularly overwhelmed. Each focus group could produce 10 to 15 pages of field notes combined with 50 to 70 pages of transcript. A critical aspect in surviving the deluge of materials is to focus the analysis. Not all questions deserve analysis at the same level, indeed some may be "throw away" questions that are designed to help set the stage of discussion for participants as opposed to collecting new insights. The challenge to the researcher is to place primary attention on questions that are at the foundation of the study. Focused analysis conserves resources, but most importantly it enables the analyst to concentrate attention on areas of critical concern. Certain questions, I've called them the key questions in Chapter 4, drive focus groups because they represent areas of primary concern from the sponsor. These are questions that are the backbone of the study.

Analysis Must Have the Appropriate Level of Interpretation

An area of concern early in the analysis process revolves around the level of interpretation that the analyst provides. The level selected must meet the client requirements but also be practical and manageable for the analyst. A helpful way of thinking about this role is to consider a continuum of analysis ranging from the mere accumulation of raw data to the interpretation of data.

The Analysis Continuum

Raw Data   Descriptive Statements   Interpretation

◄──►

On one side of the continuum is the accumulated raw data. This represents exact statements of focus group participants as they responded to specific topics in the discussion. These statements might be ordered in categories that are of concern to the client. For example, the statements might be ordered on level of support (from very supportive to not at all supportive), or on age of respondents (responses from participants in their 20s, 30s, 40s, etc.), or on a number of other factors. Another option is to place responses in categories by participant characteristics (occupational categories, gender, relationship to program, etc.). The distinctive feature of raw data is that it contains *all* of the information from the focus groups. As a result, the length is usually enormous and often frustrating to the client. Most clients want data reduction.

Midway on the continuum are descriptive statements. These are summary statements of respondent comments prepared by the analyst. When using this style, the researcher sets out to provide a brief description that is based on raw data followed by illustrative examples of raw data. Whereas the presentation of raw data usually involves including all responses, the descriptive style seeks to simplify the task of the reader by providing typical or illuminating quotes.

The decision of which quotes to include sometimes presents a problem to the researcher. The selection choice should be influenced by the purpose of the study. If the study intends to describe the range and diversity of comments, then examples should be selected with this in mind. Other times, the purpose is to provide insights of typical, common, or usual ways in which participants respond, and if so, the researcher should select quotes that are within the mainstream. In either case, the researcher should specify the means of selection.

Interpretation is the most complex role for the researcher. The interpretative side of the continuum builds on the descriptive process by presenting the meaning of data as opposed to a summary of data. Whereas the descriptive process results in a summary, the interpretative process aims at providing understanding. Clearly, the interpretative role of analysis is more complex and difficult than either presentation of raw data or descriptions of findings. Interpretation takes into account evidence beyond words on a transcript and includes evidence from the field notes coupled with other background information.

Analysis Must Be Practical   *dep vndm vp/sdew*

Practical, here, means appropriate for the situation. Focus group analysis, like qualitative research in general, must be appropriate to the situation. For some researchers, analysis is a black hole that sucks up available time and energy, confusing the analyst and jeopardizing the quality of results. Consider this analogy:

> You are driving down the highway and the car is running smoothly and quietly. Suddenly, you hear a new noise coming from the engine. You've driven this car for over a year and this sound is not one you've ever heard before. What does this noise mean? Is something about to fail? You glance at the instrument panel for clues, but there are no red lights and the gauges seem normal. Several options flash through your mind. The best you can hope for is that the noise will go away within a moment or so. Perhaps it is just something caught underneath the car that will soon dislodge. The second best option is that you drive to the service station and talk to your friendly mechanic. The mechanic looks under the hood, turns a screw, and the noise goes away. The mechanic says "No charge" and you promise to buy gas forever from that service station. Or, the mechanic after looking under the hood utters the words "Tune up," which when translated into common people talk means, "It will cost you about $200-$300 to get rid of this noise." Worst of all is when the mechanic says "Overhaul," which means the solution requires several thousand dollars and a week without the car. The point is that at the beginning when you first hear the noise you don't know what is needed for the solution. You don't know until a skillful technician diagnoses the situation using past experience and special tools to gain more information about the problem.

Focus group analysis often operates in a similar manner. At the beginning of the research study you have a hunch about the type of analysis needed, but evidence presented at focus groups can lead you to change your strategy and approach. You might anticipate a time-intensive, transcript-based analysis protocol but find that the results are readily apparent. The opposite could also be true. Analysis could be simple and straightforward if the patterns are clearly identifiable, when minimal differences exist within the group and across groups, or when participants clearly reject differing explanations and coalesce around common concerns.

The analyst is guided by practicality. Beginning hunches or plans might need to be set aside or modified to meet emerging situations. Rigidity and inflexible analysis plans can lead to excessive investigation or a superficial assessment of data that truly deserves intensive study.

The environment or situation dictates the amount of attention needed. Several factors that can influence this relate to the problem under investigation. Studies will vary in that some involve risky decisions or have limited reversibility. In others, those sponsoring the study may propose standards for credibility that differ from the mainstream of current research. Other times, practicality is most influenced by financial resources or time constraints.

Practicality must also be considered in making analysis decisions such as whether to use transcripts or computers in analysis. The attractive benefit of the computer is its consistent protocol in finding and connecting categories coupled with the confidence that available data have been exhaustively searched. Human abilities prevent us from being absolutely consistent because of fatigue in the tedious search of large data sources.

Analysis Requires Time

Focus group analysis begins earlier and usually lasts longer than analysis used in quantitative research procedures. In contrast, when numeric analysis is required the researcher waits until all data are available; these numbers are then computer coded and statistically analyzed by using accepted protocol. Also in contrast, the time spent in the analysis phase of a focus group research project spans a longer period. A distinctive feature of qualitative inquiry is that data inquiry and data analysis are simultaneous activities—they occur together. Often, novice researchers are not prepared for the amount of time needed in focus group analysis.

Analysis Is Jeopardized by Delay

Analysis delay tends to erode analysis quality. This is particularly a problem in focus group research in which the overall analysis period may last for weeks or sometimes even months. Delay is a concern for several reasons. Although comments may have been captured electronically, there are other types of input that affect analysis quality that cannot be captured by electronic means. The sense of the group, the mood of the discussion, and the eagerness with which the participants talk to each other are elements not included in the transcript. Over time, memories of these background factors fade and get confused with other focus groups. As more focus groups are conducted, the recent discussions interfere with the recollection of earlier focus groups and critical information may be lost.

As a result, several procedures are advised. First, exercise care in scheduling the focus groups. Only a limited number should be conducted in one day and a reasonable amount of time should be allocated between them. The number of focus groups per day will vary with length of the focus group, the traveling distance between groups, and the skills of the moderator. Two focus groups per day is reasonable. Second, the moderator, or more specifically the assistant moderator, should be charged with taking careful notes. Moderator notes tend to be sketchy at best because excessive time spent in capturing exact comments can limit the spontaneity of the discussion. However, the assistant moderator is able to devote full attention to capturing both what is said and the environmental factors that shed additional light on the discussion. Third, immediately after the focus group the moderator team should conduct a debriefing, and it is best to tape record this discussion. Both the moderator and assistant should share their perceptions of critical points and notable quotes that emerged from the focus group. This task serves several purposes. It captures immediate reactions following the focus group and often provides helpful insights into later analysis steps. Furthermore, for a number of moderators this is like a mental dump, where memories of the past focus group can be placed before going into the next focus group. The moderator must begin each focus group refreshed and unfettered by the comments made in the previous focus group. Having committed impressions and thoughts to a tape recorder seems to free the moderator of memories that would interfere with later discussions.

Analysis Can Move Progressively to Higher Levels

Early findings and insights can be incorporated into later focus group interviews for the purpose of confirmation or amplification. Typically, the first focus group yields a considerable amount of new information and then each additional focus group produces decreasing amounts of new insight. This phenomenon provides an advantage in analysis. The analyst can limit time spent on questions in which there is saturation (where no new information is presented) and use this time to seek reactions to emerging theories and insights. Some questions might be eliminated altogether and others are asked but the moderator carefully monitors discussion and briskly moves it on to other topics. For example: "Let me share with you some topics that have emerged from earlier groups . . . ; tell me your reactions"; or "In our earlier groups we've been hearing about . . . ; what do you think about it?"; or "We've been hearing some comments about . . . and we are not sure what to make of it; what do you think?" Care is needed to avoid the bandwagon mentality ("Everybody is telling us . . . ") but rather to invite their insights into the research process ("Help us understand . . . " or "Does this explain how it works?").

Analysis Should Seek to Enlighten

A guiding principle of analysis is to provide enlightenment, to lift the level of understanding to a new plateau. At times, focus groups point out what decision makers or research sponsors don't already know, but in other situations they confirm earlier suspicions and hunches. The analyst should ponder what new information is provided by the focus group. In my interviews with heavy consumers of focus groups a consistent trend emerges. Focus group analysts who raise the level of understanding and awareness about the problem or situation are clearly preferred. In fact, those who do not have this capacity are regularly avoided in future research.

The attention to providing enlightenment is more than just a problem of analysis. The potential for enlightenment has much to do with how the study was framed, who was selected to participate, and the nature of the questions, just to name a few of the factors. Nevertheless, the analyst can often make major contributions to this effort. Several

strategies have proven helpful in the past. One procedure is to seek
answers to these questions:

- What was known and then confirmed or challenged by this study?
- What was suspected and then confirmed or challenged by this study?
- What was new that wasn't previously suspected?

Another strategy is to compare and contrast the results with established
theory in social science. Other procedures that may assist the analyst
are to present results in terms of topologies, continuums, diagrams, or
metaphors that depict how focus group participants view the topic of
study. Topologies provide classification systems that enable users to
identify critical parts of a larger system. These topologies could emerge
either from the analyst or from the participants themselves (see Patton,
1990, pp. 393-400). Continuums are similar to topologies but represent
phenomena that are expressed in amounts or quantities. Diagrams
provide visual, symbolic images that depict relationships, flow, connections, and the like, that are critical to understanding. Metaphors also
facilitate understanding by comparing the topic under investigation to
another, often more familiar, object or thing.

Metaphors can emerge rather unpredictably, for example: Several
years ago I was involved in a project that sought to identify the training
needs for a group of professionals. About half way through the study
researchers found that focus group participants were alluding to different levels of skills. Clearly, not all skills were the same in the minds of
the participants, and there was a relationship among skills. As researchers were pondering this phenomenon and how to explain it, one of the
team members looked out the window (others claim he was daydream-
ing). It was a cold, winter day with snow on the ground. Perhaps the
sight of snow prompted his mind to wander, but an idea emerged. The
researcher said, "The training needs are like a snowman." He tore out
a piece of paper from his notebook and quickly drew a picture of a
snowman with three balls of snow. "Look," he said. "The biggest
snowball is the base—the foundation. This describes the technical skills
that the professionals say are the foundation to being credible and
conducting programs. The middle ball of snow represents methodological skills. These professionals say that they must be able to deliver, to
present and communicate their technical information. The top ball is
the head—the conceptual skills. The professionals need skills to see the
big picture, to analyze the environment, to develop strategic plans, and

to think about where it is all going." It was a flash of insight and other researchers concurred that the snowman metaphor did indeed reflect the comments of participants. (That researcher continues to spend a fair amount of time looking out the window. Who knows what new insights might be discovered there?)

Analysis Should Entertain Alternative Explanations

Analysts are cautious about their interpretations, especially in the beginning stages. The best analysis occurs in environments in which there is free exchange of ideas and alternative views are sought out and eagerly examined. It is dangerous to prematurely become committed to a particular interpretation. Colleagues are encouraged to offer rival explanations and each suggestion should be exposed to rigorous cross-examination. Over time, several explanations are likely to emerge because they are more robust and capable of providing understanding over a breadth of cases.

Analysts seek interpretations that explain a sufficient amount of the cases. They attempt to find disconfirming evidence. They make efforts to explain the outliers, the unusual cases, or those who have a minority view. It is not an indication of weakness if alternative interpretations emerge or even if no interpretations emerge. In some cases there may be no unifying explanation of participant views, except that the participants express differing views. The absence of patterns in the data can be a meaningful discovery.

Analysis Is Improved With Feedback

Analysis benefits from multiple insights and perspectives. Corrective feedback is available from four sources: group participants, co-researchers, experts who were not present in the focus group, and decision makers.

Focus group participants can provide feedback at several times, but the analyst must make efforts to seek it out. The most immediate and often most beneficial feedback occurs at the end of the focus group itself. At the end of the focus group, the moderator or assistant moderator might offer a brief summary of critical points (see Chapter 6). Participants are invited to amend or change this oral summary and then if suggestions are offered, the group is asked to confirm or correct the new ideas. Providing a succinct 3-minute summary of a 90-minute discussion is challenging but well worth the effort.

Participants can also be invited to provide feedback by drafting reports that summarize the focus group they participated in. This can be accommodated by mailing out the draft summary and then inviting comment by phone or in writing.

In some situations, where it is important for participants to be aware of the total scope of the project, the analyst may choose to send participants the draft summary (or even the full report) for all focus groups. In this situation, although participants are more limited in their ability to see the larger picture but nevertheless they should be able to see part of their group discussion within the larger report. In the public and nonprofit sector, there is another advantage of circulating this draft report. Whereas the initial focus group experience typically sparks interest in the topic, the draft summary allows participants to see the situation from multiple vantage points. It further allows the analyst or decision makers to test out the viability of recommendations.

Co-researchers are a rich source of feedback. In most cases the co-researcher is the assistant moderator, but in some situations there may be others on the research team who are close to the project. These co-researchers have the advantage of knowing about the purpose and details of the study and their background in research procedures is advantageous. Feedback from the assistant moderator is particularly beneficial. Being in the focus group and listening and observing without the pressure to ask questions or keep the discussion rolling allows the assistant to place complete attention on the conversation. As a result, the assistant moderator has proven to be an invaluable source of information in the analysis process.

Another source of feedback are experts who were not present in the focus groups. These could be individuals who are knowledgeable about the audience, the subject under investigation, or qualitative research methodology. These individuals can be beneficial not only in the analysis stage, but also as the study is being designed to comment on the questions and the recruitment strategies.

Decision makers or those who commission the study can also be a beneficial source of feedback. Indeed, these individuals typically have the most to gain or lose if the study is not on target. In the market research environment, the decision makers can watch from behind the one-way mirror and will occasionally communicate with the moderator while the group is in progress. Notes might be passed to the moderator, the moderator might take a brief break near the conclusion to check signals with the sponsors, or they might even use electronic means of communication.

Analysis Takes Special Skills

Good analysts are like good athletes. They are born with certain skills or aptitudes that give them an advantage over others, but if those skills are not refined, disciplined, and honed their talents will not reach full potential. Some analysis attributes are inherited, whereas others can be acquired in the formative years. Much of analysis seems to relate to the mental makeup of the analysts. Are they open to new ideas? Are they able to step outside of their personal experience and express ideas from the vantage point of others? Are they sufficiently secure with their own feelings to allow and even encourage others to offer divergent views? Do they have a first-rate memory?

It has been my pleasure to work with hundreds of students who have sought to conduct focus group interviews. Analysis is by far the most difficult task to learn. Analysis ability doesn't seem to be related to academic degrees, and in some cases advanced training produces a rigid doctrinaire approach that can actually limit thinking. Academic training does have several benefits, however. It emphasizes a disciplined and systematic belief structure and it establishes a protocol for accepting or rejecting evidence. It offers a host of theoretical constructs that expose the student to multiple worldviews. It is clearly beneficial if the analyst has had exposure to multiple ways of thinking and knowing. Superior communications skills, both oral and written, are also essential.

Summary

Focus group analysis is guided by certain principles about the nature of analysis, what it is and how it is conducted. These principles differ from the positivistic paradigm that has held sway in much social science research. The principles described in this chapter are not intended to be all-inclusive but rather to help the applied researcher begin to understand some of the forces inherent in qualitative analysis. Furthermore, it is from these principles that specific analysis processes emerge. These are discussed in the following chapter.

8

Process of Analyzing Focus Group Results

A statement of what data analysis is:

Data analysis consists of examining, categorizing, tabulating, or otherwise recombining the evidence, to address the initial propositions of a study. (Yin, 1984, p. 99)

A story of what data analysis is not:

Once upon a time an institution of higher learning set out to hire a new president. The governing board of the institution sought applications from far and near but because of the limited travel budget only the near applications were seriously considered. It turned out that three professors were among the final candidates to be interviewed by the board. The first was a professor of accounting, the second was a professor of engineering, and the third was a professor who regularly served as a management consultant. After completing all interviews the board was deadlocked. In an attempt to resolve the dilemma the board decided to invite all three professors back to answer one final question.

The accounting professor was the first to be asked: "What is two plus two?"

The professor immediately replied, "With great confidence I can tell you that the answer is exactly four."

The engineering professor was the second candidate to be asked the question: "What is two plus two?"

After a moment of reflection the engineer replied: "In the field of engineering we are accustomed to problems such as this. In engineering we frequently must deal with numbers that are rounded. Therefore the first two could be any number between 1.50 and 2.49 and the same is true of the second number. This means that the sum of two plus two could be any number between 3.00 and 4.98.

Finally the board invited the management consultant into the board room. The question was asked: "What is two plus two?"

The consultant slowly got up from the chair and went over to shut the door, then over to the window to close the blinds, and finally back to the board table. The consultant leaned across the table and with a low voice, slightly over a whisper, he asked: "What do you want it to be?"

Qualitative analysis is not whatever you want it to be, but unfortunately that is a perception that is sometimes held. The intent of this chapter is to present an overview of focus group analysis that is practical, systematic, and verifiable.

Analysis can be a stumbling block for qualitative researchers. The unanticipated volume of data is sobering, but more often it is the complexity of the analysis that stops the researcher cold. In some situations researchers have been accused of overlooking important evidence, ignoring critical factors, or twisting facts to meet earlier assumptions.

The Situational Analysis Process

Qualitative research must be situationally responsive. The inductive properties of qualitative research assume that the researcher makes decisions and refines the quest for knowledge en route. Sample size is clarified en route, questions are adjusted and fine-tuned en route, and analysis protocol should also be responsive to en route signals from the environment.

Situational analysis occurs when the degree of rigor in the analysis is determined by the situation, or the problem at hand, as opposed to a preordained and predetermined protocol. In situational analysis the analyst does not prejudge the type or nature of analysis needed until he or she has had sufficient exposure to data. Early estimates are made of the time and resources that may be anticipated in the study, but these are subject to later modification.

Before Conducting Focus Groups

Analysis begins by going back to the intent of the study. Indeed, throughout the analysis process the researcher should remember the purpose of the study. A key principle is that the depth or intensity of analysis is determined by the purpose of the study. At times the purpose of the study is narrow and elaborate analysis is unneeded and inappropriate. The beginning of analysis is the realization that the problem drives analysis. Difficulties emerge in both qualitative and quantitative analysis when there is a mismatch between analysis resources and the problem. This can result in elaborate analysis of trivial data or inadequate analysis in a complex problem of major concern. The researcher must remember the intent of the study and regularly weigh choices and options against two factors: available resources and the value of that new information.

In some respects beginning the focus group analysis is like standing at the entrance of a maze. Several different paths are readily apparent at the beginning, and as the traveler continues, additional paths and choices continually emerge. It is unknown to the traveler if the path will be productive until it has been explored, but the process of exploration requires an investment of effort even if it is just a peek around the corner. Survival requires a clear fix on the purpose of the study.

Reflect on the Purpose of the Study, the Resources Available, and the Investment Needed in Analysis. This environment will offer clues on the degree of rigor needed. For example, if the study is to be used to make decisions that are difficult or expensive to reverse, then a more intensive process would seem warranted. The researchers will need to estimate the resource investment needed for analysis and offer a recommended analysis strategy plus other possible strategies that involve varying amounts of resources.

Consider Analysis Implications of Focus Group Questions. The challenge to the researcher is not only to ask questions that are relevant to the study but to ask those questions in a sequence, with a level of abstractions and use of cues that maximizes the quality of analysis. Some questions are more difficult to analyze and demand more time and review of the transcript. These are typically the questions that deal with abstractions or in which language can have multiple meanings. Here the analyst needs to make trade-offs. Certain steps can simplify the analysis process but in so doing sacrifice the richness of other aspects of the study. For example, suppose a public organization wished to perform a needs assessment in order to offer services that best met local needs. These questions could be narrowed in several ways. One strategy is to restrict the breadth of needs to only those the agency has been chartered to address. Another strategy could be to provide specific cues to generate ideas in targeted areas and then to evaluate the suggestions by rating them on areas such as: importance, practicality, centrality to mission, and so on. The implication for analysis is that certain topics of discussion may be overlooked as a result of narrowing the inquiry. This is one of the decisions that must be addressed by the analyst before conducting the focus groups.

Make a Preliminary Decision on Analysis Strategy. In terms of the investment of researcher time, analysis is one of the most variable processes of focus groups. An early estimate is prudent, and those who pay for the study may be involved in the decision. The decision on reporting and the decision on analysis often go hand-in-hand. Therefore, when discussing options with the client I often recommend an analysis choice along with a style for reporting results. (Additional information on reporting is included in the following chapter.) The options for analysis are many, and each veteran researcher has favorites. One way to consider these choices is to place them on a continuum of time investment and rigor (see Figure 8.1). The choices include the following:

Option 1: Transcript-Based Analysis. Transcript-based analysis is the most rigorous and time-intensive of the choices. Tapes are transcribed and the analyst uses the transcript coupled with field notes and the discussion from the debriefing of the moderator team. For a series of three focus groups, a veteran researcher might allocate 30-48 hours for transcript preparation plus another 30-48 hours for the analysis process, which include preparation of the first draft of the report.

Option 2: Tape-Based Analysis. Tape-based analysis involves careful listening to the tape and the preparation of an abridged transcript. This abridged transcript is considerably shorter than the typical 50-70+ page focus group transcript. This transcript contains comments that directly relate to the topic at hand plus the moderator's (or assistant moderator's) oral summary at the conclusion of the focus group. As a result, the abridged transcript may be 3-10 pages long. For the series of three focus groups the veteran researcher might allocate 12-18 hours, which include the preparation of the first draft of the report. This estimate assumes that the analysis is conducted by the same individual who moderated the focus groups.

Option 3: Note-Based Analysis. Note-based analysis relies primarily on field notes, a debriefing session, and summary comments at the conclusion of the focus group. The focus group is taped, but the tape is used primarily to verify specific quotes and to transcribe the oral summary at the conclusion of the focus group. If more rigorous analysis is needed later, the tape is available for transcription. Again, for the same series of three focus groups the analyst might allocate 8-12 hours, which include preparation of the first draft report.

Option 4: Memory-Based Analysis. In this analysis process the moderator presents an oral report to the clients immediately following the focus group. Field notes might be consulted but much is derived by recall. This analysis strategy is often used in market research environments where the clients have been watching the focus group from behind the one-way mirror. Clearly, the quality of this analysis process depends on the skills, experience, and memory of the analyst. Novice moderators/analysts should not use this protocol until after they have mastered the more rigorous strategies. Memory-based analysis can be impressive when used by a veteran moderator who is an expert in the topic of discussion.

(NOTE: The process steps for these four options are included in Appendix 8A.)

Conduct Several Focus Groups. Once the initial analysis strategy has been determined, the researcher should conduct several focus groups. Several focus groups are often needed to gain a sense of how the questions are working, if they need to be revised, and the degree of convergence or divergence of the participants' comments. With this early information the researcher can better make the revised decision on analysis strategies.

Revise the Decision on Analysis Strategy, if Necessary. Changing degree of rigor in the analysis strategy may not be as difficult as it sounds if the researcher has laid the foundation with systematic data collection methods. Careful field notes and electronic recordings can be used in a variety of ways. Initially, the researcher might plan to prepare a detailed analysis based on transcripts and a careful review of field notes. After conducting several focus groups it may become apparent from the range of comments that the participants clearly articulate a narrow range of views and as a result detailed transcripts are not needed.

The Analysis Continuum

Least time intensive   Most time intensive

Least rigorous   Most rigorous

Memory-Based   Note-Based   Tape-Based   Transcript-Based

Figure 8.1. Continuum of Analysis Choices

Conduct Additional Focus Groups. Later, after *some* of the focus groups, the researcher may want to modify the question structure and timing and seek confirmation of emerging themes or ideas. Although most focus group studies consist of 3 to 6 groups, some will involve a dozen or more focus groups; indeed, some have consisted of over 50 focus groups on the same topic. In these studies the researcher has a special opportunity not present when only a handful of groups are conducted. After a reasonable number of groups, several trends are likely to appear and occasionally the researcher will identify "big ideas" that were discovered but not sought after. When this occurs, the researcher might reduce the time for some predetermined questions, and eliminate questions that are deemed unproductive, confusing, or redundant. This allows the addition of new questions that have emerged from earlier focus groups. The researcher might seek confirmation of earlier findings, or test out categories, topologies, or diagrams that were developed from previous groups.

While Still in the Focus Group

Once participants leave the focus group it is difficult, if not impossible, to tie together missing pieces of the analysis puzzle. Certain analysis functions must be performed while participants are still gathered together.

Listen for Inconsistent Comments and Probe for Understanding. One distinctive feature about focus groups is that participants occasionally change their opinions during the discussion. After listening to other points of view or hearing others explain their logic, some participants may alter or even reverse their views. This phenomenon is rarely seen in other forms of data acquisition, but it does occur with focus groups. This presents some concerns about analysis. Some have considered this a deficiency of focus group research. But it is only a weakness if we assume that people don't change opinions in real life—that we develop opinions that remain constant. Because this is hardly the case, it seems that opinion change is more of a testimony that people in the focus group are functioning in a normal, natural manner. The challenge to the researcher is to discover what is influencing the change.

Participants may have changed their views after listening to new evidence presented by a participant or different logic that was considered convincing. In some circumstances, participants have been influenced by the forcefulness of another person in the group. The analyst's task is first to identify that a change has taken place, then to determine if the participant agrees that he or she has changed, and finally to determine what prompted the change.

It is interesting to note that although the rhetoric of the participants might change they may not feel that they have modified their earlier position. This could occur for several reasons. The participants might not feel that the supposedly differing views are really different after all. I have seen some individuals in focus groups hold opposing opinions and appear to be oblivious to the discrepancy. A second factor that explains the seeming discrepancy is that the opinions are conditional. Some participants have expressed opposing views and when asked to explain they describe the condition that might lead up to both opinions. If certain factors occur they would support one side, but if other factors were present their opinion would be different.

The challenge to the moderator is to identify these inconsistencies while the participants are still in the focus group. This permits the moderator to inquire about the differing points of view: "Earlier you said _____ , and now you've indicated that _____. These seem to me to be different from each other. Help me understand how you feel about this issue."

Based on observations from a number of focus groups, it would also appear that some people have no difficulty changing opinions. If they have limited investment or commitment in the topic and if changing opinions is not perceived as a threat they may change without hesitation. Others may feel a loyalty to a point of view, feel they must defend a view, or feel caught in an adversarial encounter in which they must stake out a position and stick with it in spite of opposition.

Listen for Vague or Cryptic Comments and Probe for Understanding. Sometimes the participant comments seem logical at the moment they are said, but later the logic crumbles with critical thinking. For example, several years ago I was analyzing a series of focus groups that examined the extension service of a land grant university. One of the questions was on getting people to attend events and meetings offered by the extension service. A pattern that emerged was that additional promotion would result in increased attendance. The comments were accepted at face value and it wasn't until after the focus groups were completed that a skeptic on the research team challenged these comments. She said: "They are giving you the easy answer. It is easy in our society today to claim that promotion influences people, that if they know about it they will take advantage of it. But is that true? In areas where promotion has increased the attendance hasn't changed. If it is promotion it doesn't operate in a linear way that is directly correlated to attendance." In looking back, we should have been less willing to accept the easy answer; we should have asked for an example or probed for more understanding. It could be that people were talking about a special type of promotion, offered through a particular medium, or delivered in a unique manner. Whatever it is, we missed the opportunity because we too quickly assumed we knew what they meant.

Take Careful Notes of the Focus Groups. One of the benefits of assistant moderators is that they can devote their primary attention to taking field notes and capturing important aspects of the discussion. The field notes might include the key points in the discussion, notable quotes, and important observations (silent agreement, obvious body language, indications of group mood, irony or contradictory statements when the meaning is opposite of what was said). This information can provide insight into the nature of the discussion and may not be captured on the recording.

Consider a Final Preference Question or Brief Personal Summary. In Chapter 4, I discussed a type of ending question called the "all things considered question." This question has proven helpful in nailing down the final positions of participants, especially when their comments may seemingly have supported divergent points.

Offer a Summary of Key Questions and Seek Confirmation. This is the first opportunity for the moderator (or assistant) to offer an oral summary of the critical questions. This summary has two advantages. It is close in time to when comments were actually made and therefore least subject to memory fade. More important, however, this process allows and encourages the participants to verify that the summary is accurate and complete.

Draw a Diagram of the Seating Arrangement. While participants are still in the group, the moderator might sketch a seating diagram for the focus group. Some moderators have found this helpful in recalling the names of participants. A week or two after the focus group you may not recall the names, but you might remember where the person was seated around the table. With the seating diagram you can place a name with the memory.

Obtain Needed Background Information on Participants. The researcher can use several ways to obtain this data. One way is to note and record observable characteristics such as gender, age, race, and the like. Another way is to ask participants to complete a registration form containing biographical data prior to the focus group. Information relating to status or influence is dangerous to ask in the focus group because of the tendency of the responses to influence other participants. Therefore, information such as income, educational level, size or scope of business, degrees, or employment positions are often better obtained in writing prior to the focus group.

Immediately After the Focus Group

As soon as the focus group is concluded the moderator team should take certain steps to ensure the integrity of the data. One task, which sometimes is not easy, is to get participants to leave. In some cases participants have enjoyed each other's company and clearly are not interested in departing. Once participants have left, the moderator team should use the next 30 minutes in a productive manner. This includes the following:

Spot-Check the Tape Recording to Ensure Proper Operation. Rewind and play the tape at different points to quickly gain a sense of the quality of audio recording. If problems are apparent, the researchers might immediately plan to spend additional time resurrecting the discussion from memory.

Conduct Moderator and Assistant Moderator Debriefing. Typically, researchers will want to discuss the focus group and this can be most productive if it is tape recorded for use in subsequent analysis. First impressions are forgotten and the researcher can lose sight of these initial reactions unless they are documented. In the debriefing the moderator team might discuss the following points:

- Most important themes or ideas expressed
- Most noteworthy quotes
- Unexpected or unanticipated findings
- Comparison and contrast of this focus group with other groups or with what they had expected
- Usefulness of questions and need for revision or adjustment

Label and File All Field Notes, Tapes, and Other Materials. In a series of focus groups a considerable amount of data will be collected. Lack of labels on field notes or misplaced tapes can cause enormous frustration. Spend time on housekeeping before leaving the site to avoid major frustrations later.

Considerations in the Analysis

When conducting this analysis the researcher gives consideration to seven factors:

1. Consider the Words. The researcher should think about both the actual words used by participants and the meanings of those words. A variety of words and phrases will be used and the researcher will need to determine the degree of similarity among these responses.

2. Consider the Context. Participant responses are triggered by a stimulus—a question asked by the moderator or a comment from another participant. The researcher should examine the context by finding the triggering stimulus and then interpret the comment in light of that environment. For example, when the moderator asks an open-ended question the first participant begins recounting a specific experience. These comments then provide a stimulus for the second respondent who may overlook the larger issue and respond to a narrow aspect of the original question. In other situations the second participant, triggered by the extreme comments of the earlier speaker, deliberately and carefully attempts to provide a degree of balance in the discussion. Also, the context can change when the moderator asks a question a second time in slightly different words.

The context depends not only on the discussion but also on the tone and intensity of the oral comment. The discussion transcript greatly assists the researcher in analysis, but this written summary has an inherent limitation. The tone and inflection of the comment might be interpreted in one way when heard in a group setting and in another way when read in a transcript. For example, suppose several respondents had responded to a question with exactly the same words but with variations in emphasis on certain words.

Comment	Translation
"This was GOOD!"	(It was good.)
"This was GOOD?"	(It was supposed to be good, but wasn't.)
"THIS was good!"	(This one was good, others were not.)
"This WAS good."	(It used to be good, but not any more.)

3. Consider the Internal Consistency. Participants in focus groups change and sometimes even reverse their positions after interaction with others. This phenomenon rarely occurs in individual interviews because of a lack of interaction from other participants. When there is a shift in opinion, the researcher typically traces the flow of the conversation to determine clues that might explain the change. The shift is noted and may take on importance in the final report if opinion shifts are relevant to the purpose of the study.

4. Consider the Frequency or Extensiveness of Comments. Some topics are discussed by more participants (extensiveness) and some comments are made more often (frequency) than others. These topics could be more important or of special interest to participants. It is risky to assume that either frequency or extensiveness is equivalent to importance without additional evidence. Indeed, some comments in a focus group have been deemed by participants to be of considerable importance, yet the comments occurred with minimal frequency. While considering frequency or extensiveness, it is also wise to consider what wasn't said but was expected. This can also be risky to interpret unless the researcher has explicitly asked participants for their explanation.

5. Consider the Intensity of the Comments. Occasionally, participants talk about a topic with a special intensity or depth of feeling. Sometimes the participants will use words that connote intensity or tell you directly about their strength of feeling. Intensity may be difficult to spot with transcripts alone because intensity is often communicated by changed voice tone, talking speed, and emphasis on certain words. Individuals will differ on how they display strength of feeling and for some it will be a speed or excitement in the voice whereas others will speak slowly and deliberately. One clue to intensity is when individuals vary their past speaking pattern, for example, nontalkers start speaking, slow speakers talk faster, fast talkers speak slowly, quiet speakers talk louder, and so on.

6. Consider the Specificity of Responses. Responses that are specific and based on experiences should be given more weight than responses that are vague and impersonal. To what degree can the respondent provide details when asked a follow-up probe? Greater attention is often placed on responses that are in the first person as opposed to hypothetical third-person answers. For example, "I feel the new practice is important because I have used it and been satisfied" has more weight than "These practices are good and people in the area should use them."

7. Find the Big Ideas. The researcher can get so close to a multitude of comments and details that trends or ideas that cut across the entire discussion are missed. One of the traps of analysis is not seeing big ideas. It may be helpful to take a few steps back from the discussions by allowing extra time for big ideas to percolate. For example, after finishing the analysis the researcher might set the report aside for a brief period and then jot down three or four of the most important findings. Assistant moderators or others skilled in qualitative analysis might review the process and verify the big ideas. At times the researcher might find an unanticipated big idea that provides insight into how the consumer views the product or service. Big ideas emerge from an accumulation of evidence—words used, body language, intensity of comments—rather than from isolated comments. Look for big ideas not only in the responses to key questions but throughout the discussion.

Suggestions for Data Reduction

The analyst faces a challenge of data reduction. The amount of data collected in focus group discussions is considerable. A transcript from one focus group can easily consist of 50-70 pages. In a typical series of four focus groups the researcher is confronted with 200+ pages of single-spaced transcripts, 8 hours of tape, plus field notes. The complexity of the task can be overwhelming. The ideal solution would be for the analyst to have an excellent memory, capable of storing all details and retrieving data just when needed. Unfortunately, because of their limited memories researchers must rely on other strategies to assist in the analysis process. In order to cope with this complexity, researchers often use one or more of the following implements: tape recorders, word processors, and transcripts with scissors or colored marking pens.

Variable speed tape players save valuable time. Some tape recorders enable the researcher to play back the tape at different speeds. The recorder can be speeded up to almost twice the normal speed with minimal distortion or slowed down to about 75% of normal speed to capture exact words of a critical participant comment. The variable speed tape recorder costs a bit more than the standard cassette recorder but is well worth the extra investment.

Cassette players with double decks are helpful in transferring sections of one tape onto another tape. The advent of reasonably priced double deck cassette players enables the researcher to listen to a tape and then make a copy of selected relevant comments on the second tape deck. If needed, all responses to a particular question can be packed on the second tape. This process enables the researcher to play all responses to one question without changing cassettes. Another strategy is to use a double deck recorder to capture a collection of the most insightful quotes from participants. This second tape with selected quotes can prove helpful in oral reports. Double deck recorders are also helpful in making a backup copy of tapes.

Some researchers prefer using word processors to type significant quotes while listening to the cassette tape. The word processor allows the researcher to sort, categorize, and rearrange statements with ease. In addition, the computer provides the opportunity to add participant names or create wide margins for notes or coding.

A low technology option involves the use of scissors or colored marking pens on transcripts. If entire transcripts of the discussion are available the researcher can cut out or mark sections that relate to specific themes for later aggregation.

The analysis process is like detective work. One looks for clues, but in this case the clues are trends and patterns that reappear among various focus groups. The researcher's task is to prepare a statement about what was found, a statement that emerges from and is supported by available evidence. In preparing the statement, the researcher seeks primarily to identify evidence that repeats and is common to several participants. However, some attention is also placed on determining the range and diversity of experiences or perceptions. The researcher must identify those opinions, ideas, or feelings that repeat even though they are expressed in different words and styles. Opinions that are expressed only once are enlightening but should not form the crux of the report.

Analysis Issues to Consider

The Analyst

Ideally, the moderator or assistant moderator should also do the analysis. These individuals have had firsthand exposure to each of the discussions, observed the interactions of all participants, and likely have had the most intensive exposure to the problem at hand.

In some situations, such as when nonresearchers are recruited to moderate, the moderator may not have the analytic skills or time required to perform the analysis. Analysis of focus groups does require special skills different from the skills of moderating and requires a disciplined effort that some moderators may not possess. It is possible to separate the moderating and analysis functions and have each task performed by different individuals. To exercise this option requires careful planning and precise definition of tasks. At times, this division of labor is the preferred option.

For example, in some organizations the professionals coordinating the research effort may be ineffective as moderators because they are too well known or associated with volatile issues. It is akin to a clergyperson asking church members on Tuesday if they are following the precepts of Sunday's sermon. Occasionally, a proxy can be identified and trained to moderate the discussions. The analysis could then be conducted by the professional responsible for the research effort or by focus group experts outside of the organization who are skilled in qualitative analysis. In these situations it is necessary for the research director to specify the questioning route, arrange for the careful training of moderators, identify procedures for collecting data, and conduct a group debriefing of all moderators.

(NOTE: Appendix 8B includes an example of the process used in note-based analysis that has been successful in working with volunteers.)

Editing Messy Quotations

Most people do not talk in nice crisp statements that result in insightful quotations. In real life, people use incomplete sentences or ramble along with disconnected thoughts strung together with verbal pauses. Thus, transcripts of focus group interviews inevitably contain messy quotations. The researcher must determine the extent to which statements can be abridged or modified. An area in which editing is often needed is in the placement of periods. Run-on sentences that are understood when spoken may get confusing when read. The period often improves readability for lengthy quotes. *The most important aspect in using quotations is that the researcher captures the intended meaning of the speaker.* Sometimes the actual words do not convey the meaning—as in situations in which the speaker is trying to use humor and will say the opposite of what is intended. The researcher has an obligation to fairly and accurately present the views of the participants. In order to fulfill this obligation some minor editing to correct grammar is appropriate as long as the meaning is not changed.

Nonverbal Communication in the Focus Group

Some types of nonverbal communication are often overlooked in the analysis, especially when the researcher relies only on transcripts. The researcher should consider the energy level or enthusiasm within the group. Enthusiastic comments and excitement for the topic should be factored into statements of findings. Also, note the degree of spontaneity and the extent of participant involvement. Spontaneous comments, where probing is unneeded, may signal that people are interested in the idea. In addition, the researcher should be attentive to body language expressed during the group session. The moderator and assistant moderator should make notes of the nonverbal responses during the actual interview session, which are then considered when analyzing the results. I have favored a conservative approach in interpreting body language. Body language provides merely a first clue and verbal confirmation is needed before incorporating the concept into the analysis.

The Use of Numbers in Focus Group Results

Numbers and percentages ought to be used with caution in the focus group report. Numbers sometimes convey the impression that results can be projected to a population, and this is not within the capabilities of qualitative research procedures. Instead, the researcher might consider the use of qualifiers such as: "the prevalent feeling was that . . . " or "several participants strongly felt that . . . " or even "most participants agreed that . . . "

Information Arriving After the Focus Group

What does the researcher do with information that is relevant to the topic but obtained after the focus group interview has concluded? In one-to-one interviewing this is often a nonissue because the interview may not have a defined moment of closure. The focus group is different because in focus groups the individuals have the opportunity to hear other views and to respond. As a result, comments made after the group has adjourned cannot be countered or amplified by other individuals. In deciding what to do with this information the researcher might consider one of the primary rules of social science research: Don't disregard any information. Make note of it but also describe the circumstances under which it was received. The decision to use the information in analysis and reporting is another matter. The prudent researcher will use care and discretion in the use of this late-arriving information. In making the decision to use the information, the researcher might consider the reasons for the delay. In some cases it might simply be an afterthought of one participant on the way out of the focus group. In other situations it could be a participant who is inhibited or anxious about sharing a controversial view and chooses to communicate to the researcher in private.

Essentially there are three choices for what to do with this information. First, use it like all other information from the focus group, treating it in the same manner as the focus group data. The second strategy is to use the information in the analysis but call attention to it in the report. The third choice is to collect the information but not use it in the analysis.

Influence of Moderator or Assistant Moderator on the Participants

Nonprofit and public focus groups sometimes do not use professional moderators. The moderating may be conducted by organizational employees, clients, or volunteers. These individuals bring both advantages and disadvantages. They have background information about the organization and are familiar with the organizational culture and language. Their services can also be obtained at a minimal cost, and once they have participated in gathering information they are often more likely to carry out the recommendations. This is discussed further in Chapter 10.

Unfortunately, these internal moderators may also have disadvantages. They may occupy positions of influence or responsibility, and participants may be responding to the position held by the moderator as opposed to the moderator as a person. For example, perhaps the volunteer, unknown to the sponsoring agency, is also the local chair of a political party, an influential elder in a religious organization, or a community activist who regularly rallies support for various causes. Now, these may not be disqualifying factors, but the maxim holds that the moderator should be a neutral force in the focus group. The moderator's history or role should not influence participant comments, and if the potential exists, it is better to seek a replacement moderator.

Summary

In review, remember that the researcher is the detective looking for trends and patterns that occur across the various groups. The analysis process begins with assembling the raw materials and getting an overview or total picture of the entire process. The researcher's role in analysis covers a continuum with assembly of raw data on one extreme and interpretative comments on the other. The analysis process involves consideration of words, tone, context, nonverbals, internal consistency, frequency, extensiveness, intensity, specificity of responses and big ideas. Data reduction strategies are essential in the analysis.

APPENDIX 8A

Analysis Options Process Steps

Option 1: Transcript-Based Analysis

A. Make backup copies of tapes

B. Give the original tapes to transcriptionist for entry onto computer

C. When transcription returns, moderator or assistant listens to tapes, adds names of speakers, and completes missing data, if possible

D. File tapes, transcripts, field notes, and the like for future analysis

E. When you are ready to complete analysis, gather transcripts and field notes by categories of focus groups

F. Read transcripts and field notes one category at a time

G. Look for emerging themes (by question and then overall)

H. Develop coding categories and code the data

I. Sort the data into coded categories

J. Construct topologies or diagram the analysis

K. See what data are left out and consider revision

L. Prepare the draft report—begin with most important questions

Option 2: Tape-Based Analysis

A. Gather tapes and field notes by category

B. Review field notes by category

C. Enter abridged transcript on computer

D. Look for emerging themes (by question and then overall)

E. Develop coding categories and code the data

F. Sort the data into coding categories

G. Construct topologies or diagram the analysis

H. See what data are left out and consider revision

I. Prepare the draft report—begin with most important questions

Option 3: Note-Based Analysis (assuming multiple moderators)
A. Conduct a discussion of all moderators and assistants
B. Moderators and assistants present findings, which are tape recorded
C. Analyst asks the group to compare and contrast each successive focus group report
D. Analyst offers the group (for their confirmation) a brief oral summary of key findings
E. Later, analyst reviews the tape of the analysis discussion and the field notes, listens to selected tapes identified by moderator teams, and reviews other available material
F. Prepare the draft report—begin with most important questions

Option 4: Memory-Based Analysis
A. Moderator reviews field notes
B. Moderator mentally analyzes (points G, H, I, J, K in Option 1 above)
C. Moderator presents an oral report to client

APPENDIX 8B

Instructions to Volunteers on
Note-Based Analysis

1. Before the Focus Group Starts
Test the tape recorder. Turn on recorder—as you walk around the room, say who you are, where you are, and a description of your group. Play it back to ensure the recorder is working and begin the recording at the end of this introduction.

2. During the Focus Group
A. Listen for inconsistent comments and probe for understanding.
B. Listen for vague or cryptic comments and probe for understanding.
C. Offer a summary of key questions and seek confirmation.
D. Draw a diagram of the seating arrangement.
E. Complete the "Participation Information Form" with observed background information on participants.

3. Immediately After the Focus Group
A. Spot-check tape recording to ensure proper operation.
B. Conduct moderator and assistant moderator debriefing. Turn the tape recorder back on so the debriefing is captured on tape.
  - Identify the most noteworthy quotes.
  - Identify the important themes or ideas expressed.
  - Identify "big ideas."
  - Compare and contrast this focus group with other groups or with what you had expected.
C. Label and file all field notes, tapes, and other materials.

4. Within a Week After the Focus Group or ASAP

Find a time when you have about 4-5 hours without interruptions. It is best to do this *before* you conduct the next focus group. The second focus group will make it more confusing and difficult to recall the discussion in the first group.

A. Gather tapes and field notes by category.

B. Review field notes by category.

C. Go to end of the tape and transcribe the oral summary (best if you can enter this on a computer).

D. Go to the beginning of the tape and listen to the entire tape. As you listen, have the field notes in front of you. Capture word-for-word the exact statements of the best (notable) quotes. Identify the speakers by initials.

E. Listen to your debriefing.

F. Identify the major points. The major points will usually relate to the important questions that were summarized in the oral debriefing. The major points might include "big ideas" or "moderator insights" that are supported by the data (the comments of the participants).

G. Write the first draft of your report, which will include:

- Major Points (one or two pages typed),
- Notable Quotes (one or more pages typed).

H. Share the first draft with the assistant moderator (or moderator) for feedback and comments.

I. Discuss feedback from assistant moderator (moderator) and revise report so that it is mutually acceptable to both moderator and assistant moderator.

J. Prepare final report for sharing.

5. Attend the Reporting Session and Share Your Report

9

Reporting Focus
Group Results

Reports do make a difference! Research results are sometimes ignored because of inadequate or ineffective reporting. At times, researchers have underestimated the importance of oral and written reports. In part, this may be due to traditions within the academic community. Academic researchers have prepared reports for others within the research community but not necessarily for those who make day-by-day decisions within organizations. Their reports have often focused on uncovering theories, principles, or truths to guide future researchers and were presented in a writing style that has limited appeal. Moreover, in an academic environment, reports have traditionally been assessed by the degree of adherence to appropriate research methodology or rigor.

One professional group concerned about reporting has been evaluators. In the last several decades, evaluators have been troubled about the lack of use and misuse of evaluation results. This attention to using results is grounded in the *Standards for Evaluations of Educational Programs* as prepared by the Joint Committee on Standards for Educational Evaluation (1981). The Joint Committee underscored the importance of evaluation utility—that is, the potential for "an evaluation to serve the practical information needs of given audiences" (p. 19). The *Standards* emphasize the need for clarity, dissemination, and timeliness. In effect, the *Standards* recognizes that evaluations are to be useful to specific people for specific purposes and not merely academic exercises that add to our existing body of knowledge.

A second professional group, market researchers, have had a rich tradition in applied research and place emphasis on research results that assist decision makers. In this profession, the research effort has been designed from the beginning to produce information related to specific decisions. For example, market researchers wonder, Should we introduce the new product? Will the new product be purchased? What strategies should be used in advertising the product? Both professions, evaluators and market researchers, have contributed to our ability to communicate findings of research efforts, and this chapter draws on the methods of both disciplines.

Consider the Audience

A Tale

Once upon a time there was a special kingdom. A wise king ruled this vast kingdom. Throughout the week the king would consider the needs and problems of the realm and make weekly pronouncements, laws, and decrees intended to address his subjects' concerns. The wise king grew weary of his awesome responsibility, because his solutions didn't always work and he suspected that his weekly pronouncements were in fact weakly pronouncements.

The king was indeed wise and decided to consult his royal advisers before future decisions were announced. The royal court was ablaze with excitement and eagerly did all members provide advice to the king. Knights and wizards, ladies in waiting and ladies not waiting, all provided counsel to the king. The king was pleased for the advice was helpful, and the king grew in stature and respect among his people.

One day, when considering a particularly important decision, the king's advisers recommended that the royal researcher conduct a special study. This study would give the advisers the information they could use to help the king make the right decision. It was an important study that required much effort. Fortunately, the royal researcher was trained in all of the latest techniques. The royal researcher was eager to oblige and hastily retreated to examine the problem in more detail. The royal researcher had a special ivory tower where he practiced his craft and none had ever entered this ivy-covered structure, except for royal research assistants. After four weeks, the royal researcher came out of the tower with a comprehensive report.

The report was beautiful to behold, for it had gold edges, sandalwood covers, and pages of the finest royal parchment. However, after reading the report the king and the royal advisers became troubled because the report was not useful. It was an elegant report, but it did not provide useful answers to the difficult decisions encountered by the king and royal court. The wise king then decreed that henceforth all royal researchers must "Consider the Audience."

Modern-day kings, royal courts, and royal researchers face the same situation today. Information is needed, but all too often that which is produced is not specifically related to the problem at hand, has not involved the appropriate individuals, or is too late to be helpful. Those who plan research endeavors, including focus groups, should remember the royal decree: "Consider the Audience."

The researcher begins reporting efforts by reflecting on the audience—those who will be receiving and using the report. One of the pitfalls of reporting is fuzzy audience identification. Researchers have a tendency to write reports for amorphous groups—the organization, the feds, the board—as opposed to specific people. A helpful strategy is to reflect back on the identified users and assemble information of particular interest to these individuals. In some situations, different reports can be prepared for different users, with each report emphasizing areas of concern and interest to each user category.

Those who prepare reports tend to assume that people prefer to learn about results in the same way the researcher does. This assumption is in conflict with what is known about individual learning preferences. Evidence suggests that people differ on how they prefer to receive information. This leads us to two implications for researchers. First, they should learn as much as they can about their audiences' preferences in receiving information. Educational level, occupation, age, and other demographic data can be helpful in this inquiry. Often, the most insightful way to obtain this information is to inquire about the most memorable reports the user audience has received in the past. You might ask: What were these reports like? What took place? What about the report did you find especially helpful? The second implication is the necessity of using a variety of media. Reports can be prepared for presentation in a variety of ways: in writing or orally, or complemented with charts, photographs, audio/video tapes, tables, or figures, just to name some of the options. Procedures used are limited only by resources and creativity. Reports with multiple media help ensure that the message is effectively communicated because the combination of methods accommodates individual learning preferences and also provides reinforcement of the findings.

When preparing reports for specific people the emphasis is on clarity and understanding. As a result, the writing style is characterized by less formality, shorter words, and familiar vocabulary. Active voice is preferred to passive construction. Quotations, illustrations, or examples of concepts are encouraged. When writing for nonresearchers, the complex descriptions of analysis and technical jargon actually inhibit understanding. Complex research procedures, if used, must be explained in an understandable way to those not acquainted with such procedures.

Consider the Purpose of the Report

The process of reporting serves three functions. First and foremost, the report communicates results. The underlying principle of reporting is that the report communicates useful information to an identifiable audience for a specific purpose. For this communication to be effective the reporter must select the appropriate media, strive for clarity and precision in reporting, and place attention on the individual information needs of specific people.

Second, the process of preparing reports assists the researcher in developing a logical description of the total investigation. This function is most apparent in the preparation of written reports. Report writing is a disciplined effort that helps the researcher arrange the findings, conclusions, and recommendations in a logical sequence that can be subjected to review. This disciplined effort results in tighter logic, more precise statements, and an overall improvement in quality.

The third purpose of reporting is to provide a historic record of findings. Although the report is intended to serve more immediate needs of audiences, it also can provide a longer term reference for future studies and decisions. Concerns and problems often re-emerge, the environment may change, the recommendations for improving the program may not work, and decision makers may have need to re-examine or even replicate an earlier study. Therefore, one of the purposes of the report is to provide a document that can be subjected to examination at some point in the future.

The Nature of Reporting

Focus group reports can be of three types: written only, oral only, or a combination of both written and oral. Whenever possible, the researcher should attempt to provide the report in a combination of modes, because each method offers unique advantages. Written reports are well suited for distribution within an organization and are preferred when people are difficult to gather together. Oral reports allow for questions, clarification, and the use of taped highlights or quotations. When written and oral reports are used together, the advantages are multiplied.

The Written Report

When preparing the written report, the researcher should consider the style of the report. Focus group reports have traditionally been presented in a narrative style. The narrative report uses complete sentences and is augmented with quotes from the focus groups. An alternative is the bulleted or outline report, which uses key words and phrases to highlight the critical points. Increasingly, the bulleted report is gaining popularity because of the speed with which it can be prepared and consumed.

Besides being clear and logical, the written report must also look attractive. Poor quality printing, inadequate covers, and shoddy assembly convey undesirable impressions of the total research effort. If necessary, the researcher should seek assistance in editing the report for clarity and to be certain that there are no misspellings or grammatical errors. A recommended outline for the written report includes the following:

1. Cover Page. The front cover should include the title, the names of people receiving or commissioning the report, the names of the researchers, and the date the report is submitted.

2. Summary. The brief, well-written executive summary describes why focus groups were conducted and lists major conclusions and recommendations. The summary is often limited to two pages and should be able to stand alone. Although this section is placed first in the written report, it is often the last part written.

3. Table of Contents. This section is optional and need not be included when the report is brief. The table of contents provides the reader with information on how the report is organized and where various parts are located.

4. Statement of the Problem, Key Questions, and Study Methods. In this section, the researcher should describe the purpose of the study and include a brief description of the focus group interviews. The number of focus groups, the methods of selecting participants, and the number of people in each focus group should be included.

5. Results or Findings. Most often results are organized around key questions or big ideas in the focus group interview. The results can be presented in a variety of means: using bulleted or narrative formats, using only raw data, using descriptive summaries, or using the interpretative approach.

6. Summary of Themes. A small number of themes or key points are cited. These statements are not limited to specific questions but often tie together themes that bridge several questions, if not the entire discussion.

7. Limitations and Alternative Explanations. This section can be placed within the results category if it is brief. Limitations refer to those aspects of the study that might limit the application of findings or differing interpretations of results.

8 Recommendations. Recommendations are optional and not automatically included in all focus group reports. The recommendations are future-oriented and provide suggestions as to what might be done with the results. These recommendations can be presented in a variety of ways, sometimes in very specific terms, or in terms of general concepts, or even as suggestions.

9. Appendix. The final part of the written report is the appendix, which includes additional materials that might be helpful to the reader. For example, it is advisable to include the questioning route for the focus group and the screening questionnaire. Additional quotations may also be included in the appendix.

Overall, the written report is intended to attract and hold the attention of readers.

Begin the Written Report With a Framework

The skeleton or framework of the report is composed of the key questions that were asked or the big ideas that have emerged from the discussion. These questions and big ideas serve as the outline for the written report. They can be written using three different styles or models. The first style of presentation consists of the question or idea and is followed by all participant comments (the raw data model). The second style is a summary description followed by illustrative quotes (the descriptive model). The third style is a summary description with illustrative quotes followed by an interpretation (the interpretative model).

Here are examples of these styles from a series of focus group interviews with parents. The first example illustrates reporting of raw data. In this example, the researcher included all comments in the focus group and then arranged these into clusters or categories. The categories were selected by the researcher after reviewing all comments.

When appropriate, the comments can be arranged on a continuum such as degree of support, agreement versus disagreement, intensity, and so on. This style of reporting has the advantage of providing the reader with the total range of comments; however, the sheer length of the resulting report may discourage careful reading. The raw data model of reporting is particularly appropriate in situations in which the researcher has limited experience (such as with volunteers), when the audience is interested in receiving all comments, or when a descriptive or interpretive report follows.

REPORTING EXAMPLE 9.1. RAW DATA

What do you look for in a youth organization?

Responses from parents included:

Category 1: Quality of Leaders

Good leaders who can be a role model. (John, May 2)

The person in charge must be a good influence because children idolize their leaders. (Mary, May 2)

I would like my son in a youth organization that has a dedicated adult leader. My son needs to succeed in something other than school. I want him to have the feeling of accomplishment that comes with hard work. (Bill, May 2)

Leaders are the most important thing in a youth organization. I don't want a crank for a leader. (Esther, May 2)

I want an adult who is patient and kind to work with my kids. (Marge, May 3)

Good leaders can accept kids just as they are. These adults can have fun with kids. They can laugh with kids and enjoy the company of young people. (Sue, May 3)

When I drop my daughter off at the youth organization for the first time I watch what she does. If the leader brings her into the group and makes her feel welcome I know that is a good leader. (Richard, May 3)

I was in scouts when I was young and I still remember my scoutmaster. He had a sense of humor and always brought out the best in all of us. He always had time to listen to our problems. (Bob, May 3)

Category 2: Convenience

Low cost. I can't afford uniforms and costly trips. (Bill, May 2)

I've got four kids and I'm not going to run them to four different organizations. Either all the kids get involved in one organization or none at all. (Tom, May 3)

Any organization that we would consider must be convenient. We have certain family times and the group can't interfere with that. (Esther, May 2)

Both my wife and I work and we just don't have time to run both Jim and Jessica, our two kids, to different organizations. The youth organization has to be close enough so that our kids can walk. (Bob, May 3)

Distance from our home. The organization needs to be within walking or biking distance of our house. (Marge, May 3)

Cost is somewhat of a factor. (Richard, May 3)

Category 3: Values

You know what is most important for me is to be certain that the other parents are like me. I mean, we must have the same values on things like drinking and drugs. (John, May 2)

A wholesome environment. I want my son to be around the good kids in the community. (Bill, May 2)

A chance to get exercise and be out-of-doors. (Mary, May 2)

My son needs to be in a group setting. He has troubles getting along with others and needs to learn to cooperate and compromise. (Marge, May 3)

The only group activity my children need is the church. Everything they need is within the church. (Sue, May 2)

Category 4: Other

My daughter needs to be able to do something she can feel good about and to have the opportunity to do well. She's not sports minded and needs an opportunity to get recognition for her own talents. (Richard, May 3)

Lots of activities. I want my kid to be busy. You know what they say about idle hands. (Tom, May 3)

The next example is a descriptive summary. This style of reporting begins with a summary paragraph and then includes illustrative quotes. The quotes selected are intended to help the reader understand the way in which respondents answered the question.

REPORTING EXAMPLE 9.2. DESCRIPTIVE SUMMARY

What do you as a parent look for in a youth organization?

In each group session the parents cited a number of factors with two characteristics mentioned most often. These were the quality of adult leadership and the importance of convenience. Parents were concerned that their children were exposed to adults who understood and related well to youth. The issue of quality leadership was expressed in different ways, with attention placed more on the personal attributes rather than on the knowledge or technical expertise of the volunteer. In this community, the parents were also very concerned about youth organizations not getting in the way of family, employment, or other social commitments. Parents favored youth organizations that were convenient with their present lifestyle. Factors mentioned less frequently related to the values of the youth organization and the opportunity for youth to achieve.

Typical comments by these parents included:

The person in charge must be a good influence because children idolize their leaders. (Mary, May 2)

Leaders are the most important thing in a youth organization. I don't want a crank for a leader. (Esther, May 2)

I want an adult who is patient and kind to work with my kids. (Marge, May 3)

Low cost. I can't afford uniforms and costly trips. (Bill, May 2)

I've got four kids and I'm not going to run them to four different organizations. Either all the kids get involved in one organization or none at all. (Tom, May 3)

Any organization that we would consider must be convenient. We have certain family times and the group can't interfere with that. (Esther, May 2)

The interpretive report builds on the descriptive report by the inclusion of a section on what the data mean.

REPORTING EXAMPLE 9.3. INTERPRETATIVE

What do you as a parent look for in a youth organization?

In each group session, the parents cited a number of factors with two characteristics mentioned most often. These were the quality of adult leadership and the importance of convenience. Parents were concerned that their children were exposed to adults who understood and related well to youth. The issue of quality leadership was expressed in different ways, with attention placed more on the personal attributes rather than on the knowledge or technical expertise of the volunteer. In this community, the parents were also very concerned about youth organizations not getting in the way of family, employment, or other social commitments. Parents favored youth organizations that were convenient given their present lifestyle. Factors mentioned with less frequently related to the values of the youth organization and the opportunity for youth to achieve.

Typical comments by these parents included:

The person in charge must be a good influence because children idolize their leaders. (Mary, May 2)

Leaders are the most important thing in a youth organization. I don't want a crank for a leader. (Esther, May 2)

I want an adult who is patient and kind to work with my kids. (Marge, May 3)

Low cost. I can't afford uniforms and costly trips. (Bill, May 2)

I've got four kids and I'm not going to run them to four different organizations. Either all the kids get involved in one organization or none at all. (Tom, May 3)

Any organization that we would consider must be convenient. We have certain family times and the group can't interfere with that. (Esther, May 2)

Parents were quite willing to discuss features that a youth organization should have. Foremost among the features were factors relating to the adults in charge. Parents cited specific examples of desirable qualities that adult volunteers should have. Each parent had a notion of an ideal leader that was based on some past experience either as a child or as an adult. Other features of the youth organization were subordinate to the quality of leadership in selecting an organization. The quality of leadership was the first factor cited in all focus groups. In addition, this characteristic surfaced repeatedly in all conversations. Parents believed that quality leadership was important for two reasons. It was necessary to maintain the interest of the youth and it provided the young people with a positive role model.

A secondary, but still important, characteristic of youth organizations related to the fit within the family structure. The organization had to be convenient to the family lifestyle in terms of time and cost demands.

The raw data reporting style is faster and easier for the researcher, but this style essentially transfers the work to the readers of the report. The raw data style is recommended only as a prelude to the descriptive or interpretive styles or in situations in which the analyst has limited skills or when the audience prefers reviewing all comments. Both the descriptive and interpretive styles have the advantage of data reduction, with the interpretive procedure providing the greatest depth in analysis.

The Oral Report

Before preparing the oral report the speaker should find out how much time is available for the presentation, where the report will be given, and who the audience will be. Those receiving an oral evaluation report usually wish to discuss findings, respond to the results, or ask questions. The most successful oral reports have allocated only one-third to one-half of the time for the presentation and the remainder is spent in follow-up discussion. Therefore, a 15-minute report may include a 5-minute presentation and 10 minutes for questions, clarifications, and discussion of future action.

The first few minutes in an oral report are critical, and the speaker will need to quickly set the stage for the presentation of findings. Often the audience needs additional information as to why the study is important. The speaker should carefully lay out the framework describing why the study is important to the users. The oral presentation must be focused on the key points, citing the most important finding first, and then moving to less important findings. Within these first few moments the speaker should highlight several key factors. For example: Why was the study needed? What do we know now that we didn't know before? or How can these finding be used? It is important to quickly engage the audience, to involve them in the report, to hook them into the study and explain clearly why the research effort was important.

When planning for the oral report it is helpful to give consideration to the *ho-hum syndrome*, a predictable reaction of many decision makers. *Ho-hum* is best characterized by the questions going through the minds of the audience, such as: Do we really need this study? Don't we know this already? or Shouldn't this staff member be doing something really important instead of conducting these studies? To us, the results might seem enormously important with far-reaching implications, but to a busy decision maker they might sound like hairsplitting and avoidance of real work. Much of what we discover in program evaluation and research efforts does tend to sound like common sense, and this tendency needs to be defused in the oral presentation. Often the best procedure is to address it head-on by saying, "This study is of importance to us because . . . "

The outline used in the written report does not transfer well to oral reporting. Often researchers make the assumption that a report is a report, whether it be oral or written, and that the sequence of information presented should be consistent in both kinds of reports. Oral reporting is different and it requires some special forethought and preparation. Some communications experts have recommended that the most important points be presented at the end of an oral presentation— that lesser points build toward the most critical point. This recommendation is helpful in a number of presentation environments, but it does not work well in evaluation or research reporting. Most reporting occurs in environments in which people have time restrictions and limited patience, and in which interruptions regularly occur. In these situations conciseness is valued, and thus the most important findings are better placed at the top of the list.

A related issue concerns the number of points that should be included and the phrasing of those points. I have recommended that evaluators present oral reports with fewer than seven points. The basis of this recommendation stems from studies in cognitive psychology that suggest that most people can remember five to seven things in short-term memory. In addition, I have encouraged the use of short, active phrases to describe points as opposed to complete sentences. These brief phrases are designed to do two things: to convey the important concept and also to be easily remembered.

Visuals can effectively highlight the points. One useful tool is the briefing chart. These can be made on posterboard or foamboard and be used to highlight key points. In addition, these charts can be reproduced in smaller $8\frac{1}{2} \times 11$ handouts and shared with the audience. Michael Hendricks (1984) has found charts with smaller handouts to be helpful in oral policy briefings. Selected quotations or even brief tape recordings of actual comments can also be very effective in the oral report, but they must be used in moderation.

Sometimes the purpose of the oral report is unclear. I have observed the presentation of oral reports to organizations at which when the reporter is finished the group just looked at each other for a few awkward moments. This uncomfortable silence was then followed by some type of action typical of elected bodies. Someone usually moves that the report be approved or accepted. Then they can move on to really important matters. In these situations, the group receiving the oral report did not know why they were receiving the briefing simply because they were never told why it was being presented. At the end of the report the reporter should have indicated what action is recommended or why the report was presented, such as: to provide a briefing, to form a study committee, to continue discussion at a later time, to seek funds to implement the findings, to approve a new course of action, and so on. It is dangerous to assume that the audience will know what to do with the report.

Practice makes for better reports. The reporter should allow sufficient time to practice the oral report and to revise the written report after feedback from colleagues. Hastily prepared reports often have awkward construction, vague points, misspellings, and other aspects that limit their acceptance by users. In addition, the most qualified reporter should be selected to make the oral presentation. Some people have a natural or acquired talent for preparing written reports or presenting oral reports. Select the reporter for ability and not because of his or her role in the focus group interview. Naturally, the reporter will need to be sufficiently acquainted with both the process and findings.

Summary

In summary, not enough attention has been spent on communicating the results of focus group efforts. Reporting must be targeted to the audience and appropriate for the purpose of the study. Written reports begin with a framework that can include raw data, a descriptive summary, or an interpretative approach. These written reports can be presented in a narrative or bulleted format. One report may not be sufficient. The style of the report should match the capability of the analyst and the needs of the audience. Oral reports are structured differently from written reports, with the most important points presented first. Audiences may need suggestions on how to respond and the reporter should clearly indicate why the report is being presented.

APPENDIX 9A

Example of a Focus Group Report

This is a summary report that was prepared at the conclusion of a focus group study conducted by teens in Dakota County, Minnesota. This report is a shortened summary designed to be shared within the community and was condensed from the original 14-page report.

Listening to Youth: Reducing Alcohol, Tobacco, and Other Drug Problems in Dakota County
Focus Group Results

Introduction

In 1991, Dakota County received a 5-year community partnership grant for alcohol and other drug abuse prevention from the Center of Substance Abuse Prevention (CSAP). The grant resulted in the development of the Dakota Alliance for Prevention (DAP). This study, which was sponsored by DAP, examines the perceptions of young people in Dakota County of the problem of tobacco, alcohol, and other drug use as well as prevention efforts and campaigns. All of the focus groups, with the exception of those conducted at the Probation Services Center, were conducted by young people.

Description of the Study

The focus group participants were 83 young people who participated in 1 of 14 focus group interviews. The focus groups were conducted between March 2nd and April 8th in various parts of Dakota County. Each group was tape recorded and carefully analyzed.

Study Findings

The Most Serious Problems

A serious problem, in the minds of many Dakota County teens, is the internal family conflict between parent and child. This conflict results in miscommunication or lack of communication between parent and teen. Parents are so busy with achieving financial security that they leave out adequate time with their children. Young people value their families and worry about instability and divorce.

Alcohol use was also frequently identified as a serious problem for teens throughout the county. Other common concerns are tobacco use, violence, drugs, peer pressure, and money (both the lack of and too much).

Attitudes About Alcohol

Teens indicate that alcohol use among youth is prevalent and occurs in a wide variety of settings. Although most teens view occasional use of alcohol by older teens as acceptable, excessive use or drinking and driving are seen as unacceptable for adults and young people. Some teens consider alcohol as a gateway to harder drugs and more serious problems.

Preventive Strategies

One of the most frequently mentioned preventive strategies is the example set by parents. Teens are impressed when parents are consistent and model what they preach. But the role model is not sufficient by itself because the parent must also communicate effectively with their child. The parent must show their children that they are loved and that the parent is concerned about them.

Advice to Parents

Teens in the focus groups had some advice for improving communication with parents. Communication must include careful listening, with practical advice and avoidance of nagging or lectures. Parents might introduce the topic of chemical use in casual conversation. Parents should talk openly and honestly and use examples of consequences of what can happen with chemical use. Some teens suggested that parents should talk to their child as they would to a concerned friend. Parents could tell stories about their own experiences to make their children more at ease.

Helping Other Teens

If teens wanted to help a friend who was using alcohol or other drugs they would use several strategies. First they would spend time with them and be available to listen to their concerns. Once you've established the secure friendship you might seek additional help for them by perhaps going with them to an adult to discuss the problem. Under some circumstances they may even talk to the parents of their friend. Another strategy is to tell about bad experiences or to seek out another young person who has been a user and has turned himself or herself around.

Influential Adults

Although parents and friends are seen as the most influential people in making decisions about alcohol and other drugs, other adults can also have a major impact. Influential adults are those who show respect, fairness, and consistency in enforcing rules and provide positive role models through their own behavior. They might include school administrators, teachers, coaches, or youth workers.

Realistic Messages

Speakers who use scare tactics are sometimes effective in influencing young people. These are people seen at school assemblies or other events who tell stories that are plausible and believable yet graphically describe the consequences of alcohol, tobacco, or other drugs. Some speakers who have turned themselves around are considered credible because they speak from experience.

Rules Are Important

Teens talked about the positive influence of a supportive family or when parents make and enforce rules. Rules are important for teens but they must be approached carefully by parents. Rules provide guidelines for behavior but they must be considered reasonable by the teen to be effective. The number of rules needed depends on the child.

Keep Teens Busy

An effective preventive strategy is keeping teens busy. This could include employment opportunities or even community service to help them feel they are contributing something to others. Teens see the need for more inexpensive, accessible sports, hobbies, and recreational activities in their local communities.

Study Themes

- Teens are concerned about their families and worry about issues such as divorce.
- Alcohol is a serious problem and readily available. Other drugs are easy to obtain throughout the county.
- Teens are accepting of peers who never use or occasionally use alcohol but less so of those who use alcohol or other drugs on a regular basis. Teens view excessive use, by adults or youth, and driving after drinking as unacceptable.
- Parents are more influential than they may think but need help with communication. Teens acknowledge that most parents care but are so busy that they don't have time to listen to the experiences of the young person. By and large parents are not effective at talking to teens.
- Teens want parents, and other adults, to set and enforce reasonable rules.
- Other adults, including teachers, coaches, employers, and youth leaders, can play critical roles, but they must have earned the respect of the teens. Adults seem to be unaware of their potential influence on the lives of teens with whom they come in contact. Double standards and poor role models jeopardize the messages these adults could offer.
- Boredom and too much unsupervised leisure time accelerate chemical use among teens.
- Teens need and want factual information about alcohol and other drugs, but the intensity of school-based prevention programs declines after elementary school. Some scare tactics are effective.
- Media, music, and rock concerts present problems. Media emphasize the desirable features of alcohol and tobacco. Some music promotes use of chemicals and lack of respect of parents and authorities.

Suggestions

- Parents need to spend more time with their teens.

- Parents shouldn't give up on their children when there are conflicts and problems and should take advantage of opportunities to improve their communication skills.

- Teens can take the leadership in teaching parents to communicate with their children. Teens could model communication strategies, conduct skits of effective and ineffective dialogues, and provide helpful tips and suggestions to parents.

- Each community should inventory the availability of inexpensive, accessible, chemically free activities for teens. Local officials might work together with parents and teens in preparing this assessment. The inventory must take into account not only the absolute amount of activities but how the teens perceive them.

- Schools, churches, and other community groups should work together to develop and promote more inexpensive social and recreational opportunities for teens.

- The creation of jobs and community service opportunities for young people should be encouraged.

- Schools and communities should expand the opportunities for cross-age and peer teaching and role modeling.

- Prevention programs such as DARE should be extended through middle school.

- Members of the DAP and focus group moderators should freely share information obtained in this study. This will help raise awareness and may start actions that launch improved preventive efforts.

- The DAP should encourage continued listening efforts within the community. Listening is a beginning step in identifying workable solutions and those volunteers who participated in conducting focus groups might consider conducting future discussions. This may be of particular importance to teens. These topics are deemed important to teens and the respectful and systematic seeking of information and sharing was considered both productive and enjoyable.

The following teens contributed considerable time and effort in conducting focus groups. Thanks to:

Jennifer Berg	Dave Boyum	Matt Dempsey
Darren Lane	Hector Martinez	Kjerstin Moody
Linh Nguyen	Teri Shingledecker	Saeng Sisomphou

and to Mary Montagne, Project Coordinator, DAP, and Karen Lindberg, Maternal Child Health Program Coordinator, Dakota County.

Special appreciation is extended to the 83 teens from throughout Dakota County who willingly shared their ideas and thoughts.

APPENDIX 9B

Example of a Focus Group Report

The following report is a summary of a national focus group study on youth at risk, conducted by the Search Institute in cooperation with the National 4-H Foundation.

Reaching Vulnerable Youth: Keys and Roadblocks to Success

What makes a program successful in working with young people at risk? What roadblocks stand in the way? What staff development and training efforts would enable Cooperative Extension Service staff to offer successful extension programs to new audiences?

4-H is addressing these questions through the national Strengthening Our Capacity to Care: Staff Training for Youth at Risk project, funded by the DeWitt Wallace-*Reader's Digest* Fund.

In early 1992, more than 200 individuals participated in focus groups conducted for the national needs assessment designed as the first component of the DeWitt Wallace-*Reader's Digest* Fund grant.

The results of the needs assessment—conducted collaboratively by the Minnesota Extension Service and Search Institute—help to guide this 4-year staff development and training initiative. They also give insights to 4-H leaders across the country about what makes programs successful and what roadblocks must be overcome.

Characteristics of Successful Programs

In addition to identifying characteristics of successful youth workers, participants in focus groups were asked to identify key characteristics of successful youth programs. Some of the themes that emerged include the following:

• *Focused and Articulated Vision.* The best programs have a clearly articulated mission that is accepted and embraced by all levels of staff and volunteers and a vision of how the organization will accomplish the mission.

- *Sustained and Holistic Approach.* The best youth programs make long-term commitments to people. They integrate the whole child's needs and strengths, the family's strengths, the school's role, and a community's resources into their efforts. "Programs that do really well with young people have a tremendous amount of respect for the capacities of young people, and they value that and try to enhance and build on that capacity," said one focus group participant.
- *Supportive, Flexible Atmosphere for Staff.* In successful organizations, rules, policies, and expectations are flexible to allow for creative problem solving and to give staff freedom to undertake unusual initiatives.
- *Community-Based Collaboratives.* The best youth programs are created from the community, not superimposed from the outside. Programs meet local needs and are supported and endorsed by community partnerships.

Although focus group participants often distinguish between the characteristics of people and programs, each cannot exist without the other. Caring, nonjudgmental, creative staff cannot function as good youth workers without the support of an effective organization. Likewise, no organization can be effective without qualified people involved.

Roadblocks

Several barriers exist that often make it difficult to reach youth and families at risk. Some (the first four) are common in all youth-serving organizations. Others relate specifically to 4-H efforts.

1. *Negative Staff Attitudes.* Negative attitudes (fear, distrust, disrespect) are often based on lack of experience, knowledge, and connection with the community. Others may be rooted in prejudice, racism, or paternalism.
2. *Cautious Clientele.* Youth and families at risk may believe programs are undependable and do not address the community's real needs.
3. *Logistic Problems.* Programs can be inaccessible because of location, cost, or hours.
4. *Patronizing Philosophy.* Human service programs often operate as though experts know best what to do for disenfranchised people rather than involving them in decision making and leadership.
5. *Lack of Clear Definitions.* There is no consensus about how to define youth at risk. Most focus group participants did not feel the "everyone is at risk" definition is helpful, because it belies the wide range of factors that increase vulnerability.
6. *Inconsistent Endorsement.* This point includes several strands of concern, ranging from individual fears and insecurities about working with youth at risk to organizational concerns about support from key constituencies.

7. *Lack of Understanding of How Youth-at-Risk Programming Relates to Traditional Programming.* Focus group participants wanted common language to clarify the similarities and differences between prevention versus intervention efforts and between traditional versus at youth-at-risk programming.

8. *Uncertainty About Organizational Commitment and Support.* Focus groups expressed concern about the long-term commitment of Extension to the Youth-at-Risk Initiative. Questions about whether the Initiative will outlast funding create uncertainty.

9. *Overreliance on Formal Education.* Experienced agents noted that hiring requirements, and promotion and reward structures, are closely tied to formal educational attainment. The belief that staff is valued and rewarded in proportion to degrees earned limits the hiring pool and keeps most staff white and middle class.

10. *Lack of Relevant Product and Material Resources.* Current resources are perceived to be inappropriate for disadvantaged young people because the resources often assume an incorrect starting point for the subject matter and lack cultural sensitivity.

11. *Lack of Collaboration.* Extension has a long-standing tradition of finding what you need within the Extension system rather than working with others. Collaboration was, however, viewed by focus group participants as key to success in youth-at-risk programming.

Overcoming Roadblocks

How can the leadership in 4-H begin overcoming some of these roadblocks? Focus group participants made several recommendations for training and development:

• *Use Experimental Staff Development Strategies.* Listening to a speaker discuss the necessary ingredients for working with new audiences of young people will probably not make staff more capable or comfortable doing it. Training must be experiential to have a significant, long-lasting impact.

• *Explore Practicum of Mentoring Approaches.* Staff should be encouraged to work alongside youth workers who are experienced in working with vulnerable youth.

• *Diversify Trainers.* Trainers need to be able to "walk the walk and talk the talk," not simply offer theoretical or academic perspectives.

• *Employ a Multitiered Approach.* Staff development and training should include training for those playing various roles within Extension, recognizing that staff and volunteers have different levels of readiness and experience.

• *Build Collaborations and Coalitions.* Coalitions or collaborations can be a means of learning from those who are more experienced in working with disenfranchised youth and families. "We have to get ourselves away from the idea that people have problems and we in Extension have the answers," said one focus group participant. "We have to look at partnerships for solving problems that are community based."

• *Move Beyond "Business as Usual."* The ultimate success of the Youth-at-Risk Initiative depends on moving beyond traditional designs and models of training and development. Efforts must be made to introduce comprehensive change.

What Makes a Successful Youth Worker?

As part of the needs assessment for Strengthening Our Capacity to Care, more than 200 individuals participated in focus groups about successful youth work. Out of these focus groups grew five characteristics of an individual who is effective in working with youth, including youth at risk.

1. *Value and Respect for Clientele.* Good youth workers celebrate, build on, and learn from the young people's and families' strengths. Empathy and respect are prerequisites.

2. *Capacity for Caring Adult-Youth Relationships.* Good youth workers genuinely care about the betterment of people and can convey these feelings through relationships.

3. *Empowerment Orientation.* The best youth workers foster change by emphasizing opportunity, responsibility, and participation rather than by creating dependency or focusing on problems. They take risks to help youth build self-competence, self-confidence, and strength.

4. *Self-Knowledge.* Youth workers must know and understand themselves before facilitating another's growth. They should assess personal biases, understand their motivations, have a sense of personal worth, and be able to set boundaries.

5. *Motivation and Ability for Creative Problem Solving.* Good youth workers are good networkers and have the personal motivation and drive to continue working collaboratively to solve problems.

APPENDIX 9C

Example of a Focus Group Report

Summary Focus Group Report Prepared for Decision Makers

The following report was prepared for the Chair of the Department of Rhetoric at the University of Minnesota and a planning committee for the annual Institute for Technical Communication (ITC). In previous years, the Institute had been offered for academics. The committee wanted to change the focus and design a program that would be of interest to practicing technical communicators as well as academics. Thus, they commissioned a small market study of technical communicators from the Minneapolis-St. Paul area to gather information about their continuing education practices and needs.

Memorandum

To: ITC Planning Committee
From: Sandra Becker
Re: Focus Group Report

As you requested, I have completed two group interviews of technical communicators from the Twin Cities area. Using the membership list of the Twin Cities' Society for Technical Communicators, I invited an equal mix of managers and non-managers as well as corporate and contract writers drawn at random. The uniformity of responses between the two groups seems to indicate that the results of the interviews are reasonably reliable.

The following information provided by the groups should help you make decisions about the program, pricing, and promotional tactics for next year's ITC. Based on those findings, I offer several recommendations for your consideration.

Findings

1. Employers sponsored outside training opportunities for all respondents. Companies paid up to $200/day for courses that lasted up to 3 days. All of the courses were technical in nature.
2. Courses longer than 3 days would not be well received by employers.

3. Sponsorship and credibility of instructors, the topics of training, timing, and location were the most important factors considered by potential participants. No single factor seemed more important than others.

4. The following topics, in descending order of importance, were suggested as areas in which employers weren't providing adequate training:

   A. On-line documentation

   B. Company politics, especially the role of the writer on the design team and within the company

   C. Project management, namely, scheduling, estimating, budgeting

   D. Design, graphics, and graphics production

   E. Product evaluation

   F. The writer as teacher

   G. Product liability and the technical writer

Recommendations

1. Keep the Institute less than 4 days. One of those days (or at least a half-day) could fall on a Saturday to demonstrate to employers the seriousness of the writers' desire to participate in the program. Keep the Institute in July as you have in the past.

2. Charge over $100/day, because the market will bear a $200/day fee if the topics are of interest to potential participants.

3. Because both groups concurred about the topics listed above, I think you should incorporate as many of their suggestions as possible into the program.

4. Use their language in your promotional materials. For example, instead of listing instructional design as a topic, use their phrase—*the writer as teacher*, or simply, *teaching*.

5. Stress that the University is sponsoring the Institute and include some well-known experts on the program, because sponsorship and expertise of presenters are considered important.

I would be happy to meet with your program subcommittee to provide additional information about the topics suggested by the respondents.

PART III

Issues and Concerns

The final section of this volume addresses topics that are of particular concern to public and nonprofit organizations. Chapter 10 is an overview of how nonresearchers can effectively provide assistance in the focus group process. The uses of focus groups with special audiences is highlighted in Chapter 11. Using focus groups in special situations is discussed in Chapter 12. Contracting for outside assistance with focus groups can be frustrating, so Chapter 13 offers helpful tips in getting hired help. Finally, what does the future hold for focus groups? A Postscript offers some factors on which the future of focus groups may depend.

10

A Collaborative Approach to Focus Groups

Over the past decade, focus groups have taken on a different role in the public and nonprofit sector. For a number of years, if you wanted to conduct focus groups the only option available to public and nonprofit organizations was to hire an outside expert. The outside expert would conduct the research, present the report, and move on. More recently, a new option has been successfully used in a variety of organizations. These public and nonprofit organizations realized that study results are more likely to be successful if staff and others are actively involved in framing the problem, gathering the information, and preparing the report. If staff and outside groups were expected to later support and promote alternative policies and procedures, they needed to be involved early and in meaningful ways. This involvement had to go beyond a briefing meeting or a colorful flyer describing recent top management decisions.

The model that has evolved has been a collaborative approach that places volunteers, staff members, and nonresearchers in the center of the focus group project. These individuals are charged with conducting a study that will tap into various parts of the organization, institution, or community. These individuals are carefully recruited and possess certain talents and resources that can contribute to overall success. Outside help, if and when needed, is provided on a consulting or contractual manner.

Bonnie Bray was an employee of the State Department of Education. She was given the task of conducting a needs assessment of emotionally and behaviorally disturbed children throughout the state. The end product would potentially change legislation affecting the families of these children. Early on in the project Bonnie began to consider focus groups because she wanted parents and youth, as well as a variety of caregivers, to share their experiences, identify needs, and profit from comments of others. The budget demands of a sizable study caused Bonnie to hesitate hiring a research agency. Bonnie was skillful in getting people together and had unique talents in persuading individuals of various backgrounds to lend a hand. She already had a task force who was committed to the study and who had contacts with target audiences. Bonnie did hire outside experts but not to conduct focus groups. The experts helped prepare the questions and the recruitment protocol and conducted the analysis. The experts trained the task force to conduct focus groups throughout the state. When the report was completed, the task force used the report, which was based on their collective experiences, to formulate recommendations for action.

There were frustrating moments along the way. Coordination of people and equipment was a regular concern. But in the end the report was impressive and recommendations were not only rooted in the study but were practical and useful. The process of conducting focus groups was a benefit to the task force, but in ways that were not anticipated. Out of the process grew a common vision and commitment borne out of experiences of listening to peoples' concerns.

The collaborative approach introduces complexity and difficulty but also yields additional benefits. With the collaborative approach extra goals are now included. The goal is no longer just to produce a report of a study; the goal is expanded to include: developing skills among the participants, creating awareness among influential individuals, generating support for viable solutions, producing a believable and trustworthy report, and ensuring that recommendations are practical and useful. The process of data gathering and listening takes on more importance and may be equivalent in importance to the information that is collected.

For some, using a collaborative team to assist with a research project is a foreign idea. Since research is hard work, researchers have often assumed that others are just not interested in lending a hand. Indeed, in a number of social science research efforts, specialized backgrounds are needed and even the hired staff are sometimes lacking in critical skills. If you decide to use a team, then the study must place considerable emphasis on staff development and training. Each team member needs to know what his or her task is and then must have adequate skills with which to function.

Advantages and Disadvantages of the Collaborative Process

Before making a decision on the use of a collaborative approach, the researcher and study director should consider the advantages and disadvantages of seeking help from others. The advantages include the following:

1. It increases the talent pool. By involving a wider number of people one can tap into natural talents and skills that are essential, such as the ability to moderate focus groups or the conceptual skills in planning and analysis.
2. It provides increased connections with people who are needed to recruit and sanction the study.
3. It increases the quantity and breadth of feedback for designing and conducting the study.
4. It increases the likelihood that the results will be used because critical stakeholders helped design, implement, and analyze the results.
5. It saves immediate costs by replacing research staff with volunteers.
6. It saves longer term costs by having a trained cadre of people to call on for future studies.
7. It provides an opportunity for staff or volunteers to learn a new skill.
8. The process can be empowering. Individuals who may previously have had limited experiences in decision making and policy formulation can learn from experience how to obtain, analyze, and present information in a credible and systematic manner.

Several disadvantage can also occur.

1. Rigor may be lost. Increasing the number of moderators and analysts increases the chances for inconsistency—in analysis judgments and in moderating skills.
2. Training becomes essential to maintain quality control. Team members will require intensive training and that training must fit into their schedules.
3. Time is needed. The study will take longer, it will likely get bogged down at several points, and time will be needed to get the study back on track. For example, preparing focus group questions with a committee is agonizingly slow, but patience is usually rewarded.

4. Team members vary in skills, and at times it can be difficult to find productive slots for certain members. As a result, there is wisdom in carefully recruiting individuals who already possess critical basic skills.
5. Success will require the researcher or study director to have strong group process skills.
6. The level of motivation among the team to complete their task may vary and conflicts in schedules often occur.

In spite of these disadvantages, with proper recruitment, skillful supervision, and adequate training, the collaborative approach can yield impressive results.

Pulling It Together

When using a collaborative approach, the researcher or study coordinator will need to consider three dimensions: the tasks, the people, and the roles. First, the tasks to be completed; second, the types of people who will be involved; and third, the functions or roles taken on by individuals or groups. Let's take these one at a time. First, here are the tasks that need to be considered:

Tasks to Be Considered in the Collaborative Process

Develop the Overall Strategy. This task occurs at the beginning of the study and is often made by individuals or groups who control resources and determine policy. The task involves setting the overall strategy, sanctioning the study, or at least approving preliminary consideration. Sometimes those making this decision will want estimates of resources and brief plans of how focus groups will operate, how people will be involved, and what the expected outcomes will be.

Refine the Plan. The vision of the overall strategy needs to be translated into specific action steps. Planning skills and research skills are needed here to develop the specifics of the study, including determining target population, number and location for focus groups, and a refined estimate of needed resources.

Recruit Team Members. Enlist help from others to serve in some aspects of the study. Job descriptions may be needed to provide individuals with a sense of what is expected of them. Individuals are recruited to attend training and to make a joint decision on their future roles in the project. The roles may involve moderating but in some situations it may be best to make other assignments. It could also involve serving as an assistant moderator, recruiting participants, typing transcripts, or being a member of the advisory task force.

Determine Logistics. Plans often need even further refinement so that specific policies and procedures are clarified. This includes obtaining needed equipment and supplies, food, and locations and determining the compensation fees for participants.

Develop Questions. This step often begins with a brainstorming session followed by refinement and sequencing of questions. Expect multiple revisions in the questioning route. Some questions may be specific to one group and others may be general to all groups.

Train Team Members. Provide team members with instruction in the specific roles of moderating, assistant moderating, and recruiting. It is often best to make volunteer assignments after training. Demonstrate a focus group and encourage team members to practice the introduction.

Recruit Focus Group Participants. Someone must identify the specific individuals who will attend the focus group. These individuals must meet specifications for participation that were established earlier. This step involves an initial contact and a commitment to participate followed by oral and written reminders.

Moderate Focus Groups. Serve as moderator or assistant moderator at the focus group interview. This includes securing the needed equipment and supplies, setting up the room, hosting the interview, conducting the focus group interview, and then, following the interview, participating in a debriefing session.

Coordinate Day-to-Day Activities. This individual is the central point of information for the duration of the study. This person maintains communication with all team members, arranges substitutes when needed, and makes decisions on budgets, plans, and timing. She or he also alerts team members of new developments or modifications relating to the study.

Type-Transcribe. This individual(s) transcribes the focus group interviews using a word processor. This task is optional depending on analysis procedures.

Analyze. This task involves the identification of themes and patterns, similarities and differences, across all the focus groups. It also involves preparing a written summary of findings. In the collaborative approach, this task is sometimes divided into two levels in which moderators prepare the first level of analysis on specific focus groups. Then a second level of analysis compares and contrasts focus groups by category as well as synthesizes all focus groups within the study.

Recommend. Recommendations are future-oriented statements that specify desired activity by individuals or organizations. These statements grow out of the analysis process and are grounded in the evidence.

Report. This task involves the sharing of results with others, such as elected officials, administrators, influentials, or the general public.

People to Be Considered in the Collaborative Process

In using the collaborative approach there are several types of people or configurations of people that have been successful. These include the following:

Administrator. The administrator typically heads an agency, division, or unit and has fiscal and staffing responsibilities.

Group Coordinator. An individual who provides central coordination of the entire effort. Typically a staff person.

Advisory Task Force. This is a smaller group that has been delegated to carry out certain functions.

Staff Member. This is an employee of the organization who has been assigned to the project or willingly participates in the study.

Team Member. This is an individual who is not paid by the project. It could include a staff member from a cooperating organization who is released or assigned to work on this effort.

Inside Expert. This is a staff person with specialized expertise who works within the organization and has been assigned to work on the project.

Outside Expert. This is an individual with specialized expertise who is hired to assist with specific parts of the project.

Total Group or Assembly. This is a coalition, advisory board, or larger group that provides broad representation.

Roles to Be Considered in the Collaborative Process

The amount of involvement or decision making might vary from one task to another. For each task identified an individual or group might carry out one of the following roles:

Informal Advice. This includes suggestions or ideas on doing the task that are advisory and not binding.

Review With Optional Feedback. In this role, individuals or boards have an opportunity to look over the plan and comment. The use of this role will vary considerably by organization and administrative style. Feedback is optional.

Review With Feedback. In this strategy, comments and feedback are expected and wanted before advancing to the next stage.

Sanction the Action. This is the role of the decision maker who makes the decision and bears the responsibility.

Do the Task. This is the individual or group that carries out the responsibility.

The Three-Dimensional Matrix

These three dimensions can be represented in a matrix in which the planners can consider what needs to be done, who will be doing it, and how they will function. A sample collaboration matrix is shown in Figure 10.1.

Let's take an example and sketch out the tasks and functions. Suppose that a state department of education, at the request of the state legislature, sought to revise the rules and regulations that applied to local school districts. The collaborative focus group approach was selected

Involvement of People in Focus Group Studies

TASKS TO BE COMPLETED	WHO WILL DO IT?						
	Administrator	Group Coordinator	Advisory Task Force	Staff Member	Volunteer or Helper	Inside Expert	Outside Expert
Develop overall strategy	5						
Refine the plan	4	5	1				3
Recruit team members	2	3	5				
Determine logistics		5	2				2
Develop questions		3	3				5
Train team members		3	2				5
Recruit participants		2	2	5	3		2
Moderate focus groups		1		5	5		1
Coordinate activities	1	5	1	1	1	1	1
Type-transcribe						5	
Analyze		1		5	3	1	5
Recommend	4	5	3	3	3		2
Report	4	5	5	5	5		

Possible functions or roles of individuals or groups:
1. Informal advice
2. Review with optional feedback
3. Review with feedback
4. Sanction the action
5. Do the task

Figure 10.1. Collaboration Matrix

because it would allow a wider number of partners (the traditional interest groups of education) to participate in systematic listening around the state.

The administrator who was a high-ranking member of the department of education sketched out the overall strategy and then turned the task over to a group coordinator for implementation. The boss expected that a plan would be developed with budget and timeline, which she would sanction and then she would essentially become a bystander until the report was prepared. Because the report recommendations would likely affect policy decisions, the boss wanted the chance to review and approve both the recommendations and report in the draft stage.

Much of the detailed work fell to the group coordinator. This person was selected because of his knowledge of the system and ability to coordinate a complex and somewhat ambiguous task involving both staff and volunteers. He was in charge of day-by-day operations with specific responsibilities for refining the plan, establishing the logistics, and developing recommendations (with feedback from others).

The advisory task force was a small group of staff who had a broad network of connections in the field of education. This ad hoc group primarily provided advice but did take on specific functions of recruiting volunteers to serve as moderators.

The staff members and volunteers had similar tasks. Staff members were employees of the department who were released from other responsibilities to take on this assignment. The volunteers were members of groups, associations, or organizations that had historically been concerned about rules and regulations for local school districts. The volunteers were clearly influentials within their environment but not with the statewide visibility that would jeopardize their ability to assist in moderating the focus groups. The staff served as focus group moderators and the volunteers were assistants. Staff took leadership in analysis of individual focus groups and volunteers reviewed and offered feedback.

Inside and outside experts were used at selected points in time. An inside expert helped with typing and transcribing tapes. The outside expert was a consultant to the project and assisted in refining the plan and developing logistics. The major tasks of the outside expert were to prepare the questions, train staff and volunteers to conduct focus groups, and conduct the analysis across all focus groups.

Primary Roles of Nonresearchers

As described earlier, there are about a dozen tasks that can be performed by volunteers and nonresearchers. However, four tasks dominate the consideration: recruiting, moderating, analysis of individual groups, and reporting results.

Recruiting

Volunteers and nonresearchers can assist in recruiting focus group participants. The participants for a focus group must meet certain criteria relating to the purpose of the study, and when the criteria are quite narrow and specific, recruitment can be a major concern.

For example, suppose a community church was considering starting a child care service, a venture that had been suggested enthusiastically by parents in the church. To make the project financially self-sufficient, the service would need to draw from families outside of church membership. The child care operation would require some investment for equipment and remodeling the building. These decisions would be, for all practical purposes, irreversible. Prior to investing money in remodeling, the church might conduct a series of focus groups with parents in the community. Focus groups would be designed to provide information about desirable specifications for child care facilities as well as desirable and undesirable features of these kinds of services. The target audience for the focus groups might consist of working mothers or fathers between the ages of 30 and 40 who have children between the ages of 1 and 5. In this example, the target audience is likely found in limited numbers in the community, and, furthermore, they are apt to be people with busy schedules who are reluctant to spend several hours at a meeting. The recruitment strategy might begin with the core of enthusiastic parents. These parents might become the volunteers needed to recruit other mothers or fathers into the focus groups, and in addition, the volunteers may have helpful suggestions as to incentives for participation as well as means of getting in touch with the parents. The strategy might consist of individual contacts, telephone recruiting using community phone books that contain family members and ages of children, and referrals from knowledgeable residents in the community.

One of the positive features of volunteer assistance in recruiting is that these individuals might be able to use existing community contacts and networks in the recruitment effort. Furthermore, volunteers are likely to be familiar with the demands and pressure on prospective participants and may be able to identify persuasive and innovative recruitment strategies.

Overall, the recruitment strategy must be practical and economical and yet meet the screening criteria. One of the dangers of using non-researchers is that the recruiting could lapse into a convenience sample, in which people are selected simply because they are easy to recruit and little is known about the participants. To prevent this, planners and researchers must be explicit about the criteria and protocol but not so much so that it inhibits the volunteers' ability to use their network. Open communication and feedback is critical. An example of protocol for recruitment is found in Appendix 10A.

Moderating

Nonresearchers can also serve as focus group moderators. In some situations volunteers may actually be preferable for moderating focus groups, as in situations when limited resources do not allow for professional moderators or in groups in which, because of demographic, racial, or social characteristics, the volunteer is readily accepted because he or she is a bona fide member of the group.

In some communities, the staff members of the nonprofit organization are well-known and at times seen as the embodiment of the agency. These staff members may be seen as instructors, administrators, or advocates of valued social issues, and consequently, their role within the agency impedes their ability to moderate focus groups. For example, a county agricultural agent who has repeatedly advocated improved farming methods may want to know reasons why these methods are not being adopted. Farmers in focus groups will likely be selective in responding to inquiries of the agent moderator and may avoid sharing insights that reflect badly on the agent. For similar reasons, I have discouraged the use of volunteer moderators who are readily identified with community issues.

Moderators must be selected with care. Some people have an affinity for the task and can listen sincerely, ask open-ended questions, and probe even without special training. Because of these innate skills, careful selection of volunteers is well advised and other tasks should be arranged for volunteers not possessing the moderating skills.

Analysis

Analysis with the collaborative process can involve several different options. The choice of option will depend on the resources and staff available. The assumption is that different moderators receive common training on moderating, note taking, and the use of predetermined questions. After receiving this training, each moderator or team conducts one or more focus groups with predetermined audiences.

One decision to be made is whether to use complete transcripts or abridged transcripts in analysis. Memory-based and note-based analysis usually do not have sufficient rigor, especially if you are working with novice moderators. A continuing concern in the collaborative focus group process is excessive variation between moderators. Each moderator will have slightly different styles that could limit comparison. Thorough training will help moderators know approximately how much time to spend with each question, the degree of detail wanted in each question, and variations on question wording that are acceptable substitutes. The transcripts and abridged transcripts are recommended because they minimize individual differences in interpretation. An example of the analysis process is included in the appendixes to Chapter 8.

Another decision is who will do the analysis. The choices involve an experienced analyst who analyzes all of the focus groups or a team approach of moderators working with the expert. From a rigor perspective the single, expert analyst is the best choice, but it is likely also the most expensive. The team approach offers a cost savings, an opportunity for a team to learn about analysis, and the benefit of multiple perspectives.

The option that I have preferred is to use abridged transcripts with a team approach. Moderators and assistant moderators working together prepare a brief analysis of each of their focus groups. They use a common field note reporting form and prepare an analysis report using a predetermined outline (an example is included in Appendix 10B). When all moderating teams have completed their focus groups and have prepared reports, they meet together in a debriefing session to compare and contrast their findings. The expert analyst guides the discussion and enlists the advice of team members in identifying themes and patterns across or within groups. Following this sharing session, the expert analyst then collects written reports, field notes, and tapes, and prepares a composite report. This report is then reviewed by members of the team with feedback and revisions encouraged.

The collaborative team can play an important part in the analysis of focus group results. If these team members have had direct experience with the area of investigation then these individuals may be helpful in interpreting the findings. At times, agency professionals have selective exposure to the program being investigated, and a wider range of insights from nonstaff team members is actually essential to understanding how the total program is perceived. In other situations, findings might yield perceptions that have never been shared with agency staff, and although they may be new to the professional, they may be common knowledge to lay team members.

Oral Reporting

Nonresearchers have demonstrated considerable talent in reporting results of focus group studies, particularly when they have been intensively involved in the planning, data gathering, analysis, and recommendation stages of the study. These individuals will possess a variety of presentation skills and people contacts that ensure that the findings enjoy wide circulation. Furthermore, these nonresearchers typically possess the impression of unbiased credibility because they "volunteered" to become involved in the study. The manner of reporting takes many forms and is only limited by the creativity of the participants. In the past, teens have shared results with the city council, parents have provided testimony at the state legislature, and other volunteers have appeared on local cable television.

Training the Collaborative Team

The moderating function is one of the critical components of a focus group and to a large extent the quality of the results are directly related to the skills of the moderator. It has been my experience that careful screening plus approximately 12 hours of training have been adequate to prepare moderators for conducting focus group discussions. In these cases the moderators did not develop the questioning route or coordinate the analysis, and additional training would be needed to provide minimal competency in this area.

The training of moderators should focus on achieving competency in several types of skills, including the following:

- Smoothly handling the presession small talk and creating a friendly environment.
- Skillfully introducing the focus group and providing the ground rules and opening question.

- Asking questions without unduly referring to the questioning route and using effective follow-up probes.
- Remembering the big picture and preparing mentally.
- Maintaining mental discipline and concentration throughout the interview. Specifically, they need to think in three dimensions as they observe the discussion:
  1. The present: What is happening at this moment.
  2. The next step: Thinking one step ahead of the participants and always having a mental picture of what will occur next.
  3. The meaning of the information provided by the focus group: Are the topics being discussed addressing the critical areas needed in the study? How will this information be used?

It may be helpful to have a researcher experienced with focus groups serve as assistant moderator at the initial focus group interview and offer constructive suggestions in the post-meeting briefing.

Advice to Researchers When Using the Collaborative Approach

Over the past several decades, researchers have had limited opportunity to involve individuals in a collaborative approach. Moreover, up to now, group process skills were generally not included in core curriculum for evaluators or other researchers. As the researcher contemplates this approach, these tips may be of assistance. I am grateful to Mary Anne Casey for allowing me to borrow these from her presentation in 1991 at the American Evaluation Association (Casey, 1991).

Consider these "DOs" and "DON'Ts" when working with volunteers in focus groups:

DOs

Pick Your Volunteers Carefully. Avoid taking only those who initially show interest in the study. Often the best people need to be persuaded to participate and are those you have screened carefully and then recruited to the project. Pick volunteers who have the capacity to listen to the bad news as well as the good. Pick volunteers who are sociable. Pick volunteers who can leverage the results with decision makers or who can personally benefit from the results. Avoid volunteers who are perceived as crusaders or who have an ax to grind.

Provide Training and an Opportunity to Practice. It may be that you start with a day of training: a half-day overview of the focus group process and a half-day discussing the study. This includes discussion of the purpose of the study, the types of questions to be asked, and the target audiences. It is helpful to have the volunteers react to the design of the study. They may spot problems or have ideas on how to improve your strategy. You should also discuss what is expected of them. This could be followed by another half day when they practice the focus group introduction, work through the questioning route, recommend ways to locate potential participants, and ask questions specific to the study, logistics, and their role.

Provide Directions and Explanations Wherever Possible. Be VERY prescriptive about what you want done and how you want it done. Give detailed procedures on paper. If you want volunteers to recruit people tell them

- Your criteria for participants.
- How many participants to recruit per group.
- How many groups to recruit.
- Dates and locations.
- How to contact potential participants.
- When to contact potential participants.
- What to say.
- How to follow up (who sends a confirmation letter?).

(You may want to have your staff or one volunteer do all recruiting, minimizing opportunities for confusion. But tap into volunteers' networks to locate potential participants and times of meetings and conferences on which you may piggyback a focus group.)

Make sure volunteer moderators

- Know how to moderate.
- Have the questioning route.
- Know if they are to tape record.

- Have the equipment and know how to use it.
- Know where they are supposed to be, when, and with whom (have names and phone numbers of participants, moderator, assistant moderator, central contact person).
- Know what is expected of them as a result (for example, you may want to provide a form for field notes, suggest an audiotaped debriefing between moderator and assistant moderator, and let them know where to send the audiotape of the group and other materials).

Stress the Importance of the Study and the Importance of the Role They as Volunteers Play in the Success of the Study. People will veer from your road map. If the map is fuzzy they may get totally off track. If the map is detailed they may take only small diversions. If they understand the importance of the road map they may stay on course.

Designate a "Central Intelligence" Person. Choose either the person in charge of the study or one of his or her support people. Include this person's name and phone number on all your handouts. This is the one person all people call with questions or concerns. He or she acts as a clearing house for all scheduling information for volunteers, sites, and meetings and also collects all field notes and audiotapes. This minimizes the confusion that occurs when more than one person seems to be in charge.

Capitalize on the Interests of the Volunteers. Let them decide if they want to recruit, moderate, or assist. Let them select the groups they work with (unless there is a reason to match certain people with certain groups). Give them as many options as possible within the limits of the study. People work better if they like what they are doing.

Have People Work Together. It may be that you pair a staff person with a volunteer, or you can pair volunteers. It helps to have two people for support and backup and also for the different perspectives they bring. After the session, they can discuss what they each heard. Having two people helps diminish bias that may creep in if only one person filters what is heard.

Keep in Touch With Your Volunteers. Call them before a group to see if they need anything or have any questions. Call them after the session to find out how things went. Your concern and interest will reinforce the importance of what they are doing.

Have Someone with Experience in Qualitative Analysis Analyze Your Data. You may have to hire someone to do this. It is difficult to teach people in a short amount of time to do qualitative analysis. Even if you have a volunteer with a Ph.D., don't assume this person can analyze focus group data.

Involve Your Volunteers in a Group Debriefing. Once your data have been analyzed, bring the group together to discuss the findings and possible recommendations. They may also want to discuss their experiences in the study. They may have recommendations on how to improve the process.

Celebrate Your Volunteers' Contributions to the completion of the study and the importance of the research to your organization's goal. In one such study, the mayor of St. Paul sent personalized letters to the volunteers thanking them for their contributions. In another study, each volunteer was given a book with a personal note from the study director.

DON'Ts

Don't Abuse Your Volunteers. It may be that you require each volunteer to be involved in at least one group. However, you may want to limit involvement to three groups. Don't let them overcommit. Analysis is a huge undertaking. It is unfair to ask a volunteer (if you find one with the expertise to do it) to do this without some kind of payoff (money, course credit, authorship).

Final Thoughts

The collaborative process works, but only in the right climate. The environment must include trust, open communications, and responsible behavior. Top management must believe that the team can contribute, and the team must believe that administrators are guided by the best interests of the organization and truly want the results of the study. Those who embark on this path have found an energized and sometimes revitalized organization.

Summary

Nonresearchers can take on difficult tasks and with training and supervision perform these responsibilities in a capable manner. The primary advantage of using nonresearchers or volunteers in focus groups is not simply the cost savings, for if the costs of supervisory time and training are factored the savings may be minimal. Instead, the greatest values are the development of new skills among volunteers, skills that they can transfer to other problems; increased validity due to the volunteers' insight into interpretations; and enhanced understanding of the needs and challenges of the agency, which can result in better informed supporters.

APPENDIX 10A

Recruitment Process

Recruitment Strategies: Finding Parents in the Community

This strategy is intended to recruit parents living within a community to participate in a focus group interview.

1. Develop the specifications for participation, that is, parents who live within the school district who have at least one child of high school age. Preferably these parents should also have a child in elementary or middle school.

2. Develop the *nomination list*. Begin a file card on each person on the list with name, address, phone number, and other demographic characteristics. Several methods are acceptable for developing this list. One method is to invite recommendations from knowledgeable people in the community. Ask selected people in the community to recommend names of parents who fit the specifications. These selected people should be those who are in a position to meet or work with a number of parents in the community. For example: clergy, teachers, park and recreation officials, local merchants, police. Keep track of each person who is identified as well as the name of the person who nominated him or her. Do not take more than three names from any one person. A second method is to use community phone directories that are found in some cities. These directories list parents' names along with the names and ages of their children. With this list you can identify a random list of parents who have children. A third method is to use lists of parents with children. These lists are sometimes available from schools or community service agencies. Whatever method you use, continue until you have assembled a file with about 30-40 names for each focus group.

3. Determine the location, date, and time of the focus groups.

4. Prepare the *invitation list* from the longer nomination list. First, *randomly select* a limited number of people who might be invited.

5. Then, review the invitation list and screen out selected participants. Remove the following:

A. Your friends or relatives.

B. Any people who do not meet selection criteria.

6. Phone parents about 10 days in advance and invite one parent to attend. Invitations are given on a first-come, first-serve basis from the invitation list until eight people have promised to attend.

7. Send an official letter of invitation to those who have accepted your invitation. Include the date, time, place, and a description of the topic.

8. Remind the participants (by phone or in person) the day before of the location and time of the focus group. If someone is unable to attend, seek a substitute.

Definitions

Nomination list. A longer list of potential participants.

Invitation list. A shorter list of people who might be invited to the focus group.

Random selection. There are several acceptable ways to randomly select participants. One is to select every *n*th person from the list. If you want to select 7 out of a list of 35 people, you pick every 5th person on the list. Alternates are selected in the same manner. A second way is to give each person a number and then write each number on a slip of paper, put it into a hat, mix up the slips, and then draw out 7 slips with numbers. Select alternates in the same way.

APPENDIX 10B

Field Note Reporting Form

Information About the Focus Group

Date of Focus Group	
Location of Focus Group	
Number and Description of Participants	
Moderator Name/Phone Number	
Assistant Moderator Name/Phone Number	

Responses to Questions

Q1. The most serious problems facing families and teens?

Brief Summary/Key Points	Notable Quotes

Q2. Alcohol, tobacco, and other drug use compared to the most serious problem?

Brief Summary/Key Points	Notable Quotes

Q3. Acceptable use of alcohol?

Brief Summary/Key Points	Notable Quotes
By adults By young people under 21 Comments on the difference	

Q4. Circumstances when teens drink.

Brief Summary/Key Points	Notable Quotes
When is it likely to occur? Where is it likely to occur?	

Q5. How is alcohol obtained?

Brief Summary/Key Points	Notable Quotes

The form is continued for each question in the focus group.

11

Focus Groups
SPECIAL AUDIENCES

This chapter examines focus groups with special audiences. Three types of special audiences deserve attention. One category is groups and organizations that wish to conduct internal focus groups. A second category includes focus groups with young people. A third special audience includes focus groups within ethnic or racial homogeneous audiences.

Much of what we know about focus groups is based on white, middle-class, adult American consumers. These were the consumers that fueled the American economy with their purchases. Millions of dollars of market research efforts have been spent on determining what will sell. In more recent times researchers have been interested in other categories of people.

Focus groups have proven effective for a variety of audiences. This research procedure has demonstrated the capacity to work regardless of level of education, culture, occupation, or socioeconomic class, as long as the researcher is respectful of the limitations of focus groups. International researchers have taken focus groups to Costa Rica, Morocco, Thailand, India, and a host of other countries and have returned with positive experiences. Others have successfully conducted focus groups with migrant workers, inner-city residents, physicians, business executives, American Indians, and scores of other groups.

For a number of years the principal strategy with focus group research was to assemble complete strangers. The rationale was that strangers would have advantages similar to the anonymous survey. There would be no history between the participants and therefore participants would be free to speak their minds. They would not have met each other before the session and they would have no continuing ties at the conclusion of the session. This selection strategy was relatively easy to manage in many of the larger cities where marketing research usually takes place.

As focus groups began to be conducted for other purposes (academic research, evaluation, program development, needs assessment), researchers began to question the practicality and usefulness of using complete strangers. In many community studies it was difficult to locate strangers. Furthermore, the purpose of the study was to capture the opinions and ideas of local residents, and therefore strangers just wouldn't fit. The line on recruitment was drawn at the wrong place and needed to be redrawn.

Focus Groups With Existing Groups and Organizations

Although the focus group process is robust, there are several situations in which additional caution is needed. One area requiring caution is in using the procedure with existing groups, and especially work groups within an organization. In these environments, participants are likely to know and work closely with each other. Focus groups with these existing work groups present two challenges. The first challenge is in creating an environment in which employees are willing to openly and honestly share their concerns, anxieties, and suggestions. The organizational climate may restrict open communication and discourage or even punish alternative points of view.

The second challenge is in the analysis of results. After the researcher has overcome the first difficulty and successfully created the necessary environment, the second challenge is to determine what it means. Communication within these pre-established groups can be extraordinarily complex. The analyst cannot know all factors that influence group comments. Generally, the discussion process in focus groups is pleasant and enjoyable to participants, and usually people are quite willing to share their ideas and opinions with others. The problem is in analysis of what was shared. Were there words or nonverbal communications that have special meaning within this context? Were they being selective in what they said because of others in the group? Were they taking positions on issues simply because of certain other individuals in the group or because of some unrelated factor? The analyst cannot possibly know all dynamics or environmental factors that might have influenced participants in such a discussion.

In spite of these difficulties, focus groups can be effectively used in existing organizations and even in work groups. Mitchell Elrod, Jr. (1981) has used focus groups within organizations to study employee relations, benefits, training, supervision, current or planned marketing programs, quality control measures, and work schedules. In order to obtain this information, Elrod encourages random selection of employees at the same level in the organization who participate in a focus group during business hours, which is held outside of the office or business in a neutral location. In addition, the focus group is conducted by a professional moderator not affiliated with the organization. Elrod (1981) and his colleagues have been pleased with the results of these groups.

> To date, the moderators from our firm have had no known problem establishing an atmosphere of mutual confidence with employee groups. In fact, the overwhelming reaction has been one of gratification that "someone up there really does care what I think." (p. 31)

Focus group discussions with exceptional employees (or volunteers) can yield valuable information for organizational decision makers. A series of focus groups with exceptional staff members may produce clues that will maintain their levels of productivity, uncover their secrets of success, or provide suggestions on how the organization can improve.

Focus group interviews with front-line service people, including waiters and waitresses, repair people, retail sales, and the like, have proven helpful to a variety of organizations. These critical employees are the first to encounter the most difficult customers, what Zemke and Anderson (1990) call "customers from hell." Focus groups with the front-line staff allowed the researchers to develop categories and also solution strategies for dealing with these nightmare customers.

In-house focus groups are more productive if attention is placed on achieving a nonthreatening, permissive environment. Extra consideration must be given to explaining the purpose of the discussion to defuse potential sensitivity. In addition, it is important to remind participants that the focus group is part of a research study and not a decision or planning committee. Moderators should avoid creating the impression that the organization will change following the group discussion. Participants are reminded that the intent is to gather information from a number of employees and then share these aggregated perceptions with those who will be making decisions.

The choice of moderator should be given consideration. Moderators from outside of the agency have the advantage of being neutral, but they may be unfamiliar with the organizational culture. Internal moderators are more likely to be familiar with the organization, but they will have the challenge of engendering confidence and trust of the participants. There is not a clear advantage to either external or internal moderators. The decision of the type of moderator must be influenced by situational factors such as the topic of study, organizational complexity, the history of trust and openness within the institution, plus the capabilities of the internal and external researchers.

Participants should be grouped with care. Participants should be placed with others at the same level or status in the organization but not in the same work team. Perceptions are most important, but job titles or salary level should also be considered. Perhaps the easiest method to ensure that participants are similar in level is to assemble a list of potential employee participants and then seek feedback from several of these people about the list.

Focus Group Interviews With Young People

Focus groups have considerable potential for discovering how young people think about issues, programs, and opportunities; however, special logistic procedures and moderator skills are often essential. Focus groups with young people are different from those with adults. For example, young people are greatly influenced by the environment and may be skeptical of the moderator's claim that all opinions are wanted and that both negative and positive views are appreciated. Young people regularly find themselves in situations in which adults seemingly want feedback but then react in an unpleasant manner when contrary or negative ideas are expressed. Furthermore, youth peer pressure is powerful and can greatly shape opinions.

When considering focus groups with young people, the researcher should begin by observing them in informal settings. A number of the mistakes that occur when doing focus groups with teens and preteens are due to faulty assumptions. We assume that youth have similar preferences and habits to those of adults. The researcher should reflect on the situations when young people naturally talk and share thoughts with each other. Are adults present when kids talk? If adults are present, how do these adults relate to the youth? How large are the groups? In my observations of teens I have found that discussions take place on the floor, around a table eating pizza, on the front steps of the school, on the beach, or on the street. As a result, teen focus groups may work better if conducted outside of institutions run by adults, where adults make and enforce rules—churches, schools, and even recreation centers.

Focus groups with young people may need to be limited to 60 minutes or less, especially with preteen audiences. Young people repeatedly find themselves in environments where change or relocation takes place every 45-60 minutes. If the researcher has planned a 2-hour focus group discussion it is likely that there will be a bunch of bored kids for the second hour. Therefore, researchers should limit the questions, and, if possible, incorporate things to touch, do, or respond to. For example, a brief one-page survey early or midway through the discussion can be helpful to focus their attention on future areas of conversation.

The nature of focus group questions may need some special thought when working with young people. Dichotomous questions that can be answered with a "Yes" or "No" should be especially avoided. Adults may assume that the moderator really wants elaboration of the answer but young people often take the question more literally and give one-word answers. Moderators should avoid questions that threaten the independence and freedom of young people. For example, suppose the moderator wanted to know how decisions were made about which high school courses to enroll in. In this situation the moderator should avoid asking who makes the decision, for few teens want to admit in front of their peers that their parents influence the decision. Instead, it may be more productive to ask teens to think back to the last time the decision was made and describe what happened.

Researchers who plan youth focus groups need to be concerned about the characteristics of the participants. Of specific concern are age variation, gender differences, and group cohesion. The rule of thumb for youth focus groups has been to keep the age of the group to within two school grades. Generally, focus groups below high school age are also segregated by gender because of the rates at which boys and girls mature as well as the powerful role of cross-gender communications. When conducting youth focus groups researchers tend to prefer groups that are not pre-established. Cohesive groups and cliques may provide a rather narrow range of views that are heavily influenced by peer leaders. As a result, researchers often prefer to assemble groups who are relative strangers to each other.

Moderators conducting youth focus groups need to take more time in enabling young people to feel comfortable with each other and the environment. Adult groups typically form quickly and within a few minutes the adults seem comfortable with talking to each other. This is usually not the case with young people. The moderator might consider conducting a 15-minute get-acquainted activity at the start of the group or allowing more time for relaxed sharing of ideas before the focus group begins.

Adult permission is typically needed when conducting youth focus groups. The researcher should contact the sponsoring and cooperating organizations to determine proper protocol regarding parent or guardian approval. In some cases, when the focus group is part of ongoing organizational activity—such as when fitting within objectives of the school and also conducted during school hours—then permission may not be essential. The need for permission for youth focus groups has a double purpose. The first purpose is to meet the legal expectation of informing child and parent. The second purpose is to adequately inform the parent of the proposed focus group interview. In a number of cases, researchers have wisely gone above and beyond the letter of the law and provided considerable background information to parents or guardians.

The moderator plays a critical role in youth focus groups and therefore selection of the right moderator deserves careful thought. One of the decisions is the benefit of moderators closer in age to the participants. In several recent studies on alcohol, drug, and tobacco use prevention, focus groups consisted of youth in grades 7 through 11 and were conducted by high school age moderators. The results were impressive and convinced the sponsoring organization of the wisdom of involving youth moderators. The decisive factor in conducting successful focus groups however, is less likely to be moderator age and more likely to relate to open communication established by the moderator. The teen-led groups were successful in part because they had removed the image of adult authority, and that prompted sharing on sensitive topics. It is also likely that a skillful adult moderator who has created the permissive environment might also obtain valuable information in these situations. Some adults have a knack for getting kids to talk, probably because they exude trust, respect, tolerance, humor, and a willingness to listen. Therefore, the decision on youth versus adult moderators is a toss-up. The success is more likely due to factors other than age, such as training, application of moderator skills, and adherence to traditional focus group strategies.

Focus Interviews Within Ethnic or Racial Groups

Focus groups have being used increasingly to assess needs or test program materials for ethnic or racial groups. When conducting focus groups in the environment of such groups, it is essential that researchers understand the culture and traditions. The researcher should consider when and where people talk, who is present during discussions, how long the discussions last, who is entitled to ask questions, and what protocol is used when asking questions. These factors become the basic elements in establishing the focus group interview.

Usually one of the first areas of concern is in the characteristics of the moderator. There is an advantage in having a moderator with similar characteristics as the participants. Many of these groups have historically been controlled and guided by white people in positions of power and influence. As a result, there may be a tendency to assume that other individuals from the outside, and particularly those who are white, possess power and want information to maintain that influence. Within some groups there is a tendency to be cautious about talking to outsiders and particularly outsiders who are in power. However, the race or ethnicity of the moderator is only one of the factors that deserve consideration. Just because the moderator is of the same race or ethnicity as the participants doesn't mean that the groups will function effectively.

The researchers should use available background information to make decisions about the structure and logistics of the focus group. In some communities, it is critical that the study be sanctioned by local influentials. The blessing and support of these influentials can open doors and provide additional information critical to the study. The disadvantage is that this step takes time and often prolongs the study. Local residents can provide valuable insights in developing recruitment strategies and incentives, providing feedback, or piloting the questioning route. The decision of using a local person as a moderator often hinges on whether there is a skillful moderator available or if the researcher would need to train an individual to take on that task. A related decision is whether the focus group is done in the local language. By and large, these questions should not be answered unilaterally by the research team. The prudent strategy is to consider a task force to provide advice and counsel. In fact, for each of three different functions a small group might provide advice: securing sanction to proceed, refining the research procedures, and providing assistance with critical aspects of the study.

First, consider those individuals who can sanction the study. Without their approval the study may not be politically feasible or practically based. A task force or group of elders, influentials, or respected leaders might be invited to provide advice. Second, consider those who can best offer advice on improving the study design, offer feedback on recruitment strategies, or assist in developing questions. These individuals ensure that the focus group methodology is culturally sensitive and acceptable. These individuals may be different from the first group in that they are more similar to the target audience, more familiar with research protocol, or more familiar with the topic of the study. Finally, consider those who can assist with certain critical tasks in the focus group process, such as recruitment, moderating, or analysis/interpretation. The researcher might wish to involve talented local individuals who are willing to receive instruction, offer their advice, and assist with these tasks.

No one person speaks on behalf of any group of people, but many will try. Don't expect that one "leader" can tell you what is appropriate, offensive, tasteful, or wise. Each speaks from experiences and values, which may vary widely. It is critical to respectfully seek multiple viewpoints before making decisions on the conduct of the focus group research effort.

Summary

Focus groups are effective means of obtaining information from special audiences. The focus group is able to produce meaningful information and to do so in a manner that shows respect for traditions and uses language barriers and culture as an advantage. For focus groups to work, however, the researcher must be alert to certain modifications of the procedures. The researcher must be sensitive to establishing an environment in which these individuals feel comfortable in talking. The researcher must be understanding of varying needs for control among different populations. The researcher must approach each group with respect, seeking the wisdom the participants possess. When the researcher meets these expectations, the focus group yields impressive results.

12

Focus Groups
SPECIAL SITUATIONS

The (focus group) technique is robust, hardy, and can be twisted a bit and still yield useful and significant results. This is not an argument for laxity in group design, nor is it an apology for inadequate moderators. Rather, the point here is that flexibility rather than rigor ought to characterize the use of focus groups.

Gerald Linda, 1982, p. 98

For the casual observer, focus groups seem quite simple. They look like groups of people talking about a common topic of interest, a procedure that seems almost too simple to be called research. Successful focus groups are supposed to look easy. They are similar to the seemly effortless grace of a master gymnast or the comfortable, relaxed stride of an Olympic marathon runner. They look easy because the moderator has command of the fundamentals and executes the basic principles with comfortable precision. This aura of simplicity has resulted in abuses in qualitative research in general and focus groups in particular. An abuse that occurs with frequency is the mislabeling of focus groups. In some areas of study, "focus groups" have become the "in" word and quite a variety of group experiences have been misplaced under this rubric. This book has emphasized a somewhat rigorous approach to focus groups, in large part because of the misuses that have occurred in private market research firms, educational organizations, and nonprofit agencies.

218

Flexibility in the use of focus groups and modification of the procedures can be extremely beneficial if these changes are deliberate and factored into the analysis of results. Modifications that have merit in certain situations include periodic focus groups repeated with the same participants, focus groups with dual moderators, and telephone focus groups. In some situations a group process is used that is called a focus group but that departs dramatically from certain traditions. Most notable are media focus groups. Let's examine these one at a time.

Periodically Repeated Focus Groups

A periodically repeated focus group consists of two or more focus groups on the same topic over a period of time. For example, a community center might conduct annual or even quarterly focus groups with those using the facilities, or a state park system might conduct weekly focus groups with campers. In each of these situations the organization is able to keep abreast of users' perceptions and take corrective action as needed.

Stew Leonard's Dairy in Norwalk, Connecticut, has made it a habit of listening to customers. Every month, a group of customers is promised a $20 store gift certificate if they attend a focus group. Conducted regularly since 1983, the groups yield helpful new ideas. Leonard says:

> We get ideas in two ways: One is the suggestion box and the other is the focus group. It's always better when you hear it from customers directly. (Cushing, 1987, p. 103)

Nonprofit organizations, like private sector businesses, find that their services, clientele, and objectives change over time. Original purposes of the organization are modified and adapted by forces in the environment and these changes directly affect members or consumers. Periodic assessment of the organization via focus groups might be performed at several levels. The assessment might concentrate on overall organizational strategy or zero-in on specific features of particular interest such as new member recruiting.

Repeated focus groups can also be conducted with the same participants with a time interval between sessions. This use of focus groups is helpful in situations in which the researcher wants to track changes in perceptions over time. Another variation of repeated focus groups is to observe participants who are purposefully brought together with divergent points of view. In these groups a degree of moderator skill is required to set the stage for openness and interaction. Participants will likely need reminders that the intent is not to debate the different sides of the issue but rather to explore each point of view in greater depth. It can be illuminating to discover the logic and rationale used by the participants on each side as they present their point of view as they seek to win "converts." If the purpose of the study is to determine arguments that are convincing to those with differing points of view, then repeated focus groups are a sound choice.

Special Focus Group Structures

The structure of the focus group can be modified to accommodate two moderators—either in a dueling or a complementary role. In the dueling mode, moderators take planned predetermined sides and participants may either be assigned to or choose a side they will participate on. The primary advantage of the dueling structure is that it "legitimizes" different points of view and "invites" supporting arguments or points of view from the participants. In effect, this structure helps researchers gain an understanding of how participants construct arguments in order to be most convincing to the opposing side.

Complementary moderators work together but represent different levels of expertise with focus groups and the topic of discussion. For example, one moderator may be an expert in focus groups and a generalist, whereas the second moderator might know little about focus groups but be a specialist in the topic under discussion. In effect, this procedure allows for a subject matter expert in the focus groups, but not in a manner that will unduly influence the group. Suppose that a community center wants to build a new recreational unit and decides to conduct a series of focus groups with members of the community. The moderator with expertise in focus groups might be complemented with a moderator with an architectural background who could present background information on various ideas suggested by the participants.

A variation of the use of complementary moderators is to have the sponsor of the focus group serve as the second moderator. This might include the director of the nonprofit agency or a member of the board of directors. These situations require some degree of caution, because these individuals tend to be rather defensive and to overreact when they hear negative comments. Furthermore, if this second moderator is an individual with local prominence or in a respected position, the participants might have some inhibitions about providing candid feedback.

Focus Group Discussions on the Telephone

Focus group discussions can be conducted on the telephone—a procedure that offers some advantages in assembling people who are difficult to reach. With a conference call telephone hookup, the moderator can carry on a focus group discussion with people scattered around the country. The telephone focus group offers the advantage of allowing participants to interact over distances at a fraction of the cost of transporting the same people to a central location.

The principal disadvantages of telephone focus groups are the stifled discussion and the lack of nonverbal communication. Telephone focus groups lack the spontaneity and creativity typical of in-person focus groups. As a result, the comments are more repressed and restrained. Moreover, much is gained in focus groups by watching the participants—head nodding, signs of boredom, smiles, frowns, degree of alertness, visible interest in the topic—all of which are unavailable on the telephone. In this sense, a telephone focus group is one step above an individual telephone interview, but it will lack the richness of an in-person focus group.

A telephone focus group can be conducted with varying levels of sophistication. At one extreme, it can be conducted with limited resources and resemble a conference phone call. With more sophisticated telephone equipment, it is possible to have a console with lights and name tags to identify speakers, special switching devices that allow only one person to speak at a time, and lights that indicate when others are attempting to talk.

Media Focus Groups

The media have discovered the appeal of focus groups. Newspaper readers and television viewers like to read about or see others share opinions and ideas. These media groups only have a few common points with focus groups described throughout this book. The argument for calling these sessions "focus groups" is that questions may be focused, participants may be preselected based on established criteria, and the moderator might be skillful in conducting the group. These advantages must be balanced with certain major weaknesses. These groups are about as far as possible from other characteristics that constitute successful focus groups, particularly a permissive nonthreatening environment in which confidentiality is assured.

The purpose of these sessions is to link individuals with statements, to capture "sound bites," and to tell the world. The individual has no assurance that comments will be used in context and no recourse if they are not. The participants are at the mercy of the media, and those in the media fully expect participants to bear that responsibility. These media focus groups typically have several methodological flaws that limit their value as serious research. First, they often consist of only one focus group. Furthermore, results from this one focus group are implicitly or explicitly generalized to a wider population. Second, the sessions are not conducted in a permissive, nonthreatening environment. Video and still cameras capture images throughout the session, constantly reminding participants of their potential for publicity. Recording devices capture everything said, but only a few comments will ever be published. Third, the basis of selection is often to achieve a cross-section of residents or voters. Often limited homogeneity is present, except that they may be adult voters who reside in the same community, city, or state.

I suggest that we encourage the media to exercise some responsible caution and make a few adaptations. It would be more accurate if they called these sessions "group discussions," which would avoid some confusion to readers. If the media are serious about conducting focus groups and wish to call these sessions "focus groups," then they may wish to consider a sequential series of discussions with varying levels of formality. Slight variations could occur in groups to determine the influence of cameras and recording equipment. For example, several groups might initially be conducted in the traditional focus group procedure without cameras, with homogeneous selection, and with explicit assurances of confidentiality. If this preliminary effort does identify trends, then the next step might be to conduct a second series of focus groups with similar questions that use quotes but still assure participants of confidentiality. Then later, a third series of focus groups would allow cameras and seek public quotes. In this manner, the media could gain some sense of whether the participants modify their comments when they are "on record," taped and photographed.

Media events called "focus group" are often entertainment—not research. We should place them in the same category as television or radio stations who conduct surveys using a pay-to-call-and-vote system: "Give us a call and vote on this important issue! Tell us your opinion! We want to hear from you! The question for today is: What is a focus group? On your touch tone phone, push 1 if you think it is a group discussion, push 2 if it is a discussion that pays people to participate, or push 3 if you would like to be in a focus group."

Issues When Adapting Focus Groups

When adapting focus groups to other types of situations, the researcher should bear in mind what the focus group can do and what it can't do. Although there is elasticity in the procedure, too much stretch may jeopardize the process. When adapting focus groups consideration should be given to the following:

The purpose of the effort. It is appropriate to use focus groups to collect information, to listen, and to learn. Focus groups are not intended to teach, to inform, to tell, or have others sanction a decision.

The people involved in the process. Focus group participants are preselected. Open invitations to the public or blanket invitations to a group are not used in focus group interviews.

The nature of the discussion. A focused interview is comprised primarily of open-ended questions that allow participants to select the manner of their response. It is not an open discussion of anything of interest.

The nature of the environment. The focused interview is conducted in a permissive environment conducive to sharing, listening, and responding. It is not a place where judgments are made about the quality or worth of comments, where decisions are made, or where there are deleterious consequences for "incorrect" opinions.

Summary

Focus group interviews have been successfully used in a variety of situations. They can be conducted with the same people over a period of time, on the telephone, or with multiple moderators. All of these adaptations of focus group interviews possess the characteristics of focus groups discussed in Chapter 2. A limited number of homogeneous people are invited to participate in a focused discussion in order to provide data of a qualitative nature. The purpose is not to teach, to provide therapy, to resolve differences, or to achieve a consensus but to obtain information in a systematic and verifiable manner. With that purpose in mind, the researcher should be encouraged to "twist it a bit" and discover just how robust and hardy focus group interviews really are. Media, however, may need to examine what they have called "focus groups" and either change the name (truth in advertising) to something such as "group discussion" or make certain modification to test and ensure that comments are not influenced by the media environment. For now, these media-based "focus groups" are best classified as entertainment—not research.

13

Contracting for Focus Groups

A GUIDE FOR CONSUMERS AND CONSULTANTS

Focus groups do not have to be designed and conducted by research agencies or consulting firms. Within the past decade, a number of public and nonprofit organizations have developed the capabilities of conducting internal focus group research to augment the research that is available from external vendors. Selecting the external research firm and feeling comfortable with the cost estimate and correctly estimating the time commitment for internally sponsored projects are continual challenges. Here are some suggestions that may be helpful.

Identification of a Research Firm

The first step is to identify the potential research firms or individuals in the community that conduct focus group interviews. Marketing or advertising people in larger companies can offer advice about names of people and market research firms. Larger companies may subcontract some of their market research to local individuals and firms, and their recommendations may prove quite helpful. Another approach is to identify knowledgeable individuals and seek their advice. For example, college faculty, local evaluators, or consultants may provide helpful leads. In addition, the membership directories of professional organizations such as the American Evaluation Association or the American Marketing Association list potential consultants.

Initial Contact With Potential Contractors

Telephone calls to potential consultants will help reduce the list to manageable proportions. When making initial contacts the following information is useful:

- What experience have they had with focus groups?
- Do they specialize in certain product areas?
- Who on your staff conducts and analyzes focus groups?
- How long have they been in business?
- Will they provide a list of past clients?
- Are they willing to prepare a formal proposal, describing their procedures, timeline, and costs?

This initial telephone visit should assist in narrowing the field to those consultants who seem interested and have the requisite experience. It is often best to solicit proposals from two or three of the most promising. If time permits, it is often helpful to go to the office of the consultant for further discussions, because examples of past work can be found in vendor files. Often one can view the discussion room or, in general, size up the operation.

Making the Decision

In making the decision about contracting, cost alone is not the key factor; however, it should be considered. Consultants with past experience, a successful track record, and satisfied clients are preferred. The prospective client should give thought to the degree to which the consultant understands the specific problems or issues. This is accomplished by talking to the moderator who will be conducting the interviews and considering the rapport achieved with this individual.

The head of the research firm or the person representing the firm will not necessarily serve as moderator. The client should ask who would be doing the moderating and also request to speak to that person. The moderator should convey interest and enthusiasm for the project while also demonstrating an ability to listen and be empathetic. The client should be comfortable with the moderator's communication skills—both oral and written.

The moderator's role in the analysis is an area of special concern. The potential moderator should be asked to comment on the number of groups that would be involved and the analysis process. The moderator might be asked to explain the sequence of steps involved in analysis. One of the best ways to assess the potential of the prospective consultant is to look over past focus group reports prepared by the consultant or research firm. Some reports are proprietary and cannot be shared, but if no reports are available for inspection, it may be a signal that few have been completed. When reviewing these focus group reports, the client should identify the reporting style preferred (raw data, descriptive summary, or interpretive) for the study being considered. Several options might be available in terms of the final report. A number of consultants limit themselves to preparing reports that only highlight participant's comments. By scanning through other reports prepared by the moderator, the client can tell if the report goes beyond what was said and provides analysis.

In a number of situations the client will only need specialized assistance from the consultant. For example, preexisting groups or address lists may reduce the costs of participant recruitment. Oral-only reports, written minireports, and comprehensive written reports will each have differing costs.

How Much Should It Cost?

The costs for focus group interviews vary considerably depending on a number of factors such as location, type of audience, selection process for participants, and number of groups.

When estimating costs, I have found it helpful to calculate separately the costs of each of five focus group aspects: planning, recruiting, moderating, analysis, and other costs.

Planning

The first category and often most difficult to estimate is planning the focus group study. This planning step involves three components:

conceptualizing the study, developing the questions, and planning the logistical arrangements. These components are difficult to estimate because of the wide variation of time needed between one study and another. The client may have preconceived ideas of whom to involve, the questions, or the location. In some studies these notions may not be practical or desirable, but in other studies the client will have a sound grounding in focus group research and have thought through much of the planning stage. In some studies it is difficult to bring closure to the questions, especially when a task force or advisory committee is involved. The entire planning step can sometimes be completed in less than 8 hours, whereas in other studies that involve multiple clients on complex topics the planning time can approach or exceed a full week.

One of the decisive factors that influence the time needed is the approach used by the consultant. In some research situations, one person makes most if not all the decisions about the study. This executive understands the problem, has a grasp of what focus group research can offer, and speaks on behalf of the organization. At other times, there are multiple clients such as a board, task force, or committee who must become committed before proceeding with the study. This second scenario occurs with some frequency in the public and nonprofit sector. As a result, many questions are asked and the consultant in effect becomes a teacher, helping the team contribute their understanding of the problem, insights into the target audiences, and suggestions on questions and logistics.

For beginning researchers this planning stage can become a black hole that sucks up time, resources, and consultant profit. It can be frustrating to move a group to consensus on study procedures or questions when the group is divided or historically doesn't deal well with consensus. A number of focus group researchers and applied researchers in general have agonized over this dilemma. Some strategies that should be considered include these:

- Talk to client decision makers about the time involved in the planning stage at the beginning of the study and offer some options that can reduce the frustration for all partners.
- Provide an open-ended hourly contract for the planning stage to allow for formative modifications of the study. In this way the client is aware of the additional costs of prolonged discussion and negotiation and is willing to assume these additional costs.

- Estimate an additional amount of time for the planning stage to accommodate the collegial discussion.
- Include a set amount of added expense for each member of the planning or advisory task force. (A colleague charges an additional $1,000 for each committee member involved in the research project.)
- Set a time when closure will occur on questions and delineate the type of input that each committee or task force can offer. At the beginning of the study, specify who will make final decisions and the timetable for those decisions.

Recruiting

Recruiting participants to the focus group can occur in several ways. The recruiting can be conducted by the researcher, volunteers, or an outside group or agency, each of which will depend on the telephone as the principal means of contact. The efficiency of telephone recruiting depends on having a sufficiently large pool of potential contacts, being able to make telephone contact with individuals on the list within a reasonable number of calls, and the willingness of the individuals to participate.

These telephone contacts might be classified into categories based on the study characteristics and incentives to participate. The categories include "willing" prospects who readily agree to attend the session, "hesitant" prospects who are less willing to attend, and "difficult" prospects who are the least willing to attend the focus group. The "willing" prospects are those who are positively disposed toward the topic or organization, and about 20% to 40% of those contacted agree to participate in the focus group interview. This also assumes that the participants have been prescreened, which is to say that they have met necessary sociodemographic or other behavioral characteristics for attending the focus groups. Rarely will the researchers find over 50% of the potential participants agreeing to participate, unless the sessions are conducted during work hours with the participants granted time off to attend or if the focus groups "piggyback" on existing events or activities. In some situations, the recruitment will be difficult, with less than 10% of those contacted agreeing to participate.

A second method of recruitment is through the use of volunteers. Volunteers are a valuable resource for public and nonprofit organizations and their potential for recruitment is often overlooked. Volunteers have been known to make extraordinary efforts in assisting with focus group studies. One of the ways that volunteers can contribute to a focus group study is by identifying potential participants and then contacting selected participants to attend the focus group interview. This strategy is often mutually beneficial for both researcher and sponsoring organization because it minimizes time and costs of the outside consultant and identifies a specific area in which volunteers can make valuable contributions. For this strategy to work effectively, the researcher must establish well-defined guidelines on how to identify potential participants and also how to extend the invitation to attend the focus group interview.

The third recruitment method is to seek assistance from an outside group or agency. It begins with the researcher establishing screening criteria for participation and then sharing these criteria, along with recruitment protocol, with the recruiting agency. These agencies could be one of the scores of market research firms around the country that specialize in focus group recruitment. A number of these organizations have hundreds of names on file of people who possess certain sociodemographic characteristics. Other times, these firms use random telephone interviewing to screen potential participants. Price of recruitment is directly related to the number of screening characteristics and the difficulty of recruiting the prospective participants. Nonprofit organizations can also call on "sister" or collaborating agencies for help in recruitment. Occasionally, when a study is of interest or concern to another agency, the sponsoring agency can invite a second agency to participate in the study by helping with recruiting and thereby gaining access to subsequent results. At times, other nonprofit organizations may assist by identifying potential focus group participants simply out of support for another agency.

Whatever means is used for recruiting participants, the researcher will still need to develop criteria and specifications for follow-up letters of invitation and the protocol for telephone reminders the day before the focus group.

The time needed for recruitment will depend largely on how difficult it is to locate prospective participants and on their willingness to accept the invitation. The costs dramatically increase as screening criteria are added. For example, it would be relatively easy to identify women who are employed outside the home, but it would be increasingly difficult if you specified additional criteria, such as age between 25 and 35, preschool children, and college graduates.

Moderating

The easiest estimate to make is likely the time needed to moderate a focus group. In a typical focus group of 2 hours, the moderator might plan for approximately 6 hours—3 each for both the moderator and the assistant moderator. Typically, the moderating team will need to arrive early, at least 30-45 minutes before participants arrive, to set up equipment and arrange the room. After the focus group, the team may need to spend another 30 minutes in debriefing the focus group. The travel time to the focus group site must also be included. One of the ways public and nonprofit organizations conserve resources is to identify a staff member or volunteer to serve as assistant moderator.

Analysis

Next to planning, analysis is the second black hole for estimating time and resources. The estimates are difficult because the researcher does not know how soon or in what manner the key findings will emerge. In some studies, the analyst may need to review the transcripts multiple times, comparing and contrasting participants' comments until central themes emerge. Other times, themes and patterns emerge quickly and clearly. As suggested in the earlier chapter on analysis, situational analysis calls for developing an analysis plan (with a budget estimate) and then amending that plan based on early focus group results. Because this is not always possible or practical, the researcher may wish to err on the side of additional rigor and then use selective shortcuts when and where feasible. The choices consist of analysis based on transcripts, tapes, notes, or memory. Let's examine the time expectations of each option.

Transcript-Based Analysis. With this option, the researcher carefully examines all evidence, including transcripts, field notes, debriefing discussion, oral summary statements, as well as the audio or video recordings. Veteran analysts often spend about 5 to 6 days conducting the analysis of a series of three to six focus groups. As the number of focus groups increases, the time demands do not increase at a corresponding rate. The comparison is depicted in Figure 13.1. Veteran analysts offer several tips to beginning analysts. Additional time should be added to the estimate if these conditions are present: If you've never analyzed focus group reports before, add 35% more time; If you have a committee that has to approve the final draft, add 20% more time; if you are preparing recommendations, add 20% more time.

Groups	Analysis Time Needed
3-6 focus groups	5-6 days
9-12 focus groups	7-12 days
15-24 focus groups	14-18 days

Figure 13.1. Time Estimate for Transcript-Based Analysis
SOURCE: J. Migler & R. Krueger, 1992

It often requires about 10-14 hours of clerical time to transcribe one focus group. This assumes that the typist will not be interrupted, that the tape is of reasonable quality with minimal background noise, and that the typist has adequate equipment and skills.

Tape-Based Analysis. With tape-based analysis the researcher listens to the tape, prepares an abridged transcript, and consults field notes, debriefing discussion, and oral summary statements. A brief summary, often with bulleted format, is prepared for each focus group. This typically requires between 4 and 8 hours per focus group.

Note-Based Analysis. Note-based analysis involves the moderator or assistant moderator in preparing a brief report based on the field notes, debriefing discussion, and oral summary statements offered in the focus group. This type of analysis may require approximately 2 to 3 hours per focus group.

Memory-Based Analysis. The advantages of memory-based analysis are in the immediacy and speed with which it can be provided. These sessions are equivalent to the debriefing session between the moderator and assistant moderator following the focus group, only they also involve the client. These sessions usually last less than 1 hour.

Other Costs

Other costs must be added to the cost of focus group research. Included are costs for the following:

- Travel expenses for moderator team
- Travel expenses for participants
- Honorariums

- Food
- Room charge
- Child care
- Equipment rental or purchase
- Tapes/batteries/name tents/handouts
- Phone costs
- Office supplies, duplication, postage

The costs of focus group projects can and do vary considerably and can range from nothing (where all time and expenses are included in other budgets or where it is donated) to $3,000 or more for each focus group. Typically, the budget estimates provided by consultants will not itemize individual parts of the process, but they might provide cost estimates for various options in reporting or recruiting.

Contracting for Special Needs

At times, the client will have focus group needs that necessitate a special contract, such as designing the study, staff training, moderating, diagnostic feedback to moderators, or audits of the draft or final reports.

Contract for Designing the Focus Group Study. Much of the success of the study depends on how well it is planned and designed. An outside expert might develop a plan that is carried out using staff and resources internal to the contracting organization. The expert might be under contract for several days to obtain background information on the purposes of the study, develop a questioning route, identify the sampling strategy, prepare the telephone screening survey, train a small core of moderators, and outline a master plan for implementing the study.

Contract for Diagnostic Feedback to Moderators. Focus groups are typically conducted over a time span of several weeks and consist of a number of different discussion groups. It is often valuable to receive diagnostic feedback early in the series of focus groups in order to identify strengths of the moderator and areas needing improvement for future focus groups. Without this coaching, moderators tend to repeat unproductive moderating activities and thereby limit the amount and quality of participant discussion. This diagnostic feedback can be provided in several ways. The preferred way is by observing the moderator in a focus group and then providing feedback. A second method calls for listening to the focus group tape (while reviewing the transcript, if available), examination of the field notes, and analysis report prepared by the moderating team. Using this information, the reviewer provides feedback to the moderator.

Contract for an Outside Audit of the Focus Group Report. A written report is prepared at the conclusion of the focus group interviews. The outside audit consists of an outside expert reviewing the draft report and suggesting changes as needed prior to publishing the final focus group report. Experts review all available raw materials from the focus groups, including tapes, transcripts, field notes, analysis reports prepared by moderators of individual focus groups, and a double-spaced draft of the final report. After reviewing the raw materials, the consultant makes notations and suggestions directly on the draft report with an indication of the level of importance of each of the suggested changes. When changes are needed, the expert does not draft the revision but rather provides an outline of what might be included. This draft with suggestions is then returned for future revisions, as needed. The expert auditor also prepares a cover letter that can be inserted into the report. This letter provides an official judgment about the quality of the analysis process.

Summary

The decision to contract for outside help in conducting focus groups is typically motivated by several factors: the desire to maintain quality control in the process; the lack of internal staff to conduct the study; or the need for a neutral party to conduct the study. Of these factors the most difficult to monitor is quality control, because cost alone is not the indicator of quality. Experts who are experienced with focus group procedures can often provide the elements that result in quality: an appropriate sampling strategy, a well-developed questioning route, skillful moderating, and systematic analysis. However, some of the most beneficial focus group studies have been conducted by internal staff members with very limited budgets. Several aspects of the focus group budget are relatively easy to estimate, such as time needed for recruitment and moderating along with the miscellaneous costs of actually conducting the group. However, estimating the time needed to plan and analyze the focus group is difficult.

APPENDIX 13A

Planning Worksheet
for Focus Groups

1. Planning

Conceptualizing the study (1-20 researcher hours)
Development of questions (4-30 researcher hours)
Logistical arrangements (1-16 researcher hours)

Researcher Planning Time _____ **hours**

2. Recruiting

A. Recruiting (Consider these choices)
  1. By the research team
     a. Development of telephone script and follow-up letter (1-3 researcher hours)
     Phone recruiting (estimate about 10-15 calls per hour)
        (1) "Willing" prospects (3-5 calls for each confirmation)
        (2) "Hesitant" prospects (5-10 calls for each confirmation)
        (3) "Difficult" prospects (10+ calls for each confirmation)
  2. By volunteers
     a. Researcher prepares criteria and trains volunteers on how to recruit (2-8 researcher hours)
  3. By a group or agency
     a. Researcher prepares criteria and specifications (2-4 researcher hours)
B. Follow-up letters (2 clerical hours per group)
C. Follow-up phone reminders (1 clerical hour per group)

Phone Recruiter or Clerical Time _____ **hours**
Researcher Recruiting Time _____ **hours**

3. Moderating

    A. Travel time for moderator team

    B. Moderator time per focus group (3 hours per group)

    C. Assistant moderator time per focus group (same as moderator)

                    Researcher Moderator Time _____ **hours**

4. Analysis

    A. Determine the level of rigor desired

        1. Rigorous: Very careful attention to transcripts, field notes, debriefing, and summary statements, with limited review of tapes. Here are some estimates from analysis through production of first draft of report:

Scope	Time Requirement
3-6 focus groups	5-6 days
9-12 focus groups	7-12 days
15-24 focus groups	14-18 days

    BUT

    Add 35% more time if you've never done it before

    Add 20% more time if a committee has to approve draft

    Add 20% more time if recommendations are needed

        2. Less rigorous or less complex topic (4-8 researcher hours per focus group)

        3. Least rigorous or least complex topic (1-2 researcher hours per focus group)

    B. Transcripts of focus groups (10-12 clerical hours per group)

    C. Revisions for final draft (2-20 hours)

    D. Oral report(s) (1-4+ researcher hours)

               Time Required for Clerical Help _____ **hours**

           Researcher Analysis and Reporting Time _____ **hours**

5. Add Other Costs

Travel expenses for moderator team $ _____

Travel expenses for participants $ _____

Honorariums $ _____

Food $ _____

Room charge	$ _____
Child care	$ _____
Equipment rental or purchase	$ _____
Tapes/batteries/name tents/handouts	$ _____
Transcription costs	$ _____
Phone costs	$ _____
Office supplies, duplication, postage	$ _____

Total Other Costs $ _____

6. Final Calculations

Total Other Costs $

Total Clerical Time_____ Hours × Hourly Rate of $_____ = $_____

Total Researcher Time _____ Hours × Hourly Rate of $_____ = $_____

Grand Total Cost $_____

Postscript

THE FUTURE OF FOCUS GROUPS

What is the future of focus groups? Are they simply a trendy procedure that will evaporate within a few years, or will they last? The answer depends on several factors.

The future of focus groups will depend on a sound recognition of the limits of the procedure. Focus groups can be a refreshing and appealing means of obtaining information. If anything, they have some seductive qualities that tempt researchers and decision makers to use them in unwarranted situations. They are seductive in several ways: the results are understandable, the participants typically enjoy the opportunity to participate, and the process creates a favorable impression that the sponsoring organization really cares enough to listen to people. These are major advantages, but they can also tempt users to misuse and abuse the technique.

Focus groups provide a special type of information. They provide a richness of data at a reasonable cost. They tap into the real-life interactions of people and allow the researcher to get in touch with participants' perceptions, attitudes, and opinions in a way that other procedures do not allow. Decision makers have needed this type of information in the past, they need it now, and because of the increased pressure for accountability, they will be need it even more in the future.

There is a hunger to be heard. All around this country, and in a number of other countries, people want and expect to have more control over their futures. They expect politicians, decision makers, bosses, and others who exert power and influence to pay attention. At the same time, politicians and assorted decision makers say they are listening and that they have received and understood the messages. However, for many, these have been hollow words. A prevailing notion in many nations is representative democracy. Elected officials are really supposed to represent us. The captains of industry are supposed to be concerned about the needs and aspirations of their employees. It is interesting that many leaders in both the public and private sector spend more time talking than they do listening.

Never before has there been such a push for organizations to listen. Never before has there been such a need to listen. Institutions and organizations need rebirth and people have valuable ideas for change and improvement.

It's tough to be a decision maker. I've met many extremely talented managers and administrators who truly have the best interests of employees and customers at heart. They really want to listen. They assume that people are able to discuss and logically come up with a conclusion in a reasonable and sequential manner. More often the discussion turns out to be confusing, with multiple values and opinions and no discernible consensus. Petty rivalries, personality differences, and old battles are fought again and again in these hearings or committee meetings. Employees and customers present differing points of view, and since a decision has to be made, it is no surprise when the manager pushes ahead and takes action.

The focus group, by itself, is not the answer, but it can contribute in a meaningful way. It is a systematic and disciplined approach that emphasizes understandable rules and respect for other views. Each person is important and is encouraged to present his or her views and then listen and respond to others. Although consensus sometimes occurs, it is not expected. The focus group helps people hear themselves and receive feedback from peers. This process keeps us grounded in reality.

References Cited

Albrecht, Terrance L. (1993). Understanding communication processes in focus groups. In David L. Morgan (Ed.), *Successful focus groups* (pp. 51-64). Newbury Park, CA: Sage.

Alkin, Marvin C., Daillak, Richard, & White, Peter. (1979). *Using evaluations.* Beverly Hills, CA: Sage.

Anderson, Leith. (1986). Is Baptist important in our church's name? *The Standard, 76*(5), 25, 27, 29.

Andreasen, Alan R. (1983). Cost-conscious marketing research. *Harvard Business Review, 83*(4), 74-79.

Andrews, Amy. (1977, July 11). How to buy productive focus group research. *Advertising Age,* pp. 128,147,148.

Axelrod, Myril D. (1975, March 14). 10 essentials for good qualitative research. *Marketing News,* pp. 5-8.

Bellenger, Danny N., Bernhardt, Kenneth L., & Goldstrucker, Jac L. (1976). Qualitative research techniques: Focus group interviews. In *Qualitative research in marketing.* Chicago: American Marketing Association. (Also reprinted in James B. Higginbotham & Keith K. Cox (Eds.), *Focus group interviews: A reader.* Chicago: American Marketing Association, 1979.)

Bennett, Amanda. (1986, June 3). Once a tool of market researchers, focus groups gain wider usage. *The Wall Street Journal,* p. 1.

Bernstein, L., Harris, J., & Meloy, R. (1989, May). Focus groups improve billing practices, patient relations. *Healthcare Financial Management, 43*(5), 57-60.

Brown, Judith E., et al. (1992). Development of a prenatal weight gain intervention program using social marketing methods. *Journal of Nutrition Education, 24*(1), 21-28.

Business and Higher Education Report, American Council on Education. (1991, Spring). New report reveals "troubling differences" between experts and the public. *Educational Record, 72*, 2, 48.

Casey, Mary A. (1991). *Volunteers improve focus groups.* Paper presented at the meeting of the American Evaluation Association, Chicago, IL.

Casey, Mary A., Leske, Gary, & Krueger, Richard A. (1987, February). *Marketing agricultural education.* Paper presented at the meeting of the Agricultural Education Central States Research Conference, Chicago, IL.

Chesterton, Gilbert K. (1951) The invisible man. In *The Father Brown omnibus.* New York: Dodd, Mead.

Coe, Barbara J., & MacLachlan, James H. (1980). How major TV advertisers evaluate commercials. *Journal of Advertising Research, 20*(6), 51-54.

Cook, Michele. (1986, December 3). Zoo looking for a new lab tag: Maybe it's a pet peeve. *St. Paul Pioneer Press Dispatch*, p. 1D.

Covey, Stephen R. (1989). *The 7 habits of highly effective people.* New York: Simon & Schuster.

Cushing, Marguerite. (1987, June). Focus groups: What's in them for supermarkets. *Progressive Grocer,* pp. 103-106.

Diamond, William D., & Gagnon, Jean P. (1985). Obtaining pharmacy class feedback through the use of focus group interviews. *American Journal of Pharmaceutical Education, 49*(1), 49-54.

Elrod, J. Mitchell, Jr. (1981). Improving employee relations with focus groups. *Business, 31*(6), 36-38.

Glaser, Barney G., & Strauss, Anselm L. (1967). *The discovery of grounded theory: Strategies for qualitative research.* Hawthorne, NY: Aldine de Gruyter.

Grossman, Jack H. (1979, January 12). Qualitative research model can help probe. *Marketing News*, p. 10.

Grunig, Larissa A. (1990, June). Using focus group research in public relations. *Public Relations Review, 16*(2), 36-49.

Guba, Egon G., & Lincoln, Yvonna S. (1989). *Fourth generation evaluation.* Newbury Park, CA: Sage.

Hanafin, Teresa M. (1989, December 2). Developers take a new read on their market. *Boston Globe*, p. 45.

Hendricks, Michael. (1984). Preparing and using briefing charts. *Evaluation News, 5*(3), 78-80.

Joint Committee on Standards for Educational Evaluation. (1981). *Standards for evaluations of educational programs, projects, and materials.* New York: McGraw-Hill.

Jourard, Sidney M. (1964). *The transparent self.* Princeton, NJ: Van Nostrand.

Katz, Daniel, Gutek, Barbara A., Kahn, Robert L., & Barton, Eugenia. (1975). *Bureaucratic encounters.* Ann Arbor, MI: Institute for Social Research, University of Michigan.

Kelleher, Joanne. (1982). Find out what your customers really want. *Inc, 4*(1), 88, 91.

Labaw, Patricia. (1985). *Advanced questionnaire design.* Cambridge, MA: Ballinger.

Langer, Judith. (1979, September 21). 12 keys to unlock qualitative research on sensitive subjects. *Marketing News*, pp. 10, 20.

LaPiere, Richard T. (1934). Attitudes and actions. *Social Forces, 13*, 230-237.

Lazarfeld, Paul. (1986). *The art of asking why.* New York: The Advertising Research Foundation. (Original work published in 1934 in *The National Marketing Review.*)

Leaming, George. (1991). Discussing price isn't done in "polite" focus groups. *Marketing News, 25*(11), 16.

Linda, Gerald. (1982). Focus groups: A new look at an old friend. *Marketing & Media Decisions, 17*(10), 96, 98.

Mariampolski, Hy. (1984). The resurgence of qualitative research. *Public Relations Journal, 40*(7), 21-23.

Merton, Robert K., Fiske, Marjorie, & Kendall, Patricia L. (1990). *The focused interview*, 2nd ed. Glencoe, IL: The Free Press. (Original edition published in 1956.)

Miller, Cyndee. (1991). Focus groups: A useful crystal ball for helping to spot trends. *Marketing News, 25*(11), 2.

Morgan, David L., & Spanish, Margaret T. (1984). Focus groups: A new tool for qualitative research. *Qualitative Sociology, 7*(3), 253-270.

Mueller, Marsha R., & Anderson, Eugene. (1985). *Report of three focus group interviews held with commercial farm families in northwestern Minnesota*. St. Paul, MN: University of Minnesota, Agricultural Extension Service, Office of Special Programs.

Office of the Inspector General. (1990, June). *Crack babies*. OEI-03-89-01540. Washington, DC: Health and Human Services, Office of Evaluation and Inspections.

Patton, Michael Q. (1990). *Qualitative evaluation and research methods*. Newbury Park, CA: Sage.

Peterson, Roland L., & Migler, Jerry R. (1987). *Adjusting post-secondary agriculture curriculum to promote educational access: An experiment*. St. Paul, MN: University of Minnesota, Department of Vocational and Technical Education.

Reynolds, Fred D., & Johnson, Deborah K. (1978). Validity of focus group findings. *Journal of Advertising Research, 18*(3), 21-24.

Rice, Stuart A. (Ed.). (1931). *Methods in social science*. Chicago: University of Chicago Press.

Roethlisberger, Fritz J., & Dickson, William J. (1938). *Management and the worker*. Cambridge, MA: Harvard University Press.

Rogers, Carl R. (1942). *Counseling and psychotherapy*. New York: Houghton Mifflin.

Schmit, Julie. (1993, June 1). Deep secrets told among passengers. *USA Today*, pp. 1B-2B.

Strauss, Anselm, & Corbin, J. (1990). *Basics of qualitative research: Grounded theory and procedures and techniques*. Newbury Park, CA: Sage.

Study: Money not the only motivation for respondents. (1991). *Marketing News, 25*(11), 17.

Van de Vall, Mark, Bolas, Cheryl, & Kang, Tai S. (1976). Applied social research in industrial organizations: An evaluation of functions, theory, and methods. *Journal of Applied Behavioral Science, 12*: 158-177.

Weiss, Carol H. (1976). Policy research in the university: Practical aid or academic exercise? *Policy Studies Journal, 4*(3), 224-233.

Winski, Joseph M. (1992, February 10). Addicted to research, Nick shows strong kids' lure. *Advertising Age*, pp. S1, S22.

Yin, Robert K. (1984). *Case study research*. Beverly Hills, CA: Sage.

Zeithaml, Valerie A., Parasuraman, A., & Berry, Leonard L. (1990). *Delivering quality service: Balancing customer perceptions and expectations*. New York: The Free Press.

Zemke, R., & Anderson, K. (1990). Customers from hell. *Training, 27*(2), 25-33.

Bibliography

Readers may wish to consult the following sources for additional information on focus group interviewing.

Education, Training, and Social Sciences Publications

Baucom, J. (1991). Focus group survey of working newly graduated nurses. *Recruitment and Retention Report*, *4*(7), 1-3.

Bers, T. H. (1989). The popularity and problems of focus group research. *College and University*, *64*(3), 260-268.

Bers, T. H., & Smith, K. (1988). Focus groups and community college research: Lessons from a study of nontraditional students. *Community College Review*, *15*(4), 52-58.

Bertrand, J. T. (1992). Techniques for analyzing focus group data. *Evaluation Review*, *16*(2), 198-209.

Bloch, D. P. (1992). The application of group interviews to the planning and evaluation of career development programs. *Career Development Quarterly*, *40*(4), 340-350.

Brodigan, D. L. (1992). Focus group interviews: Applications for institutional research. *AIR Professional File*, *43*(Winter), 7.

Brown, J. E. (1992). Development of a prenatal weight gain intervention program using social marketing methods. *Journal of Nutritional Education*, *24*(1), 21-28.

Buttram, Judith L. (1990). Focus groups: A starting point for needs assessment. *Evaluation Practice*, *11*(3), 207-212.

Engleberg, I. N., & Cohen, M. C. (1989). Focus group research in the Community College. *Community/Junior College Quarterly of Research and Practice*, *13*(2), 101-108.

Farber, B. J., & Wycoff, J. (1991). Bringing the customer into focus. *Training*, *28*(5), 41-44.

Hartman, R. I. (1988). Feedback through focus group interviews. *Journal of Career Planning and Employment, 69*(1), 77-80.

Howard, E., Hubelbank, J., & Moore, P. (1989). Employer evaluation of graduates: Use of the focus group. *Nurse Educator, 14*(5), 38-41.

Jacobi, M. (1991). Focus group research: A tool for the student affairs professional. *NASPA Journal, 28*(3), 195-201.

Javidi, M., Long, L. W., Vasu, M. L., & Ivy, D. K. (1991). Enhancing focus group validity with computer assisted technology in social science research. *Social Science Computer Review, 9*(2), 231-245.

Krugman, D. M., Shamp, S. A., & Johnson, K. F. (1991). Video movies at home: Are they viewed like film or like television? *Journalism Quarterly, 68*(1-2), 120-130.

Larson, C. L., & Preskill, H. E. (1991). Organizations in transition: Opportunities and challenges for evaluation. *New Directions for Program Evaluation*, (49), 1-92.

Lederman, L. C. (1990). Assessing educational effectiveness: The focus group interview as a technique for data collection. *Communication Education, 39*(2), 117-127.

Lengua, L. J., & Roosa, M. W. (1992). Using focus groups to guide the development of a parenting program for difficult-to-reach, high-risk families. *Family Relations, 41*(2), 163-168.

Manning, S. S. (1990). Ethical decisions: A grounded theory approach to the experience of social work administrators. *Dissertation Abstracts International, A: The Humanities and Social Sciences, 51*(5), 1775-A.

Mitra, A. (1992, November). Use of focus groups in questionnaire design. Paper presented at the American Evaluation Association, Seattle, WA.

Morgan, D. L. (1989). Adjusting to widowhood: Do social networks really make it easier? *Gerontologist, 29*(1), 101-107.

Nix, L. M., Pasteur, A. B., & Servance, M. A. (1988). A focus group study of sexually active black male teenagers. *Adolescence, 23*(91), 741-751.

Nowack, K. M. (1991). A true training needs analysis. *Training & Development Journal, 45*(4), 69-73.

O'Donnell, J. M. (1988). Focus groups: A habit-forming evaluation technique. *Training & Development Journal, 42*(7), 71-73.

Schwaller, M. B., & Shepherd, S. K. (1992). Use of focus groups to explore employee reactions to a proposed worksite cafeteria nutrition program. *Journal of Nutrition Education, 24*(1), 33-36.

Sevier, R. (1989, Winter). Conducting focus group research. *Journal of College Admissions* (122), 4-9.

Sink, D. W. (1991). Focus groups as an approach to outcomes assessment. *American Review of Public Administration, 21*(3), 197-204.

Stein, M. L. (1989). Focus groups. *Editor & Publisher, 122*(27), 22.

Taylor, J. M., & Ward, J. V. (1991). Culture, sexuality, and school: Perspectives from focus groups in six different cultural communities. *Women's Studies Quarterly, 19*(1-2), 121-137.

Unger, J. (1990). Focus group evaluation of hospital recruitment materials. *Recruitment and Retention Report, 3*(10), 3-4.

Ward, V. M., Bertrand, J. T., & Brown, L. F. (1991). The comparability of focus group and survey results: Three case studies. *Evaluation Review, 15*(2), 266-283.

Widdows, R. (1991). The focus group interview: A method for assessing users' evaluation of library service. *College and Research Libraries, 52*(4), 352-359.

Zemke, R., & Anderson, K. (1990). Customers from hell. *Training*, *27*(2), 25-33.

Health, Nutrition, and Medicine Publications

Barker, G. K., & Rich, S. (1992). Influences on adolescent sexuality in Nigeria and Kenya: Findings from recent focus group discussions. *Studies in Family Planning*, *23*(3), 199-210.

Basch, C. E., DeCicco, I. M., & Malfetti, J. L. (1989). A focus group study on decision processes of young drivers: Reasons that may support a decision to drink and drive. *Health Education Quarterly*, *16*(3), 389-396.

Crockett, S. J., Heller, K. E., Merkel, J. M., & Peterson, J. (1990, April). Assessing beliefs of older rural Americans about nutrition education: Use of the focus group approach. *Journal of the American Dietetic Association*, *90*(4), 563-567.

DesRosier, M., & Zellers, K. (1989). Focus groups: A program planning technique. *Journal of Nursing Administration*, *19*(3), 20-25.

Dickin, K. L., Binchan, R. K., Purdue, S. E., & Obinya, E. (1991). Perceptions of neonatal tetanus and immunization during pregnancy: A report of focus group discussions in Kaduna, Nigeria. *International Quarterly of Community Health Education*, *11*(4), 371-383.

Diehl, S. F., Moffitt, K. A., & Wade, S. M. (1991). Focus group interview with parents of children with medically complex needs: An intimate look at their perceptions and feelings. *Children's Health Care*, *20*(3), 170-178.

Dignan, M., Michielutte, R., Sharp, P., Bahnson, J., Young, L., & Beal, P. (1990). The role of focus groups in health education for cervical cancer among minority women. *Journal of Community Health*, *15*(6), 369-375.

Elbeck, M., & Fecteau, G. (1990). Improving the validity of measures of patient satisfaction with psychiatric care and treatment. *Hospital and Community Psychiatry*, *41*(9), 998-1001.

Hart, G., & Rotem, A. (1990). Using focus groups to identify clinical learning opportunities for registered nurses. *Australian Journal of Advanced Nursing*, *8*(1), 16-21.

Kendall, P., & Stone, M. B. (1992). IFT focus groups find consumers favor biotechnology and increased R&D funding. *Food Technology*, *46*(7), 38.

Kingry, M., Tiedje, L., & Friedman, L. (1990). Focus groups: A research technique for nursing. *Nursing Research*, *39*(2), 124-125.

Klein, J., Forehand, B., Oliveri, J., Patterson, C., Kupersmidt, J., & Strecher, V. (1992). Candy cigarettes: Do they encourage children's smoking? *Pediatrics*, *89*(1), 27-31.

Lassiter, S. (1991). Special focus groups. *Journal of Neuroscience Nursing*, *23*(3), 143.

Lewis, C. J., & Yetley, E. A. (1992). Focus group sessions on formats of nutrition labels. *Journal of the American Dietetic Association*, *92*(1), 62-66.

Mayer, D. (1992). Florida hospital. *Healthcare Forum*, *35*(5), 75-80.

McCarthy, P. R., & Lansing, D. (1992). What works best for worksite cholesterol education? Answers from targeted focus groups. *American Dietetic Association*, *92*(8), 978-981.

Mesters, I., Pieterse, M., & Meertens, R. (1991). Pediatric asthma, a qualitative and quantitative approach to needs assessment. *Patient Education Counseling*, *17*(1), 23-34.

Nyamathi, A., & Shuler, P. (1990). Focus group interview: A research technique for informed nursing practice. *Journal of Advanced Nursing, 15*(11), 1281-1288.

Richter, J. M., Bottenberg, D. J., & Roberto, K. A. (1991). Focus group: Implications for program evaluation of mental health services. *Journal of Mental Health Administration, 18*(2), 148-153.

Robbins, K., & Holst, R. (1990). Hospital library evaluation using focus group interviews. *Bulletin of the Medical Library Association, 78*(3), 311-313.

Shepherd, S. K., Sims, L. S., Cronin, F. J., Shaw, A., & Davis, C. (1989). Use of focus groups to explore consumers' preferences for content and graphic design of nutrition publications. *Journal of the American Dietetic Association, 89*(11), 1612-1614.

Stone, R., & Waszak, C. (1992). Adolescent knowledge and attitudes about abortion. *Family Planning Perspectives, 24*(2), 52-57.

Sussman, S., Burton, D., Dent, C. W., & Stacy, A. W. (1991). Use of focus groups in developing an adolescent tobacco use cessation program: Collective norm effects. *Journal of Applied Social Psychology, 21*(21), 1772-1782.

Trenkner, L. L., & Achterberg, C. L. (1991). Use of focus groups in evaluating nutrition education materials. *Journal of the American Dietetic Association, 91*(12), 1577-1581.

Walker, L. B. (1989). Focus group confessions. *American Baby, 51*(9), 22,40.

Marketing, Business, and Advertising Publications

Abelson, H. I. (1989). Focus groups in focus. *Marketing Communications, 14*(2), 58-61.

Baker, S. L. (1991). Improving business services through the use of focus groups. *RQ, 30*(3), 377-385.

Bloom, N. (1989). Have discussion groups had their day? *Industrial Marketing Digest, 14*(2), 147-153.

Brandt, D. R., Reffett, K. L. (1989). Focusing on customer problems to improve service quality. *Journal of Services Marketing, 3*(4), 5-14.

Byers, P. Y., & Wilcox, J. R. (1991, December). Focus groups: A qualitative opportunity for researchers. *Journal of Business Communication, 28*(1), 63-78.

Calo, N. G. (1988, October 24). Focus group data can be used immediately, but carefully. *Advertising Age*, p. 24.

Caplan, S. (1990). Using focus group methodology for ergonomic design. Special issue: Marketing ergonomics: VI and VII. *Ergonomics, 33*(5), 527-533.

Cunningham, L. (1990, January 8). Electronic focus groups offer 3-way capability. *Marketing News*, pp. 22, 39.

Day focus groups have design input. (1988). *Editor & Publisher, 121*(22), 23.

DeNicola, N. (1990). Debriefing sessions: The missing link in focus groups. *Marketing News, 24*(1), 20, 22.

Donaton, S. (1992). As kids speak, magazines read 'tween lines. *Advertising Age, 63*(6), S4, S16.

Donnelly, J. H., Gibson, J. L., & Skinner, S. J. (1988). The behaviors of effective bank managers. *Journal of Retail Banking, 10*(4), 29-37.

Englander, T. (1989). Stew Leonard's: In-store Disneyland. *Incentive, 163*(1), 26, 30.

Farhi, P. (1991). What do trend forecasters know that you don't? *Working Woman, 16*(4), 72-75,108.

Fedder, C. J. (1990). Biz-to-biz focus groups require a special touch. *Marketing News,* *24*(1), 46.

Forges, C. A. (1991). Circle of housewives as appraisers of innovations and product improvements in quick frozen foods. *Marketing & Research Today, 19*(3), 152-159.

Foxman, L. D., & Polsky, W. L. (1990). Keep good clerical employees. *Personnel Journal, 69*(9), 26, 28.

Gendelev, B. (1991). Making your marketing data usable. *Direct Marketing, 53*(9), 32-34.

Giges, N. (1988). Consultant aims to tame focus groups. *Advertising Age, 59*(6), 46.

Goerne, C. (1992). Trendspotters draw on various research tools to stay trendy. *Marketing News, 26*(1), 6.

Gold, E. M. (1992). Conference call services get sophisticated. *Networking Management, 10*(4), 44-48.

Gordon, W. (1990). Ask the right questions, Ye shall receive the right moderator. *Marketing News, 24*(1), 42-43.

Green, A. (1990). Bank marketers focus on focus groups. *Bankers Monthly, 107*(4), 32-35.

Greenbaum, T. L. (1988, August 29). It's possible to reduce cost of focus groups. *Marketing News,* p. 43.

Greenbaum, T. L. (1989a). Focus groups: Helpful or harmful? *Bank Marketing, 21*(3), 26-27.

Greenbaum, T. L. (1989b). Murder at the focus group, or: Kill the idea, not the messenger. *Marketing News, 23*(19), 43-44.

Greenbaum, T. L. (1990a). Focus group spurt predicted for the '90s. *Marketing News, 24*(1), 21-22.

Greenbaum, T. L. (1990b). What the '90s will hold for focus group research. *Advertising Age, 61*(4), 26.

Greenbaum, T. L. (1991a). Do you have the right moderator for your focus groups? Here are 10 questions to ask yourself. *Bank Marketing, 23*(1), 43.

Greenbaum, T. L. (1991b). Doing your own focus group is like fixing your own plumbing. *Marketing News, 25*(11), 8-9.

Greenbaum, T. L. (1991c). Outside moderators maximize focus group results. *Public Relations Journal, 47*(9), 31-32.

Greenbaum, T. L. (1993). Focus group research is not a commodity business. *Marketing News, 27*(5), 4.

Gruenwald, G. (1991, May 27). Focus groups can be useful but not for decision making. *Marketing News,* p. 16.

Hall, C. (1989). Travel: Motel 6—King of the road. *Marketing & Media Decisions, 24*(3), 80-86.

Hayward, W., & Rose, J. (1990). "We'll meet again . . . ": Repeat attendance at group discussions—Does it matter? *Journal of the Market Research Society (UK), 32*(3), 377-407.

Henderson, N. R. (1990). Focus groups for the last decade of the twentieth century. *Applied Marketing Research, 30*(2), 20-23.

Henderson, N. R. (1992). Trained moderators boost the value of qualitative research. *Marketing Research: A Magazine of Management & Applications, 4*(2), 20-23.

Hooper, M. C. (1989). In crisis or calm, focus groups hit the mark. *Association Management, 41*(3), 116-119, 184.

Hunsaker, K. (1991). The focus group. *Association Management, 43*(8), 53-57,107.

Johnson, B. C. (1990). Focus group positioning and analysis: A commentary on adjuncts for enhancing the design of health care research. *Health Marketing Quarterly, 7*(1, 2), 153-168.

Johnson, S. (1992). Increasing participation in focus groups. *Recruitment and Retention Report, 5*(5), 6-8.

Klein, E. (1989). What you can and can't learn from focus groups. *D&B Reports, 37*(4), 26-28.

Knack, K. J. (1989). Circuit design's focus group meeting: What are the primary issues of concern facing the industry today? *Circuit Design, 6*(10), 47-52.

Lafayette, J. (1990). Interpublic updates focus groups. *Advertising Age, 61*(16), 54.

Langer, J., & Miller, S. (1985). The ideal focus group facility. *Journal of Data Collection, 25*(2), 34-37.

Long, S. A. (1991). Pretesting questionnaires minimizes measurement error. *Marketing News, 25*(11), 12.

Lysaker, R. L. (1989). Data collection methods in the US. *Journal of the Market Research Society (UK), 31*(4), 477-488.

Mariampolski, H. (1988, October 24). Probing correctly uncovers truth behind answers in focus group. *Marketing News*, pp. 22, 26.

Mariampolski, H. (1989). Focus groups on sensitive topics: How to get subjects to open up and feel good about telling the truth. *Applied Marketing Research, 29*(1), 6-11.

McDonald, W. J., & Topper, G. E. (1988). Focus-group research with children: A structural approach. *Applied Marketing Research, 28*(2), 3-11.

McKenna, C. K. (1992). Nominal and focus groups work well together. *Marketing News, 26*(1), FG-2, FG-15.

Miller, C. (1990). Network to broadcast live focus groups. *Marketing News, 24*(18), 10, 47.

Miller, C. (1991). Anybody ever hear of global focus groups? *Marketing News, 25*(11), 14.

Nasser, D. L. (1988). Workshop: How to run a focus group. *Public Relations Journal, 44*(3), 33-34.

Nelson, J. E., & Frontczak, N. T. (1988). How acquaintanceship and analyst can influence focus group results. *Journal of Advertising, 17*(1), 41-48.

Nichols, N. (1989, May 16). Fear and loathing in a Chrysler focus group. *Adweek's Marketing Index*, p. 61.

Pagnucco, D. J., & Quinn, Robert. P. (1988, August 29). "Natural group" interviews: Alternative to focus group. *Marketing News*, p. 44.

Palshaw, J. L. (1990). A few perils of marketing research. *Medical Marketing & Media, 25*(12), 92-93.

Potts, D. (1990). Bias lurks in all phases of qualitative research. *Marketing News, 24*(18), 12-13.

Ringo, S. A. (1992). Only a real pro has skills to be a moderator. *Marketing News, 26*(1), FG-1-FG-2.

Rucker, T. (1992). Economic conditions force cost cuts in focus groups. *Marketing News, 26*(1), 20, 21.

Schoenfeld, G. (1988). Unfocus and learn more. *Advertising Age, 59*(22), 20.

Schwarz, R. M. (1991). Attention to details keeps clients coming back. *Marketing News, 25*(11), 6-7.

Shalowitz, D. (1992). What do your employees want? You'd be surprised. *Business Insurance, 26*(17), 7.

Shapiro, S. (1990). Focus groups: The first step in package design. *Marketing News, 24*(18), 15, 17.

Solomon, G. D. (1988). Can focus groups provide market insight? *Advertising Age, 59*(7), 18.

Spethmann, B. (1992a). Focus groups key to reaching kids: These aren't pint-size adults, so interaction counts as much as the question. *Advertising Age, 63*(6), S1, S24.

Spethmann, B. (1992b). In sessions, kids say the darndest things. *Advertising Age, 63*(6), S1, S24.

Stiansen, S. (1988, December). How focus groups go astray. *Adweek*, pp. 4-6.

Tuckel, P., Leppo, E., & Kaplan, B. (1992). Focus groups under scrutiny. *Marketing Research: A Magazine of Management & Applications, 4*(2), 12-18.

Vitale, D. (1991). Focus group "retreat" promotes teamwork behind the mirror. *Marketing News, 25*(11), 2.

Wade, R. K. (1993). Screener questions by recruiters clear deadwood from focus groups. *Marketing News, 27*(5), 9.

Winski, J. M. (1993). "Addicted" to research, Nick shows strong kids' lure: Agency exec says net hits the hot button. *Advertising Age, 63*(6), S2, S22.

Wolff, M. R. (1988). Focus groups for the market-driven. *Bottomline*, pp. 55-56.

Wooldridge, P. M. (1991). Focus group respondents deserve a little empathy. *Marketing News, 25*(11), 6-7.

Yovovich, B. G. (1991). Focusing on customers' needs and motivations. *Business Marketing, 76*(3), 41-43.

Ziff, K. (1990). Focus group "art" reveals in-depth information. *Marketing News, 24*(18), 7, 20.

Miscellaneous Publications

Advertising Research Foundation. (1985). *Focus groups: Issues and approaches.* New York: Advertising Research Foundation.

Bartos, R. (1986). Qualitative research: What it is and where it came from. *Journal of Advertising Research. 26*(3), RC3-RC6.

Calder, B. J. (1977). Focus groups and the nature of qualitative marketing research. *Journal of Marketing Research, 14*(3), 353-364.

Carlson, P. (1993). Hocus focus. *The Washington Post Magazine*, pp. 15-17, 28-30.

Corn, D. (1991, January 21). The focus group: Helping big oil polish its image. *Nation, 252*(2), 49-51.

Desvousges, W. H. (1988). Focus groups and risk communication: The science of listening to data. *Risk Analysis, 8*(4), 479-484.

Desvousges, W. H. (1989). Integrating focus groups and surveys: Examples from environmental risk studies. *Journal of Official Statistics, 5*(4), 349-363.

Edwarda, L. (1992). The focusing of the president 1992. *Village Voice, 37*(25), 25-29.

Eisenstodt, J. L. (1992). Off-site meeting planning: A to Z instructions for the inexperienced manager. *Human Resources Professional, 4*(4), 56-61.

Ember, L. (1990). Focus groups to aid writing of acid rain report. *Chemical & Engineering News, 68*(21), 28.

Feig, B. (1989). How to run a focus group. *American Demographics, 11*(12), 36-37.

Goldman, A. E. (1962, July). The group depth interview. *Journal of Marketing*, pp. 61-68.

Higginbotham, J. B., & Cox, K. K. (Eds.). (1979). *Focus group interviews: A reader.* Chicago: American Marketing Association.

Johnson, T. (1991, September 1). Focus Pocus. *The Philadelphia Enquirer*, pp. 11-26.

Krueger, R. A. (1984, October). *Focus group interviewing as an evaluation tool.* An unpublished paper presented at the Evaluation Research Society & Evaluation Network 1984 Annual Meeting, San Francisco, CA.

Krueger, R. A., & Hutchins, A. C. (1986). Group interviews focus on good design. *Architecture Minnesota, 12*(5), 25.

Krueger, R. A., Hutchins, A. C., & Olney, G. D. (1985). *Focus group interviewing for architects and interior designers.* St. Paul, MN: Research in Design.

Krueger, R. A., Mueller, M. R., & Casey, M. A. (1986). *An assessment of farm credit mediation.* St. Paul: University of Minnesota, Minnesota Extension Service.

Lahue, P. M. (1988). Focus group studies plans to franchise Carlton Lodge. *H&MM*, pp. 3, 33.

Langer, J. (1991). Focus groups. *American Demographics, 13*(2), 38-39.

Levy, S. J. (1979). Focus group interviewing. In J. B. Higginbotham & K. K. Cox (Eds.), *Focus group interviews: A reader* (pp. 34-42). Chicago: American Marketing Association.

Manning, H., Hock, R. E., & Milstead, J. (1990). Focus group research: A case study. *Bulletin of ASIS, 17*(1), 7-10.

Rowan, M. M. (1991). Bankers beware! Focus groups can steer you wrong. *Bottomline, 8*(4), 37-41.

Welch, J. L. (1985a). Researching marketing problems and opportunities with focus groups. *Industrial Marketing Management, 14*(4), 245-253.

Welch, J. L. (1985b). Focus groups for restaurant research. *The Cornell Hotel and Restaurant Association Quarterly, 26*(2), 78-85.

Wells, W. D. (1974). Group interviewing. In R. Ferber (Ed.), *Handbook of marketing research* (pp. 2-12). New York: McGraw-Hill. (Also reprinted in J. B. Higginbotham & K. K. Cox, *Focus group interviews: A reader.* Chicago: American Marketing Association, 1979.)

Index

About the Author

Richard A. Krueger is Professor and Extension Evaluation Leader at the University of Minnesota. He holds the baccalaureate degree in history from Bethel College (1964), the master's degree in public affairs from the University of Minnesota (1971), and the doctorate in education from the University of Minnesota (1979). He has worked on a variety of evaluation projects, including those relating to nutrition, rural economic recovery, chemical dependency, community development, and volunteer participation. He regularly teaches evaluation classes at the University of Minnesota, where he serves as adjunct professor in the College of Education. In his role as Extension Evaluation Leader, he provides statewide leadership in program evaluation for the Minnesota Extension Service.

He drives a motorcycle, which he tries to repair even when it isn't broken, reads books as often as he can, enjoys good stories and has been known to tell a few of his own, and finds relaxation by shopping for tools at the hardware store. Maybe you've met him there.